Reports on
Investment Approval and FDI in India

Published in 2004 by

ACADEMIC FOUNDATION
4772-73 / 23 Bharat Ram Road,
(23 Ansari Road), Darya Ganj,
New Delhi - 110 002.

Phones : 23245001, 02, 03, 04.

Fax : 011-23245005

e-mail : academic@vsnl.com

www : academicfoundation.com

Reports on Investment Approval & FDI in India
ISBN 81-7188-337-0

Laser-Typeset at AF's DTP Division.

Printed at Print Perfect, Mayapuri Industrial Area, New Delhi.

From the Publisher

THIS publication brings together three important Reports relating to reforming investment approval and procedures and foreign direct investment.

With a view to ensuring that scarce resources are used effectively, the Government of India appointed a Committee in September 2001 to examine extant procedures for investment approvals and implementation of projects and suggest measures to simplify and expedite the process of both public and private projects.

The Committee has discussed the upstream issues entailed in various stages — from identification of Government and public sector projects and schemes up to the investment approval.

The Committee's recommendations on various upstream issues are covered in Part I of the Report entitled Report on Reforming Investment Approvals and Implementation Procedures — Government and Public Sector Projects (May 2002).

Part II of the Report Downstream Issues: Implementation and Operation (November 2002) contains recommendations on the downstream issues i.e. from the stage of investment approval to the implementation of projects and their operational phase.

In addition to Planning Commission Report on FDI (Chairman: N.K. Singh) which has been separately published by Academic Foundation, there are two other relevant reports on FDI which we have included in this publication. Parliamentary Standing Committee Report on Foreign Direct Investment (Rajya Sabha Secretariat, New Delhi, May 2003) and Report of the Committee on Compilation of Foreign Direct Investment in India (Oct., 2002) which also includes the First Action Taken Report (June 2003).

With a view to bringing the present FDI reporting system of RBI in alignment with the international reporting system, Government, in consultation with RBI had constituted a committee comprising officials from RBI, the Department of Industrial Policy and Promotion (DIPP), Government of India, in May 2002, to study the conceptual and methodological issues including data gaps involved and make necessary recommendations to strengthen the collection, compilation and reporting of FDI data. The report of the Committee submitted in October 2002 including First Action Report, June 2003 are covered in this publication.

We hope all these relevant reports put together will prove handy and useful to the readers interested in the subject.

Contents

Report on Reforming Investment Approval and Implementation Procedures

Part – I

Investment Approval Procedures —
Government and Public Sector Projects

(May 2002)

Contents

Part – I

Investment Approval Procedures — Government and Public Sector Projects, May 2002

LIST OF ANNEXES

Foreword

IN pursuance of the need felt by the Government to recast their investment approvals and regulations framework with a view to ensuring that the scarce resources are used effectively, a Committee to examine extant procedures for investment approvals and implementation of projects and suggest measures to simplify and expedite the process of both public and private projects was set up by the Cabinet Secretariat, Government of India in September 2001. A sub-group of that Committee was to specifically look into various issues relating to investment in schemes and projects in the private sector.

The Committee, besides having a number of interactive sessions among its members, also met in smaller groups for detailed deliberations. Separately a study was also commisioned with McKinsey & Company on "Strengthening the Investment Approvals Mechanisms" for Government projects.

The Committee has discussed the upstream issues entailed in the various stages, viz., from identification of Government and public sector projects and schemes up to the investment approval. The Committee's recommendations on various upstream issues are covered in Part-I of the report. The recommendations on the downstream issues would be covered in the second part of the report to be presented separately.

The Committee acknowledges the invaluable contribution of Shri V. N. Kaul who, as convenor, till his elevation as Comptroller & Auditor General of India guided its initial deliberations. Shri A.K. Basu, Shri C.M. Vasudev and Shri K.V. Irniraya, during their tenure as Members, contributed significantly in arriving at many of the recommendations.

New Delhi
May 2002

Sd/

Shyamal Ghosh
P.V. Jayakrishnan
Vinod Vaish
Pradip Baijal
S. Prabhakaran
C.S. Rao
N.S. Sisodia
B.K. Misra
Dr. Rakesh Mohan
Dr. Pradipto Ghosh
V. Govindarajan (Convenor)

Executive Summary

GOVERNMENT considered that there was a need to recast the project approvals and regulatory framework with a view to speeding up the process and ensuring that scarce resources are deployed effectively and accordingly a Committee was set up by the Government in September 2001 to examine the extant procedures for investment approvals and implementation of projects and suggest measures to simplify and expedite the process for both public and private investment. A Sub-Group of that Committee was to look into issues specifically relating to investment in schemes and projects in the private sector. Separately, the Indian Oil Corporation commissioned a study with McKinsey & Company on "Strengthening of Investment Approvals Mechanism" in Government. The Committee had the benefit of considering their report while finalising its own recommendations.

While the procedures for approval of public and private projects are different, with public projects appraised and approved at appropriate levels in the Governmental/Organisational set up and private projects requiring financial closure, the requirements of various permissions and approvals as well as the regulatory framework during implementation and operation are similar for both types of projects. The committee in part-I of the report has largely focused on the various upstream issues relating to issues that arise from conceptualisation to the stage of investment approval. The sub-group, on the other hand, is examining, at length, various downstream issues hampering implementation of projects, i.e., issues that arise from the stage of investment approval to implementation. Part-I of the Committee's report deals with the upstream issues. The downstream issues, which are common to both the public and private sector projects, will be covered in Part-II of the report, to be presented separately.

Besides delays in approval of projects and in getting necessary permissions for implementation, poor quality of project formulation and appraisal has also been identified as a major roadblock in timely implementation of the projects. Failures to upfront identify and address issues such as land availability, environmental & social impact, involuntary settlements, etc., affect project implementation at a later stage.

The Department of Expenditure, in February 2002, during the course of deliberations of the Committee enhanced the appraisal and approval powers at various levels. The approval powers have been revised after 1992. Higher powers have been delegated to some Ministries, Empowered Commissions, and Navratna & Miniratna PSEs.

Capacity Constraints and their Effect on Projects

Inadequate capacity among the existing staff engaged in the formulation, appraisal and evaluation of projects is identified as a major reason behind poor quality of projects.

The fear of audit and inordinately long time taken in concluding investigations also impact the working of personnel engaged in projects.

Project Evaluation

The findings of the evaluation studies of completed projects would be an important input while formulating new projects.

Proposed Project Cycle

The Committee has proposed a generic structure of the detailed project report. Revised project cycle that involves formulation and appraisal of projects by experts and its approval at the Government level has also been recommended. (Annex-VIII). The time frame for appraisal of projects under the revised project cycle is available at Annex-IX.

Main Downstream Issues

The Sub-Group on 'Simplification of Procedures for Projects in the Private Sector' is separately looking into the downstream implementation issues. Part-II of the Committee's report, on the downstream issues, would be presented separately. Some of the major issues that also impact the project approval, regulatory environment and investment decisions of investors are as under:

Review of Extant Laws

A plethora of laws and regulations govern the approval, implementation and operation of projects. Simplification of the procedural requirements prescribed under various Acts has not kept pace with the liberalization and changes in the structure of the economy. Multiplicity of laws regulating related aspects of project administration, inspection and reporting requirements make the administration as well as compliance difficult.

Regulatory Environment for Projects

Regulatory and reporting requirements under different Acts require prolonged interface between the authorities and the project. A study jointly conducted in January 2002 by CII and World Bank on 'Competitiveness in Indian Manufacturing' based on firm level survey has shown that about 16 per cent of the management time in India is spent on dealing with Government officials on regulatory and administrative issues. The study also notes that States with better investment climate impose lesser burden on the management.

Transparency in Project Approval Process

Lack of transparency in the prevailing systems for approvals and of regulations impose a burden on the project promoters often leading to delays in getting necessary approvals for implementation of projects. Greater transparency in the regulatory framework through easy availability of specific information about the procedural and documentary requirements, agencies responsible for issuing such approvals, time frame prescribed for decision, etc., would reduce delays.

Role of State Governments

States have a crucial role in project implementation, as States implement most of the legislations regulating projects. Strengthening Single Window Approval Mechanism, introducing 'Single Composite Application Forms', simplifying interface between regulatory authorities and entrepreneurs and greater use of IT, among others, facilitate implementation and operation of projects.

Recommendations

Full text of the recommendations is contained in Chapter-VIII. The recommendations in brief are:

A. Upstream Issues

I. Procedural

i. Project Appraisal Unit (PAU) may be established in the Planning Commission as the primary appraising agency for all public projects entailing investment of Rs. 25 crores and above. Projects from Navratna/Miniratna PSEs involving budgetary support or contingent liability on the part of Government or beyond their approval authority would also require appraisal by PAU. This limit may also be made co-terminus with Plan period requiring review every five years.

ii. The PAU may be established by strengthening the existing PAMD with experts recruited for specific fields to the extent necessary. Services of experts from other departments/agencies/other sources, etc., may be availed for sector specific requirements.

iii. TORs for preparing the detailed project reports would also be reviewed and approved by the PAU.

iv. The powers delegated at various levels may be made co-terminus with the Plan period requiring a review every five years. Enhanced powers could be delegated to Ministries dealing with larger projects.

v. In view of the expert review of the detailed project report, the requirement of pre-PIB may be dispensed with for projects with outlays up to Rs. 500 crores.

II. Project Management and Evaluation

i. Project management skills need to be strengthened by identification of a core team for its implementation, strengthening coordination with concerned Ministries/ Departments and training the personnel on the best practices on project management.

ii. In order to avoid repetition of effort in monitoring of projects by the Administrative Ministries and MSPI, it is necessary that the monitoring in the Ministries and MSPI be networked permitting on-line monitoring. The Monitoring unit in the MSPI would need to be strengthened for monitoring and concurrent evaluation of projects.

iii. MSPI may conduct post project evaluation of selected public projects with investment of Rs.100 crores and above and other priority sector projects. Each detailed project report must specifically mention whether the results of previous projects are available and how these have been used in project design.

III. Capacity Building

i. The requirements of the detailed project report and the criteria for meeting these requirements may be specified by the PAU to enable the Ministries to assess the areas where capacity building is required.

ii. Project formulation skills in the Ministries and PSEs need to be upgraded and specialization promoted. Orientation trainings may be organized for the existing staff with assistance from Multilateral Financial Institutions. (MFIs)

iii. Members of the Facilitation Teams, to be established in the Administrative Ministries, to be given orientation training through IIMs and other Management Institutes of repute on modern project management and best practices.

iv. Existing staff responsible for project evaluation may be given orientation training on different evaluation methodologies.

v. Training and reorientation of functionaries in various Government departments/agencies on e-governance and computer usage. Officers of the level of Section Officer and above to undergo compulsory usage focused computer training.

vi. Industry specific skills for various processes as well as sector specific skills for specific sectors like financial services need to be strengthened within the audit/vigilance agencies.

vii. While capacity-building initiatives would be an ongoing exercise, measures to address the deficiencies in the existing set up need to be completed in a time bound manner, say one year.

a. Downstream Issues

I. Procedural

i. The extant laws need re-casting to bring down the number of clearances, processing time and complexities in administration by making the system transparent and easy to comply with Acts which have outlived their utility may be scrapped. Provisions dealing with similar objectives need to be brought under one Act for ease of implementation and compliance.

ii. A detailed analysis of each approval requirement needs to be carried out for re-engineering of the regulatory process as under:

   a. Automatic permission upon filing of documents (Traffic Light approach)

   b. Deemed approval upon expiry of the period prescribed for approval.

   c. Grant of approval by outside agencies authorized for granting such approvals.

   d. Approvals statutorily required.

iii. Greater transparency in the administration of approvals is required for information on investment policies, sectorwise approval requirements, agencies responsible, procedural requirements and prescribed time frame, etc.

iv. Greater use of IT in administration of approvals and information to citizen, gradually leading to electronic transactions with regulatory authorities, is necessary.

II. Institutional Arrangements

i. Industrial Investment Facilitation Board (IIFB) may be established to facilitate the grant of approvals to projects with investments of Rs.100 crores and above. Time limits for the grant of various non-statutory approvals may be prescribed by IIFB in consultation with the concerned Administrative Ministries. IIFB may also take up re-engineering of the regulatory processes in consultation with the concerned Ministries.

ii. Cases involving excessive delays in approvals may be referred to a Group of Ministers to be constituted for consideration and resolution of such cases.

iii. Facilitation Teams may be established in Administrative Ministries for major projects in the infrastructure and priority sectors for identifying and removing bottlenecks and ensuring better co-ordination among concerned Ministries/Departments.

iv. Empowered 'Single Window System' may be introduced at the State level to monitor and implement the single window concept.

1

Introduction

IN pursuance of the need felt by the Government to recast their investment approval and regulation framework with a view to ensuring that the scarce resources are used effectively, the Cabinet Secretariat vide its Order no. 212/9/2001-CA.IV dated on 24.9.2001 set up a Committee with Shri V.N. Kaul, Secretary, Ministry of Petroleum & Natural Gas as convenor, to examine the extant procedures for investment approvals and implementation of projects and suggest measures to simplify and expedite the process for both public and private investments. A copy of the Order dated 24.9.2001 setting up the Committee is at Annex-I.

1.2 Following the appointment of Shri V.N. Kaul as Comptroller & Auditor General of India, Shri V. Govindarajan, Secretary (IPP) was designated as the convenor of the Committee vide Cabinet Secretariat Order dated 19.3.2002.

1.3 A Sub-Group, with Shri V. Govindarajan, Secretary (IPP) as convenor, was also constituted to look into various issues relating to investment in schemes and projects in Private Sector. A copy of the Order constituting the Sub-Group is enclosed as Annex-II.

1.4 The Committee in its first meeting on 4.10.2001 decided the modalities of deliberations, integration of various inputs including the Base Papers of concerned Ministries and Public Sector Enterprises, case studies commissioned by Prime Minister's Office, studies commissioned by Ministry of Statistics & Programme Implementation (MSPI) and reports of previous committees and studies.

1.5 Separately, the Indian Oil Corporation commissioned a study on 'Strengthening of Investment Approvals Mechanism' for

Government projects with M/s. McKinsey&Company. A copy of the Executive Summary of this report is enclosed as Annex-III.

1.6 The Committee subsequently met on 14.3.2002, 8.4.2002 and 22.4.2002 to deliberate upon the issues and recommendations. In addition, the committee also met separately in small groups for detailed discussions.

1.7 The committee has examined the extant procedures for the investment approvals and implementation of projects. These recommendations would be equally relevant to projects/programmes/schemes. Projects entail a set of interrelated activities aimed at achieving desired objectives by producing specified and recognizable end results with specific resources within a specified period of time. In the case of schemes, investment, implementations and the flow of output are almost concurrent. Programmes are collections of smaller projects of schemes. For this reason, concurrent evaluation is more commonly employed in programmes and schemes, whereas in the case of projects terminal and post-evaluation methodologies are normally adopted. While the economic rate of return is a relevant concept in projects, in the case of social sector schemes the output may be less amenable to assignment of monetary value and hence the concept of cost-effectiveness becomes relevant.

1.8 Part-I of the report contains recommendations on reforming the investment approval mechanism in Government. Part II of the report on simplification of procedures for implementation of projects is under finalisation and will be presented separately.

1.9 The committee has examined the extant procedures for the investment approval and implementation of projects/programmes/schemes. In the report, the term project has been used in a generic sense and includes programme/scheme for the purpose of this report. These recommendations would apply equally to the projects/programmes/schemes.

1.10 The Committee acknowledges the valuable contributions and suggestions made by various Ministries, Public Sector Enterprises and consultants. A complete list of references and contributions of the Ministries, PMO, Institutions and consultants is available at Annex-IV

1.11 The Committee acknowledges the special contribution by Shri V.N. Kaul who, as convenor, till his elevation as Comptroller & Auditor General of India guided the initial deliberations of the Committee. Shri A.K. Basu, Shri C.M. Vasudev and Shri K.V. Irniraya, with their rich experience, provided valuable inputs and contributed significantly in arriving at many recommendations.

1.12 The Committee also wishes to place on record the contributions of Shri M.S. Srinivasan, Joint Secretary and Shri Umesh Kumar, Director of the Department of Industrial Policy & Promotion, whose untiring efforts have helped us; meet the stringent deadlines in the preparation and presentation of this report.

2

General Issues Related to Approval and Implementation of Projects

PART-I of the report of the Committee has concentrated mainly on the upstream issue relating to Government and Public Sector projects, i.e., issues that arise from the conceptualization to the stage of investment approval. The Sub-Group has separately been looking into the downstream issues, i.e., those from stage of investment approval to the implementation of the project and also some of the operational issues. Recommendations on simplification of procedures for various approvals will be covered in Part-II of the report. The issues covered under the upstream and downstream categories are :

Upstream Issues

2.2 The issues that arise from the stage of conceptualisation of the project to the investment approval in the case of public projects are covered under upstream issues. These would also include any permission, license, approval, etc., necessary before investment approval.

Downstream Issues

2.3 Downstream issues, on the other hand, would include all the implementation and operational issues starting from the stage of investment approval in case of a public project or financial closure in case of private project up to the commencement of commercial production. It would also include the various statutory approvals/clearances required for commissioning the project. Downstream operational issues would include the operational phase of the project after its commissioning.

Causes Behind Poor Quality of Project Decisions & Delays in Implementation

2.4 The Government of India and its PSEs together invest almost Rs. 130,000 crores annually in projects and schemes in infrastructure, social development and industrial development sectors. With progressive liberalization of the economy and opening up of a large number of sectors to private and Foreign Direct Investment, the private sector has a major role in investment, which will assume even greater significance in the years ahead.

2.5 It has, however, been observed that liberalization of the economic policy and changes in the structure of the economy has not translated fully into attracting greater investments due to a variety of reasons. Existing procedures of project formulation, appraisal & approval particularly for government projects, inadequacies in the existing management system and inadequate skills in project formulation, appraisal and management are some of the major reasons behind delays in the investment approvals and implementation of projects. Some of the main upstream factors affecting these projects are:

Process Related

- Significant time lag between the grant of 'in principle' approval and submission of detailed feasibility report for appraisal.
- Poor quality of project formulation resulting in delays in decision-making and implementation in many cases. Issues that should have been identified and addressed at the formulation stages, but were missed out, also cause delays in implementation, overruns, need for revision of cost estimates and a fresh set of approval.
- Multiplicity of agencies, viz., DOE, EFC, PIB, etc., for project appraisal leading to delays in decision-making. Many agencies provide inputs at the stage of project appraisal often resulting in overlap and redundancy in their roles.
- Involvement of many agencies at the stage of project formulation and appraisal also makes it difficult to fix responsibility.

- Delays in project appraisal and approval beyond the prescribed time.
- Absence of professional project management approaches that have evolved recently, particularly in the private sector. This includes cross-functional teams to determine best project configuration, early identification of key personnel to manage the project, skill based staffing, continuity of project teams and rigorous evaluation.
- Inadequate use of IT in decision-making.

Organisational Issues

- Weak performance management systems in the Government and public sector resulting in lack of urgency to adhere to decision-making time limits or to be held accountable for results. Weak target setting and evaluation.

Capacity Constraints

- Lack of specialized skills in project formulation and appraisal.
- Absence of professional advice on project formulation and appraisal.
- Limited codification of knowledge and maintenance of database, compendium of standard appraisal techniques and documentation formats.

3

Extant Procedure for Formulation, Appraisal and Approval of Public Sector Projects

Project Cycle

A public sector project, either of Government or its agencies viz. PSEs, etc., has to pass through many stages from its conceptualization to approval before it is taken up for implementation. Private projects on the other hand have to get permissions, as required, and achieve financial closure before these could be taken up for implementation. While there is this difference in the approval mechanism, the subsequent stages for implementation of the project are similar for both public and private projects in terms of the approvals/permissions required and other reporting, record keeping and statutory requirements.

Project Cycle of Public Project – Conceptualization to Implementation

3.2 A project in the public sector would typically go through the following cycle from conceptualization to implementations at the Central Government level. Similar stages exist at the State level with the approval level being much less than that at the Central level. Very often the projects get approved at the level of the Chief Minister and the State Finance department usually has a greater say in the appraisal and approval of the projects and the elaborate process of approval at the Cabinet level which exists in Government of India is generally non-existent at the State level.

Identification of Project

3.3 A project is identified based on the National and State priorities, sectoral setting and competing claims from other activities and sectors. Concerned Ministries in the Centre/State Governments identify specific projects with the help of public sector enterprises and other expert agencies. Approval of the Planning Commission and separately of the Administrative Minister/FM/CCEA is required for launching a new plan scheme in the Central Sector or a new Centrally Sponsored Scheme. Planning Commission has laid down a two-stage process, first an 'in-principle' approval, followed by a full Planning Commission approval after the project/scheme has been appraised by EFC/PIB. Based on the pre-feasibility report, the project is considered for 'in-principle' approval by the Planning Commission for inclusion in the Plan.

Project Preparation

3.4 Project preparation is the next stage of the project cycle involving analysis of the technical, financial and institutional considerations, alternate strategies and the selection of the best alternative.

3.5 For infrastructure projects in Power and Coal, this exercise is part of Stage-1 clearance. For Stage-1 clearance, a fair estimate of the cost is prepared after considering technical, financial and institutional parameters including the study the various alternatives and the best alternative. In this stage the project has to obtain all statutory clearances, particularly relating to environment and techno-economic clearance by CEA, CWC, etc. The document thus prepared also referred to as pre-feasibility report. During this stage, preliminary activities including preparation of full feasibility report and obtaining necessary statutory clearances and basic land acquisition are taken up.

3.6 The feasibility report is a more detailed exercise and may take up to two or three years depending upon the size and complexity of the project. The feasibility report covers all aspects of the project including a more realistic estimate of cost and benefits, fund flow for the project, etc. The project preparation is usually carried out using the expertise available within the Ministry/PSEs or by outsourcing to professional bodies.

Project Appraisal

3.7 Appraisal of the project involves a detailed analysis on technical, economic, financial and institutional parameters. Appraisal process starts after the feasibility report in the prescribed format has been prepared and circulated to all the institutional members of SFC/EFC/PIB. All projects above Rs. 15 crores also required appraisal by the Project Appraisal and Monitoring Division (PAMD) of Planning Commission and Plan Finance Division of the Department of Expenditure. A time limit of 4 weeks has been prescribed for appraisal of projects by PAMD.

3.8 Ministries/Departments are required to obtain the following approval/clearances before the proposal is submitted for appraisal :

a) 'In-principle' approval of Planning Commission for inclusion of the project in the Five Year Plan/Annual Plan.

b) Provision of adequate funds, required for implementation of the proposal.

c) Comments/concurrence of Financial Adviser of the Ministry for proposal is enclosed along with the EFC/PIB memo.

3.9 After inter-ministerial consultations, the proposal is considered by the Expenditure Finance Committee (EFC) or Public Investment Board (PIB), as the case may be, which takes a final view on the viability of the project/scheme and makes suitable recommendation to the approval authority.

3.10 In case of proposals to be approved by SFC, Planning Commission has simplified the procedure. The Ministry/ Departments can convene SFC meetings without inviting Planning Commission representatives provided the scheme has been included in the Plan (in principal approval) with adequate funds.

3.11 A total time schedule of 20 weeks has been prescribed for appraisal by EFC/PIB under the present procedure as per the details available at Annex-V

Project Approval

3.12 After appraisal, the project is taken up for consideration for approval after budgetary provisions have been made. Till February 2002, the Minister of the concerned Ministry was the competent authority to sanction projects/schemes involving outlay of less than Rs. 20 crores. The Minister of the concerned Administrative Ministry and the Finance Minister were the competent authority to sanction projects/schemes with outlay between Rs. 20-50 crores. CCEA was the competent authority for projects/schemes with outlays over Rs. 50 crores. With enhanced delegation of powers effective from 18th February 2002, projects/ schemes involving investments above Rs. 100 crores now require approval of the cabinet. A copy of the order dated 18th February 2002 by Department of Expenditure enhancing the delegation of authority at various levels is at Annex-VI.

Implementation

3.13 After approval, the project is taken up for implementation. This often requires a number of approvals/permissions, both statutory as well as non-statutory, to be taken from both Central as well as State Departments/Agencies. Besides direct supervision of the implementing agency, the concerned Ministry and the Ministry of Statistics and Programme Implementation (MSPI) also monitor and supervise central projects. Similar arrangements exist at the State level for State projects.

Evaluation

3.14 Evaluation, with respect to the objectives set out for the project, is carried out by the project authorities in the prescribed format after project's completion. Often these evaluation studies are not systematically used for taking lessons for future projects due to lack of organisational arrangements either in the concerned Ministry or MSPI Ministry of Statistics and Programme Implementation.

3.15 The extant project cycle, as discussed above, is shown in the flow chart available as Annex-VII.

Approval of Projects at Stage Level

3.16 The process is almost similar for projects approved at the State level with the Planning and Finance departments normally appraising the projects and the approval at the level of the Chief Minister through the Finance Department.

4

Review of the Extant Process of Appraisal and Approval

IT is seen that apart from the bottlenecks created due to delays in approvals of projects and in obtaining various permissions / approvals, poor quality of project formulation and its appraisal also impact implementation of projects. Inadequacies in the project formulation and appraisal often lead to cost and time overruns and the inevitable requirement of revision in the project cost estimates making a fresh round of approvals necessary, further delaying its implementation.

Project Formulation

4.2 While delays in the approval of projects, and in obtaining other permissions necessary for their implementation, continue to be a constraint, poor quality of project formulation and its appraisal have been identified as major roadblocks in implementation of projects. Failure to identify any constraints in the availability of essential requirements of land, environmental impact, etc., at the time of project formulation itself could cripple the implementation of the project at a later stage.

4.3 Project preparation commences after inclusion of the proposal in the Plan. While some departments/PSEs have reasonably well developed project formulation skills internally, others generally avail services of professionals. The project document prepared either internally or by the experts engaged for this purpose is appraised at appropriate level under the delegated powers. Inadequacies in the DPR noticed at the stage of appraisal would require such issues to be revisited. The Ministry/Line

Agency would draft the TOR for the DPR. Since most projects would have their own specific issues to be addressed, it would not be possible to prescribe a generic TOR for the DPR.

4.4 It is vital that the TORs for the DPR drafted by the sponsoring Ministry/Line Agency are reviewed by the experts at the stage of finalizing the TOR itself so that the requirements of the final DPR can be addressed in the TOR at this stage itself. This would avoid complications later at the stage of project appraisal, and save considerable time.

4.5 The project documentation, besides covering the justification for the project/scheme, various alternatives, economic and financial returns, implementation alternatives, etc., must also address other critical issues which impact project implementation, viz., land acquisition, environmental & social impact, involuntary settlements, etc. A generic structure of the DPR is covered at greater length in Chapter-V.

4.6 Project formulation, including pre-feasibility studies, and drafting of TORs being specialized jobs, require special skills and expertise. Capacity building measures for the personnel entrusted with the responsibilities of project formulation, therefore, assume special significance. Besides skill up-gradation of such personnel, services of outside experts may be availed as may be necessary.

Strengthening the Project Appraisal Mechanism

4.7 The need for creating specialization in the project appraisal mechanism can hardly be over-emphasized. Rigorous examination of the project proposal by experts would not only improve the project content but would also ensure best utilization of investment. In view of the resource constraint, prioritization of the projects/schemes is necessary so that only financially viable projects providing adequate returns are taken up. Multiplicity of schemes with similar objectives leading to the resources getting thinly spread also needs to be avoided. This requires strengthening of the project appraisal process. It is proposed to provide for an expert body for appraisal of all public sector projects involving investment exceeding Rs. 25 crores by setting up a Project Appraisal Unit (PAU) in the Planning Commission.

4.8 The PAU would be set up by strengthening the existing PAMD in the Planning Commission with the addition of experts recruited from relevant fields. Setting up of a new body is not envisaged. PAU will comprise an in-house core team of experts in the fields of financial management, economics, environmental and social impact analysis etc. Experts from other Departments/agencies may be co-opted into PAU for specific sectoral analysis. If such expertise is not available in the Governmental set up, PAU may employ the services of outside experts as may be considered necessary. The PAU would, besides appraisal of all public projects involving investments of Rs. 25 crores and above, also prescribe and review the TORs for the preparation of DPRs for such projects. The financial limits for appraisal of projects by PAU may be made co-terminus with the Plan period to be reviewed every five years.

Expediting the Approval Process

4.9 The project proposal after appraisal is taken up for approval at appropriate levels under the prevailing delegation of powers. In the case of Navratna/Miniratna PSEs greater powers have been delegated. It has been experienced that after appraisal, approval of the public projects does not take long and generally no bottlenecks except the delegation of authority have been experienced.

4.10 The Cabinet Secretariat had prescribed guidelines in June 2000 for inter-ministerial consultations after EFC/PIB stage for obtaining investment approval. Delays in these consultations also contribute to delays in approval of projects.

4.11 Delays in formulating proposal for Revised Cost Estimates and bringing it before the appraisal forum and approval authorities also contribute to delays in the implementation of projects besides cost and time overruns.

4.12 McKinsey in their report have recommended converting some of the critical Ministries into Commissions and conferring greater powers on other Ministries and PSEs. These issues are covered in the following paragraphs.

Empowered Commissions in Select Ministries

4.13 McKinsey's report has recommended establishing 'Empowered Commissions' in place of the existing Ministry structure in 3-4 high priority sectors with large project investments. The model of converting existing Ministry Structure into Commissions has been recommended to provide for faster decision-making, clearer individual roles and greater operational flexibility. Under these recommendations, such Commissions would have both full time and part time Directors from concerned Ministries apart from professionals and would be authorized to take decisions on individual projects once the overall budget has been finalized.

4.14 The Committee, after careful consideration, is of the opinion that the concept of 'Empowered Commission' in place of the existing Ministry structure may not be appropriate as the Commission model would only replace the existing approval mechanism, which has not been a constraint in the project cycle. Projects requiring statutory clearances will also not be suitable for the 'Commission' model as all the statutory approval from concerned authorities would still be required before the project can be approved by the Commission. It is felt that with greater emphasis on the project formulation and its appraisal, the project approval process would get considerably streamlined. The powers delegated for appraisal and approval of projects have been enhanced in February 2002 and the Committee is separately recommending making these co-terminus with the Plan period to be revised at least every five years. This would further simplify the project approval process. Under these circumstances, the Commission model for select Ministries will not be suitable. Instead enhanced powers may be delegated to such Ministries for clearance of projects with scrutiny and appraisal of such projects by the PAU.

Enhancing the Approval Authority of Ministries

4.15 The Committee had examined at length the need for greater delegation of financial powers at various levels. Under the prevailing procedures, approval authority of a project would depend upon its estimated cost. Till February 2002, projects with investments exceeding Rs. 50 crores required approval by CCEA. This limit applied from 1992 when the Transaction of Business Rules were amended to enhance the outlay limit for investment proposal by CCEA from Rs. 20 crores to Rs. 50 crores. Even when delegation of power for appraisal forum was revised in 1997, no changes in the delegation of power for investment approval were made.

4.16 The Committee appreciated the need for a revision in the delegation of power and was examining this issue. During the course of deliberations of the Committee, the Department of Expenditure has, vide its order dated 18th February 2002, taken action to revise the delegation of powers at various levels. The comparative position of the appraisal and investment approval powers applicable from 1992 and revised in February 2002 is shown below :

4.17 Appraisal Authority:

Project/Scheme Outlay		*Approval Authority*
Earlier Limit (From 1992)	Present Limit (From 18th February 2002)	
Up to Rs. 1.5 Crores	Up to Rs. 5 Crores	Ministry in normal courses
Above Rs. 1.5 Crores but less than Rs. 15 Crores	Above Rs. 5 Crores but less than Rs. 25 Crores	Standing Finance Committee (SFC) of Ministry.
Rs. 15 Crores and above but less than Rs. 50 Crores	Rs. 25 Crores and above but less than Rs. 100 Crores	Expenditure Finance Committee (EFC) chaired by Administrative Secretary.
Rs. 50 Crores and above but less than Rs. 100 Crores	Rs. 100 Crore and above but less than Rs. 200 Crores	Expenditure Finance Committee (EFC) chaired by Secretary (Expenditure).
Rs. 100 Crores and above	Rs. 200 Crores and above	Public Investment Board/ EFC chaired by Secretary (Expenditure). Project Scheme where financial returns are quantifiable will be considered by PIB, others by EFC.

4.18 Approval Authority:

Project/Scheme Outlay		*Approval Authority*
Earlier Limit (From 1992)	Present Limit (From 18th February 2002)	
Less than Rs. 20 Crores	Less than Rs. 50 Crores	Administrative Minister
Rs. 20 Crores and above but less than Rs. 50 Crores	Rs. 50 Crores and above but less than Rs. 100 Crores	Administrative Minister and the Finance Minister
Rs. 50 Crores and above	Rs. 100 Crores and above	Cabinet/CCEA

4.19 The powers for approval of revised estimates and incurring expenditure on pre-investment activities have also been revised. Cases requiring expenditure on project preparation activities higher than the prescribed norms are considered in the Committee of PIB (CPIB). A copy of the Department of Expenditure's order No. 1 (3)/PF.II/2001 dated 18th February 2002 is available in Annex-VI.

4.20 The Committee is of the view that these limits would be appropriate for the time being but would need to be reviewed periodically. It is recommended that these powers might be made co-terminous with the Plan period and reviewed every five years.

Authority Delegated to the PSEs

4.21 Substantially enhanced powers have been delegated to the Navratna/Miniratna PSEs. It is, however, recommended that projects of Navratna/Miniratna PSEs involving budgetary support, contingent liability on the part of the Government or exceeding the delegated authority to the Miniratna PSEs should also be subjected to appraisal by the PAU, as in the case of other public projects.

5

Recommended Project Cycle and Detailed Project Report

THE present project cycle suffers from the deficiency of non-appraisal of the project by experts. Appraisal at the level of EFC/PIB is official level appraisal, which is in practice more a part of the approval mechanism than a scientific appraisal of project proposal. It is vital that the DPR is examined by experts before the proposal is taken up for consideration for approval. Based on the analysis of issues hampering project formulation, appraisal and approval, the following project cycle is proposed:

Project Identification : Feasibility Report

5.2 The project preparation may be considered to commence with the preparation of the feasibility report by the Ministry/LA, which will form the basis for its inclusion in the Plan. The feasibility report would essentially address the same policy issues as the DPR to be prepared later for appraisal, viz., need and justification for the project, alternatives, economic and financial returns, initial environmental and social impact analysis, extent of land acquisition and involuntary resettlement, evaluation of past projects and how these would be used in project design, implementation arrangement, phasing of expenditure, etc. Concerned Ministries/Line Agencies would be responsible for preparation of the feasibility report. Professional assistance may be taken as may be necessary. It would be useful to associate the concerned Ministries from the stage of preparation of feasibility report itself.

Inclusion in the Plan

5.3 After preparation of the feasibility report, approval of the Planning Commission and separately of the Administrative Minister/FM/CCEA is required for launching a new Plan scheme in the Central Sector or a new Centrally Sponsored Scheme. Planning Commission has laid down a two-stage process– first an 'in principle' approval followed by a full Planning Commission approval after the project/scheme has been appraised by EFC/ PIB. After the 'in principle' approval, the scheme is included in the Plan of the Ministry/Department. Ministry of Finance adopts the Ministry and scheme wise allocation of funds, carried out by the Planning Commission, for inclusion in the budget proposals.

Review and Approval of TOR

5.4 After the 'in principle' approval of the Planning Commission and inclusion in the plan, DPR is to be prepared. This work may be outsourced to professionals in case sufficient expertise is not available within the Ministry/PSE/LA. In order to avoid inadequacies in the TORs used for preparation of DPRs, it is recommended that the draft TORs prepared by the Ministry/LA are reviewed and vetted by the PAU in the Planning Commission. In order to reduce the number of references to the Planning Commission/PAU, it is recommended that the draft TOR be sent to the Planning Commission/PAU at the stage of seeking 'in principle' approval along with the feasibility report.

Preparation of Draft DPR

5.5 Following the approval of TOR and 'in principle' approval of the project/scheme, the concerned Ministry/Line Agency would take up preparation of the draft DPR. The capacities of the personnel engaged in preparation of the DPRs in the Ministries/ Line Agency would need to be upgraded and to the extent necessary skills are not available within the Ministry/Line Agency, services of professionals may have to be outsourced. Multilateral Financial Institutions (MIFs) may be requested for meeting such training needs under their technical assistance programmes. The DPR must address all issues related to the justification, financing and implementation of the project. A typical generic structure of the DPR is discussed at length later in this chapter.

Review of Draft DPR by the PAU

5.6 The draft DPR would be appraised in the PAU. For this purpose site visits may also be undertaken, if necessary, to confirm the assumptions made and data employed in the DPR. After appraisal by the PAU, the concerned Ministry/Line Agency will prepare the final DPR incorporating the suggestions proposed by PAU. A time limit of 4 weeks is considered sufficient for the appraisal of projects by PAU. It is necessary that the DPR be sent to the relevant Ministries only after its appraisal by experts in PAU so that a final and complete project proposal only is sent to the Ministries.

Inter-Ministerial Consultations

5.7 DPR after incorporating at suggestions by PAU, would be circulated to the relevant Ministries who would be given a reasonable time, of say 15 days, for their comments before official level appraisal.

5.8 Under the extant process, appraisal of projects with quantifiable financial returns take place at three stages: consideration of feasibility report at Pre-PIB meeting, appraisal of final proposal by the competent authority and final consideration by PIB. Under the recommended project cycle, since the project would have been subjected to expert scrutiny and appraisal before inter-ministerial consultations, the requirement of pre-PIB may be dispensed with for projects with investments up to Rs. 500 crores.

Official Level Appraisal and Approval

5.9 The DPR along with the appraisal note would be sent to the PIB. The PIB, which is an official review mechanism, will consider whether or not the project acceptance criteria have been met, and examine the differences of opinion, if any, between the sponsoring ministry and the PAU, but will not require either agency to revise its technical findings/views and may also factor in other non-technical considerations in its analysis. The PIB will then present the full picture giving both points of view and its own recommendation to the decision making authority, viz., the Cabinet Committee on Economic Affairs, for consideration and decision.

5.10 Inadequate allocation of funds has also been identified as a major factor behind cost and time overrun in projects. It would be necessary that at the stage of seeking approval of the competent authority, the sponsoring Ministry provides a list of all approved projects, their planned phasing of expenditure, actual expenditure and the proposed budget allocation for examination of the adequacy and justification of budgetary allocation.

5.11 Environmental and other clearances are required for some projects before these can be considered by PIB for official level appraisal and such clearances are, therefore, upstream clearances. Environmental Impact Assessment would need to be carried out and environmental clearance obtained before the project can be taken up for Stage-II clearance by PIB. Simplification of procedures for environmental and other clearances will be covered in Part-II of the report.

5.12 The recommended project cycle, as discussed above, is shown in the flow chart available as Annex-VIII. The time frame proposed for the appraisal of the projects under the recommended project cycle is at Annex-IX.

5.13 The Committee is of the opinion that greater emphasis on project formulation and expert appraisal would improve the quality of projects and also anticipate and address at the stage of project formulation itself issues, which may later affect its implementation. While the project formulation and approval stages would involve additional efforts and perhaps time, the qualitative improvement in the project formulation and appraisal by experts would help in reducing overall delays in the implementation of projects. The recommended time frame (Annex IX) prescribes a time period of 16 weeks for the appraisal of project. Wherever the recommended time frame is not adhered to at any stage, the concerned organization should work out an appropriate trigger mechanism to take the matter to the next higher level for timely decision making.

5.14 It is recommended in this context, that the Ministry of Finance, Department of Expenditure may formulate, in generic terms, a comprehensive set of project acceptance criteria for different categories of projects and get it approved by the CCEA. The technical appraisal by PAU and official review by the PIB will both consider the project proposals with reference of these criteria.

Generic Structure of Detailed Project Report

5.15 The Committee recommends that the DPR for projects may adopt the following generic structure :

1. Need for the project: What are the policy objectives to be realized by the project? These objectives must be ranked in order of importance.
2. Project benefits and target population, expected distribution of project costs and benefits among its primary beneficiaries and other groups.
3. Lessons learned from the review and post-evaluation of similar projects implemented earlier, how the project proposes to benefit from these lessons/evaluation studies of past project in the sector and how these are reflected in the project proposal.
4. General description of the project. What it does and how? What alternatives to the project have been considered? Reasons for selecting the proposed alternative. Alternative locations, basis for prioritization of the location.
5. Technologies involved in the project. Formal evaluation of the candidate technologies and reasons for the technological choice.
6. Financial and economic analysis of the project and realistic assessment of 'with' and 'without' project situation.
7. Means of financing the project : This section would cover evaluation and prioritization of alternative financing means, amount and phasing of contributions from various sources, viz., Government, financial institutions, Multilateral Financial Institutions, contribution by the beneficiaries, requirement of Government guarantee, etc.
8. Social (including equity) impact analysis of the project, beneficiaries participation in the preparation and implementation of the project, adverse social impact of the project, if any, and measures proposed for their mitigation, impact of the project on the weaker sections of the society and the strategy for their involvement.
9. Environmental impact analysis of the project to cover main environmental impacts of implementation of the

project and measures proposed to mitigate adverse impacts, whether the Environmental Impact Assessment (EIA) has been carried out.

10. Issues in land acquisition for the project: Whether the project involves any acquisition of land, whether such land acquisition could have been avoided, whether any diversion of forest lands is envisaged, whether other alternatives have been considered and examined.
11. Resettlement plan (in case involuntary resettlement is involved).
12. Responsibilities of different agencies for project implementation : This section should include the estimated period of implementation, organisational arrangements envisaged for implementation of each project component, participation of beneficiaries and other organizations in project implementation, arrangements for co-ordination such as Steering Committee, arrangements for maintenance of the project assets after the project is completed, etc.
13. PERT/CPM chart for project implementation.
14. Proposed 'zero date' of project commencement taking into account other approvals, if any, required before implementation can commence.
15. Identification and assessment of project risk and how these are proposed to be mitigated.
16. Parameters for project monitoring and post-evaluation, organizational arrangements for monitoring such as Project Monitoring Unit (PMU), midterm review, concurrent and/ or post-project evaluation.
17. Success criteria for the project : This should indicate the key performance indicator for measuring the success of the project in meeting its objectives.

5.16 While the above generic structure for the DPR would suffice the requirements of a typical project, the concerned Ministries may provide sector, specific additional information in the draft TOR for preparing the DPR.

6

Project Management, Facilitating Mechanisms, Capacity Building & Evaluation

EVEN after a project has been approved for being taken up, it still requires a large number of approvals/clearances for its implementation and commissioning. Annex-X shows the types of clearances required for project implementation. While most of these approvals would be required after investment approval, some like environmental clearance, techno-economic clearance, coal and fuel linkages, etc., are required for investment approval and would, therefore, be a part of upstream issues. Procedural simplification for various approvals including environmental clearance, is being covered in Part II of the report. Smooth and timely implementation of projects requires considerable handholding till their commissioning. This need is markedly higher in case of private projects where considerable delays and obstacles are met with during the course of getting these approvals from regulatory authorities.

6.2 At present the Foreign Investment Implementation Authority (FIIA) functions in Government of India for assisting the FDI approval holders in obtaining various approvals and resolving their operational difficulties. FIIA has been interacting periodically with the FDI approval holders and following up their difficulties for resolution with the concerned Administrative Ministries and State Governments. It has been observed that such an interactive mechanism is very effective and useful in articulation and resolution of difficulties and bridging the communication gap between regulatory authorities and foreign investors.

Strengthening Facilitation Mechanism

6.3 It is necessary that institutional facilitation arrangements are in position for projects other than FDI projects also. It is recommended that an Industrial Investment Facilitation Board (IIFB) be set up to follow up implementation of all projects with investment above Rs. 100 crores, both in the public and private sectors.

6.4 Secretary, Department of Industrial Policy & Promotion, Government of India, would be the Chairman of the IIFB with Secretaries of the Ministries of Law, Power, Labour, Small Scale Industries, Environment & Forests and Road Transport & Highways as members. IIFB could co-opt officials of concerned Ministries/ State Government, as needed depending upon the projects considered. IIFB would follow up the cases of delays in the grant of approvals in respect of projects with investments of Rs. 100 crores and above. In addition, any investor experiencing difficulties in obtaining approvals may also approach the Board irrespective of the investment limits. IIFB would also set up a sub-committee to prescribe time limits for grant of various non-statutory approvals in consultation with the concerned Administrative Ministries.

6.5 IIFB would refer cases involving excessive delays in approvals to a Group of Ministers to be constituted for consideration and resolution of such cases. The GoM could co-opt the Minister of the concerned Department.

6.6 IIFB should interact at least once every three months with the investors on the factors impending implementation of projects and scope for further simplification of procedures. While IIFB would continue to look after specific cases of foreign investment where project promoters encounter difficulties in implementation.

Facilitation Teams for Mega and Priority Projects

6.7 Facilitation Teams (FTs) may also be set up in the concerned Administrative Ministries for facilitating the implementation of projects with investments above Rs. 100 crores and for other priority projects/schemes of the Ministry. FTs would be looking after both public and private projects including their upstream approval requirements, viz., environmental, forest clearances, etc. The FTs under the Chairmanship of Secretary of the Administrative

Ministry will include the internal Financial Advisor, concerned Joint Secretary, representatives of Ministries/ State Government involved in regulatory clearances besides representatives of the Ministries of Environment & Forest for projects requiring environmental/forest clearances. FTs would guide the project from approval to implementation and identify bottlenecks and remove them. FTs will review the progress of implementation and ensure better co-ordination among the Ministries/State concerned with the implementation of the project.

Project Management

6.8 Management of the projects can be strengthened by a number of measures such as identification of a core team of personnel, strengthening co-ordination with other Ministries/ Agencies responsible for granting necessary approvals, developing project formulation and appraisal skills, outsourcing specialized skills where these are not available in the department or other organizations, etc. This would also require changes in the existing tendering, vendor rating systems as well as developing sectors specific skills in the audit and investigating agencies.

Project Monitoring

6.9 While concerned Administrative Ministries and the Facilitation Teams would monitor the implementation of their projects, MSPI would monitor the implementation of projects with proposed investment of Rs. 25 crores and above and prepare consolidated reports. In order to avoid repetition of effort in the Administrative Ministry and MSPI, it is necessary that the monitoring in the Ministries and MSPI be networked permitting on-line monitoring. The Monitoring unit in the MSPI would need to be strengthened for monitoring and concurrent evaluation of projects.

Role of Civil Services

6.10 Capacity building and creating a strong performance culture in the civil services would improve the efficiency and effectiveness of decision making in the Government. Besides highlighting the need for capacity building in the civil services, McKinsey's report has suggested introduction of the system of participative performance evaluation and performance linked compensation. While measures for capacity building for project formulation, appraisal, implementation and evaluation are being covered in the following recommendations on capacity building, making recommendations on the specific civil services reforms is not within the mandate of the Committee.

Capacity Building

6.11 Weaknesses in the project formulation and appraisal and lack of specialization in these areas have a great influence on the quality of projects. Besides causing delays at the stage of project formulation and appraisal itself, the project might need midcourse corrections resulting in both cost and time overruns and need for a fresh round of appraisal and approval.

6.12 The PAU as the specialized project appraisal body will essentially be created by strengthening the present PAMD in the Planning Commission by recruiting experts from appropriate fields. These qualified personnel would provide expert inputs to the PAU along with outside experts to be engaged for specific sectoral analysis on need basis. The existing staff in the PAMD would be playing a critical role by virtue of their vast experience of handling public projects. Such staff, despite their professional qualifications, would need orientation training for project formulation and appraisal. Multilateral Financial Institutions (MFIs) may be requested for meeting such training needs under their technical assistance programmes.

6.13 Members of the Facilitation Teams (FTs), to be set up in the Administrative Ministries to facilitate the implementation of projects, would need to be trained in modern project management techniques. IIMs and other Management Institutions of repute may be requested to conduct short-term courses for members of the FTs to provide a comprehensive orientation to the modern project management techniques and best practices in project management. Completion of such trainings may be made a pre-requisite to participation of the concerned officers in the Facilitation Teams.

6.14 In order to derive maximum benefits from the economic reforms and to attract greater investments, the work culture in Government also needs to be changed in line with the present day technologies and practices. Besides promoting specialisation, position-specific training for staff in key positions, skill upgradation, performance management and access to the best practices in project management would be necessary. Regular training of the staff at cutting edge level is necessary to bring about and sustain this attitudinal change.

6.15 Officials at and above the level of Section Officers must be imparted training in the use of computers on most commonly used application packages and any specific package related to the department.

6.16 The Committee recommends that the requirements of the DPRs and the criteria for meeting these requirements may be specified by the PAU as the expert body for appraisal of projects. It would thereafter, be up to the individual Ministries to internally assess the areas where capacity building is required and take appropriate steps for capacity building in these areas. While capacity-building initiatives would be an ongoing exercise, measures to address the deficiencies in the existing set up need to be completed in a time bound manner, say one year.

Greater Use of IT Tools

6.17 Despite heavy investments by Government in the basic information technology infrastructure, its benefits have not percolated down to the cutting edge level. While the use of basic information technology infrastructure like computers is far greater today than it was a few years back, its application in day to day operational issues varies from Department to Department and State to State. IT is being used extensively for intra department communication and sharing of information in some Departments but its use across Departments and for real time processing of information is still rather limited.

6.18 With the basic hardware and communication system in place, the work culture in the Governmental set-up needs to be aligned to information technology mode. This would require an integrated inter-Ministry as well as intra-Ministry effort. The operating systems and procedures as well as office procedures would need to be redesigned so that they become amenable to information technology tools. Electronic transmission and sharing of information, both within and across the Departments, online discussions and clarifications through e-groups, virtual online team rooms, etc., could be some of the immediate steps towards reducing delays in transmission of information and examination across Departments. This would also require standarsation of the data requirement among the Departments dealing with the subject.

6.19 It would be necessary that a roadmap for the use of IT in information sharing and decision-making be laid down. This would involve the role of each of the Administrative Ministries for the up-gradation of their internal systems and hardware, wherever required, and standardization of database. At the second stage interconnecting Ministries and State Governments and systems for online decision-making will be required.

Project Evaluation

6.20 Feedback from the completed projects, particularly on the deficiencies in project formulation, appraisal and difficulties in implementation is an extremely useful input for future projects. Institutional arrangements are, therefore, necessary for the post project evaluation of completed projects. In order that the evaluation is free from bias, it would be necessary that the evaluation be conducted by an appropriate independent agency, outside of the parties associated with the formulation, appraisal and implementation of the project including those responsible for various approvals/clearances.

6.21 It is recommended that post-project evaluation of selected projects, with investment of over Rs. 100 crores and projects from priority sectors to be identified by CCEA, is conducted by the MSPI. DPR must also cover the post-project evaluation methodologies.

6.22 A centralized evaluation unit for project evaluation may be set up in MSPI by redeploying the existing personnel assigned for similar functions in the Planning Commission, after giving them reorientation training on evaluation methodologies. Persons with necessary expertise may be co-opted from other Ministries/ Agencies avoiding any conflict of interest. Post project evaluation being a professional exercise would require skills similar to the project formulation stage and expert inputs would be required.

Since post-project evaluation would require services of experts, as much outsourcing to expert agencies as is possible should take place.

6.23 It is important that the findings of the post-evaluation studies are used at the time of formulation of new projects to avoid recurrence of the past deficiencies. It is, therefore, important that institutional arrangements are in place to utilize the experience of evaluation of past projects in new projects. It is recommended that the DPR for any project must invariably include a reference to the previous evaluation studies on the subject and how the lessons therefrom have been integrated in the project proposal.

Modifying the Role of Audit/Vigilance Agencies

6.24 McKinsey in their report have suggested modification in the role of audit and vigilance agencies to prevent overlap, setting up the Referral Boards before initiation of prosecution by investigating agencies and to reduce 'audit load' on implementing agencies. After detailed discussions on these recommendations, the Committee appreciates the need for a mechanism for prior review of cases before initiation of formal investigations. It feels that Independent Advisory Boards, comprising retired civil servants and persons of impeccable integrity, for tendering advice before prosecution by policing agencies would be extremely useful in case of Ministries like Defence, having major procurements. Similarly it is felt that an overall time frame must be specified within which the investigation needs to be closed. The Committee, however, feels that these issues need in-depth examination and possibly another group may look into these issues in consultation with concerned agencies.

6.25 The Committee agrees with McKinsey's recommendation on the need for strengthening the specific functional skills within the audit and vigilance agencies. Sector groups created by CVC for insurance and banking need to be extended to other activities and agencies. It is felt that such skills need not be sector specific but instead be process-specific such as procurement of goods, contracting for public works, etc. Where no material deficiencies with regard to prescribed processes are observed, a presumption that the implementation agency has acted correctly must follow. Sector-specific skills would be necessary for financial sector.

7

Project Implementation

Downstream Issues

EVEN after the investment approval in case of a public project and financial closure in case of private projects, numerous Acts and Regulations govern their implementation and subsequent operation. While the economic reforms initiated in the past decade have liberalized the entry restrictions and permitted easy entry into most sectors with virtual abolition of the 'license raj', procedural reforms for various approvals/permissions required have lagged behind. While some efforts have been made towards simplification of procedure under the relevant laws through delegation of greater authority, the very rationale behind continuing with the requirement of many of these approvals/ permissions in the present economic and technological scenario has not been addressed. Such bottlenecks continue to hamper implementation of not only private but also public projects. Some of the major impediments encountered in the implementation and operation of projects are:

- Multiplicity of laws governing the same or similar set of issues.
- Requirement of separate clearance/approval from same authority.
- Requirement of approvals from multiple authorities for an activity.
- Outdated procedural requirements lagging behind technological advancements.
- Too many points of contact between the project promoter and regulatory authorities.

- Lack of transparency in the administration of clearances/approvals.
- Large number of returns to be filed/registers to be maintained during the operational phase of the project.
- Little use of IT across departments and lack of communication among departments/agencies.

7.2 The Sub-Group on 'Simplification of procedures for Projects in the Private Sector' is separately looking into these issues in greater detail and recommendations on downstream issues will be presented separately in Part-II of the Committee's report. Some of the issues such as reforms in legislative framework, effective facilitation mechanism, etc., also influence the upstream issues as the statutory approval requirements also impact the project approval. Similarly, proactive facilitation mechanisms at the Central and State levels would help obtain necessary permissions quickly. This would also raise the confidence of the investors, which will be a critical factor influencing future investment decisions.

Reforms in Legislative Framework

7.3 Approval, implementation and operation of project are also subject to compliance with the requirements of numerous Acts administered by various offices of a number of Departments, both at state and Central level. While many approvals like Techno-Economic Clearances (TEC) for power projects, Environmental clearances, etc., require statutory procedural requirements to be complied with, in many other cases, legal requirements of registration and permissions, etc., are necessary.

7.4 Besides the complex procedural requirement for various approvals and delays involved in getting these approvals, separate laws regulating similar activities further complicate the regulatory environment. For instance separate laws regulate the payment of wages, bonus, gratuity and minimum wages. Similarly separate laws exist for various aspects related with the safety of the establishment, welfare of labour, protection of environment, etc.

7.5 Many legislation regulating the industries were enacted over 50-100 years ago reflecting the guiding spirit and objectives prevailing at that time. Even after a near total transformation in the economic and technological environment, the regulatory framework has not changed much. With the passage of time and growing concerns on issues related to environment, security, safety, public health, natural resource management, etc., the regulatory framework has become more complex with increased interface between the regulatory authorities and the entrepreneur.

7.6 The plethora of laws and regulations existing in India need recasting for streamlining of project clearances aiming at:

i. Reduction in number of clearances and interlinkages.
ii. Consolidation by avoiding overlap and obsolescence.
iii. Reduction in complexities and processing time.
iv. Amenability to IT tools, facilitate computerization and networking.
v. Transparency of procedures and grievance redressal mechanism.
vi. Ease of compliance and monitoring.

7.7 The extant laws regulating the industry need to be reviewed and consolidated. Laws that have become redundant and are no longer relevant in the liberalized economic scenario may also be considered for repealing. Consolidation of legislative framework would facilitate its compliance and implementation. The Sub-Group will be making detailed recommendations on these issues in Part-II of the Report.

Regulatory Environment for Projects

7.8 A large number of regulatory and reporting requirements such as periodic renewal of license/permission, elaborate and complex system of maintaining records and registers, inspections by number of regulatory bodies, filling returns, etc., also govern any project.

7.9 A study conducted in January 2002 by the CII-World Bank on 'Competitiveness in Indian Manufacturing' based on firm level survey has shown that in India about 16 per cent of management time is spent on dealing with Government officials on regulatory and administrative issues. This is a direct measure of the regulatory burden and compares poorly with Latin America & OECD Countries and China.

7.10 Responses from the firms have also shown that the frequency of visits by regulatory authorities varies according to the investment climate in the states with the states having better investment climate tending to impose lesser burden on the management than other states. The average number of visits per year by Government Officials has been as low as 5.5 in Tamil Nadu and 5.9 in Delhi compared to 13.4 in Andhra Pradesh, 14.9 in Punjab. Uttar Pradesh accounts for the highest average numbers of visits per year by government officials at 43.1 whereas the average for the 10 surveyed States is 11.5. While the average regulatory burden on SMEs is less than the large units, the regulatory burden per employee is over 14 times more in the SMEs compared to large units.

7.11 The study has also shown that the mean delay at customs while importing is 10.3 days in India compared to 7 days in Thailand and South Korea. The impact of such delays shows up prominently in sectors like textiles, which imports raw material and exports finished apparel. The average delay at customs is 11 days while importing and 4.5 days in exporting. The total delay of 15.5 days accounts for almost one third of the average production cycle of 45 days. This, besides creating attendant problems of working capital requirement, also adversely affects the competitiveness of the product in international markets.

Re-engineering of Regulatory Processes

7.12 In the above background, a fresh look into the entire regulatory processes related to various aspects of project clearances and its subsequent operation has become necessary. The extant regulatory processes would need re-engineering to cater to the present economic and business requirements.

7.13 In order to simplify the regulatory environment, re-engineering of the regulatory processes under different Acts and regulations would be necessary for :

a. Automatic permission upon filing of documents. (Traffic Light approach)

b. Automatic approval upon expiry of the period prescribed for approval. (Deemed Approval)

c. Approval from competent outside agencies authorized for granting such approvals. (Outsourcing Approval)

d. Approvals statutorily required.

7.14 The Finance Minister, in his 2002-2003 budget speech, has announced an incentive fund for Rs. 500 crores for incentivising initiatives of undertaking regulatory reforms at State level. Funds under some other special projects could also be linked with the re-engineering of the regulatory processes at the State level.

7.15 It is recommended that the proposed Industrial Investment Facilitation Board (IIFB) may also take up re-engineering of the regulatory processes and incentivising the states for undertaking regulatory reforms in consultation with the Ministries administering different legislations, in a time-bound manner. The IIFB may avail the services of experts as considered necessary.

Interface Between Project and Regulatory Authorities

7.16 By minimizing interaction between project and regulatory agencies for inspections, reporting and other regulatory requirements, the operating environment for projects will be conducive to growth. The number as well as frequency of inspections can be reduced by clubbing duties of different inspecting authorities and by sending representatives of concerned departments as a team. With advancement in technologies and experience gained by the industry, it should be possible to revise the frequency of various clearances, permissions or duration of licenses. The authority for periodic inspections can also be given to accredited certifying agencies that would be responsible for various statutory compliances by the units inspected. The requirement of maintaining registers and reporting can be rationalized with greater use of electronic filing. The Sub-Group is looking into these issues at greater length.

Transparency in Approval Process

7.17 Lack of precise information on the procedure and documentary requirements for various approvals, agencies responsible for granting such approvals, etc., also delays the approval and implementation of projects. The process of approvals from various Departments/Agencies of the Government needs to be made more transparent. By clearly spelling out the policy framework for investment approvals, procedural requirement, agency responsible for such approvals, and time frame for decision making on the department's website and making it public through other modes, the regulatory environment can be made more transparent. The Sub-Group is looking into these issues at greater length.

Initiatives by State Governments

7.18 Pro-active role of State Governments is necessary for removing impediments in the implementation of projects. While most legislation regulating the approval and regulatory framework are Central, their implementation is at the State level. Case studies commissioned by the PMO have also shown that over 70 per cent of the implementation issues actually pertain to the State Governments.

7.19 Many progressive States have of late shown strong commitment to removing impediments in the way of smooth implementation of projects by strengthening the Single Window Mechanism, introducing 'Single Composite Application Forms', simplifying the interface between regulatory authorities and the entrepreneur and by greater use of IT in the regulatory framework and reporting methods.

7.20 Single Window System would need to be established and strengthened at the State level in order to cut down delays in the grant of various approvals/permissions. This, along with the introduction of Single Composite Application Forms for necessary clearances, could remove most of the difficulties in getting necessary approvals. Single Window System would need to be sufficiently empowered to translate the single window concept into reality. Since different departments/agencies are responsible for the grant of approvals, the Single Window System to be effective should be able to monitor the grant of approval and intervene in case the concerned departments/agencies fail to grant these approvals within the prescribed time.

7.21 At the State level also facilitation mechanisms would be required where periodic interactions with the investors on any specific difficulties being encountered in the implementation of projects and need for simplification of procedures could be discussed.

7.22 The Government of Andhra Pradesh is considering extension of the Labour Laws (Exemption from Furnishing Returns and Maintenance of Registers by Certain Undertakings) Act, 1988 to establishments employing up to 100 persons and extending the self-certification scheme to ESI and EPF Acts and to provide for compounding fee for minor offences under Labour Laws. Self certification in labour laws now available only for infotech, biotech and export oriented units is proposed to be extended to all industrial units except in case of hazardous industries. Dissemination of information on such measures to other states for possible emulation of such good practices could be considered. The Sub-Group is looking into these issues at greater length, and its recommendations would be included in Part-II of the report.

8

Recommendations

THE recommendations of the Committee on upstream issues, i.e., from conceptualization of the project to investment approval are contained in this Part-I of the report. The recommendations on the downstream issues, i.e., from investment approval to implementation of the project and its operational phase would be presented in Part-II of the report to be presented separately.

8.1 Project Formulation and Appraisal

i. The project formulation stage must flag all issues, which are likely to affect its implementation later, such as land acquisition, environmental impact, diversion of forest land, social impact, etc. A generic structure of the feasibility report has been suggested at paragraph 5.15.

(Paragraph: 5.15)

ii. A Project Appraisal Unit (PAU) may be established in the Planning Commission as the primary appraising agency for all public projects with investment exceeding Rs.25 crores. PAU will also review the TORs for preparing the DPRs of projects. Projects requiring appraisal by PAU would need to get their TORs for preparing DPRs cleared by the PAU. In order to reduce the number of references to the Planning Commission/PAU, it is recommended that the feasibility report and draft TOR for the DPR may be sent simultaneously to the Planning Commission/PAU. The financial limit for appraisal of project by PAU may also be made co-terminus with plan period necessitating a review every five years.

(Paragraph: 4.7, 4.8, and 5.4)

iii. TORs for preparing DPR and also the DPR for projects of Navratna/Miniratna PSEs involving either budgetary support or contingent liability on the part of the Government or exceeding the approval authority of such Navratna/Miniratna PSEs should also be appraised by the PAU like other public projects.

(Paragraph: 4.21)

iv. The PAU would be set up by strengthening the existing PAMD staff in the Planning Commission with the addition of suitable experts, for the financial, economic, environmental appraisal of projects. The Unit may avail the services of specialists available with other departments. Services of outside experts may also be availed as may be required.

(Paragraph: 4.8)

v. Wherever the recommended time frame is not adhered to at any stage, the concerned organization should work out an appropriate trigger mechanism to take the matter to the next higher level for timely decision making.

(Paragraph: 5.13)

8.2 Project Approval

a. Increased Delegation of Powers to the Ministries

i. While the Committee was deliberating on this issue, the Department of Expenditure has, on February 18, 2002, issued orders enhancing the powers delegated to various levels for appraisal and approval of projects and revised estimates. The Committee feels that these limits would be appropriate for the time being but would need to be reviewed periodically. It is recommended that these powers might be made co-terminous with the plan period requiring a review every five years. Enhanced powers could be delegated to Ministries dealing with larger projects.

(Paragraph: 4.14 & 4.20)

ii. At present, all projects being posed to PIB are considered in the pre-PIB meetings. Since the feasibility report/DPR would be subjected to an expert appraisal where any inadequacies in the proposal would be addressed, the pre-PIB process may be dispensed with in respect of projects with the outlays up to Rs. 500 crores and such proposal may be considered by PIB directly after appraisal by PAU and inter-ministerial consultations.

(Paragraph: 5.8)

b. Powers of the PSEs

i. The Navratna and Miniratna PSEs already enjoy higher levels of delegation of powers and proposals of Navratna PSEs not requiring any budgetary support do not require the approval of the Government. There is no need for any change in the powers delegated to the Navratna/Miniratna PSEs. As stated at paragraph 8.1(iii), projects from such PSEs involving either budgetary support or contingent liability on the part of the Government or exceeding the approval authority of such Navratna/Miniratna PSEs should also be appraised by the PAU like other public projects.

(Paragraph: 4.21)

c. Acceptance Criteria

i. The Ministry of Finance, Department of Expenditure may formulate, in generic terms, a comprehensive set of project acceptance criteria for different categories of projects and get it approved by the CCEA. The technical appraisal by PAU and official review by the PIB will consider the project proposals with reference to these criteria.

(Paragraph: 5.14)

8.3 Project Evaluation

i. Independent evaluation of selected projects with expenditure of Rs. 100 crores and above and other priority projects must be carried out by MSPI to identify deficiencies in formulation, appraisal and implementation of projects.

(Paragraph: 6.21)

ii. Findings of the evaluation studies must be used at the time of formulating new projects and each feasibility report/DPR must specifically mention in a separate section whether results of previous evaluation of similar projects are available and how these have been used while formulating the project.

(Paragraph: 6.23)

8.4 Capacity Building

i. The requirements of DPR and the criteria for meeting these requirements may be specified by the PAU. It would, thereafter, be up to the individual Ministries to identify areas where capacity building is required.

(Paragraph: 6.16)

ii. Project formulation skills in the Ministries and PSEs need to be upgraded and specialization promoted. Personnel responsible for project formulation in Ministries/ PSEs would require orientation training. MFIs may be approached for assistance in training the personnel under their technical assistance programme. Services of experts for project formulation may be availed as considered necessary.

(Paragraph: 5.5)

iii. Existing staff in the PAMD with requisite qualifications would need to be given orientation for project appraisal. MFIs may be approached for assistance in training such personnel under their technical assistance programme.

(Paragraph: 6.12)

iv. Members of the Facilitation Teams (FTs) to be set up in the Administrative Ministries to facilitate implementation of projects would need to be trained in modern project management techniques and best practices in project management. IIMs and other Management Institutions of repute may be requested to conduct short-term courses for the members of the FTs to provide a comprehensive orientation to the modern project management.

(Paragraph: 6.13)

v. Existing Staff for project evaluation in the Planning Commission and the MSPI to be utilized in the Centralised Evaluation Unit in the MSPI would need to be given orientation training on evaluation methodologies.

(Paragraph: 6.22)

vi. Officials at and above the level of Section Officers must undergo compulsory usage based training in the use of computers on most commonly used application packages and any specific package related to the department.

(Paragraph: 6.15)

vii. Specific functional skills need to be developed within the audit and vigilance agencies. Such skills may be either process-oriented as in the case of procurement of goods, contracting of works and services, etc., or sector-specific as in financial sector.

(Paragraph: 6.25)

viii. While capacity-building initiatives would be an ongoing exercise, measures to address the deficiencies in the existing set up need to be completed in a time bound manner, say one year.

(Paragraph: 6.16)

8.5 Project Implementation-Downstream Issues

Once the public project receives the approval or a private project achieves financial closure, the requirement of other statutory and non-statutory approvals is similar. The Sub-Group on 'Simplification of Procedures for Projects in the Private Sector' is looking into the downstream issues for projects in private and public sectors. The Committee will be presenting its recommendations on the downstream issues separately as Part-II of the report. Some of the main issues, which also impact investment approval, are:

I. Procedural

i. Reforms in Legislative Framework: The extant laws regulating the industry need to be reviewed and consolidated. Laws that have become redundant and are no longer relevant in the liberalized economic scenario may also be considered for repealing. Consolidation of legislative framework would facilitate its compliance and implementation.

(Paragraph: 7.7)

ii. Re-engineering of the Regulatory Environment: A detailed analysis of the each approval requirement needs to be carried out for re-engineering of the regulatory process as under:

   a. Automatic permission upon filing of documents. (Traffic Light approach)

   b. Deemed approval upon expiry of the period prescribed for approval.

   c. Grant of approval by outside agencies authorized for granting such approvals.

   d. Approvals statutorily required.

   The 'Industrial Investment Facilitation Board', proposed for being set up as a central facilitation body, may take up this task to be completed in consultation with concerned Administrative Ministries in a time bound manner. Services of experts may also be availed as considered necessary.

(Paragraph: 7.13 & 7.15)

iii. Transparency in Administration of Approvals: A net-enabled information system should be developed to provide information on investment policies, sector wise approvals required from both Central and State Governments, the agency responsible for approval, its contact address, procedural requirements for the approvals, prescribed time frame, etc. To begin with such net-enabled information system could be developed by each department of the Central and State Government as part of their website. This could subsequently be interconnected across departments to provide all related information from one point.

(Paragraph: 7.17)

iv. Greater use of IT: Central Government as well as State Governments must take up e-governance measures by laying down a road map for the use of IT in information sharing and decision making by upgrading their internal systems and standardization of database and subsequently interconnecting Ministries and State Governments.

(Paragraph: 6.19)

II Institutional Arrangements

i. An Industrial Investment Facilitation Board (IIFB) may be established in the Department of Industrial Policy & Promotion, for follow-up of the grant of approvals by the Ministries and Agencies of Central Government. The Board would review the grant of approvals to projects with investments of more than Rs. 100 crores. In addition any investor experiencing difficulties in obtaining approvals may also approach the Board irrespective of the investment limits.

(Paragraph: 6.3 & 6.4)

ii. Secretary, Department of Industrial Policy & Promotion, Government of India, would be the Chairman of the IIFB with Secretaries of the Ministries of Law, Power, Labour, Small Scale Industries, Environment & Forest and Road Transport & Highways as members. IIFB could co-opt Officials of concerned Ministries/State Government, as needed depending upon the projects considered. IIFB would setup a sub-committee to prescribe time limits for the grant of various non-statutory approvals in consultation with the concerned Administrative Ministries.

(Paragraph: 6.4)

iii. IIFB would refer the cases involving excessive delays in approvals to a Group of Ministers to be constituted for consideration and resolution of such cases. The GoM could co-opt the Minister of the concerned Department.

(Paragraph: 6.5)

iv. IIFB should interact at least once every three months with the investors on the factors impeding implementation of projects and scope for further simplification of procedures. While the Board would be looking at specific difficulties faced by projects in private sector, the Foreign Investment

Implementation Authority (FIIA) would continue to look after specific cases of foreign investment where project promoters encounter delays in implementation.

(Paragraph: 6.6)

v. Facilitation Teams comprising representatives of Ministries involved in the regulatory clearances and the concerned State Government may be established for projects, both public and private, with outlays of Rs. 100 crores and above and other priority projects to be identified by CCEA, for coordination and follow up with different agencies for issue of necessary approvals.

(Paragraph: 6.7)

vi. Establishment of empowered Single Window Mechanism at the State level either under a special legislation or through alternate arrangements such as amendment in the Rules of Business, etc., needs consideration. The State Level Single Window Agency should be empowered to lay down the time frames for approvals, review the issue of approvals by concerned agencies/departments, accord approvals in case concerned departments/agencies do not grant these approvals in the predetermined time frame, and also give appropriate directions to the concerned agencies/departments.

(Paragraph: 7.20)

Annexures

ANNEX – I

No.212/9/2/2001-CA.IV
Government of India/Bharat Sarkar
Cabinet Secretariat/Mantrimandal Sachivalaya
Rashtrapati Bhavan

New Delhi-110004, the 24th September, 2001.

Office Memorandum

In pursuance of the deliberations of the meeting held on 4th September, 2001 under the Chairmanship of the Prime Minister, to discuss a fiscal stimulus initiative for the economy, it has been decided to set up a Committee to examine the extant procedures for investment approvals and implementation of projects and suggest measures to simplify and expedite the process for both public and private investment.

2. The Committee will comprise the following:

1. Shri V.N. Kaul, Secretary, Ministry of Petroleum and N.G. Convenor
2. Shri P.V. Jayakrishnan, Secretary, Ministry of Environment and Forests
3. Shri A.K. Basu, Secretary, Ministry of Power
4. Shri C.M. Vasudev, Secretary, Department of Expenditure
5. Shri Shyamal Ghosh, Secretary, Department of Telecommunication
6. Shri Vinod Vaish, Secretary, Ministry of Labour

7. Shri Pardip Baijal, Secretary, Department of Disinvestment
8. Shri V. Govindarajan, Secretary, Department of IPP
9. Dr. Rakesh Mohan, Adviser to FM and Chief Economic Adviser, DEA
10. Shri K.V. Irniraya, Secretary, M/o Statistics & Programme Implementation
11. Dr. Pradipto Ghosh, Additional Secretary, PMO
12. Shri N.S. Sisodia, Additional Secretary, Cabinet Secretariat-Member Secretary

3. While the above Committee will suggest measures to simplify the procedures, a Sub-Group headed by Secretary, IPP will make specific suggestions regarding effecting simplification to procedures relating to private investment. These suggestion would be incorporated in the main report.

4. The Committee will be serviced by the M/o Statistics & Programme Implementation.

5. The Committee will submit its report by 31st January 2002.

Sd/-

(C.K. Mishra)
Director
Tel. No. 379-2204

ANNEX – I-A

No.212/9/2/2001-CA.IV
Government of India/Bharat Sarkar
Cabinet Secretariat/Mantrimandal Sachivalaya
Rashtrapati Bhavan

New Delhi the 19th March, 2002.

Office Memorandum

Reference this Secretariat OM of even number dated the 24th September 2001 regarding setting up a Committee to examine the extant procedures for investment approvals and implementation of projects and suggest measures to simplify and expedite the process for both public and private investment.

2. Shri V. Govindarajan, Secretary, D/ Industrial Policy & Promotion, will be the Convenor of the said Committee, with immediate effect in place of Shri V. N. Kaul, Secretary, Ministry of Petroleum & Natural Gas, who has been appointed as Comptroller and Auditor General of India.

3. Other terms and conditions of the Committee remain unchanged.

Sd./-
(Ravi Mittal)
Director
Tel. No. 379-2204

To

All members of the Committee.
All Ministries/Departments.

Copy for information to:

(i) Shri V. N. Kaul, C&AG of India.
(ii) Shri Brajesh Mishra, Principal Secretary to the Prime Minister.

Sd./-
(Ravi Mittal)
Director
Tel. No. 379-2204

ANNEX – II

No. 5/5/2001-FIIA
Government of India
Ministry of Commerce & Industry
Department of Industrial Policy & Promotion
Udyog Bhavan, New Delhi.

Dated, the 9th October, 2001.

Office Memorandum

In pursuance of the Cabinet Secretariat's O.M. No. 212/9/2/2001-CA.IV dated 24th Sept. 2001 regarding fiscal stimulus initiative for the economy, it has been decided to set up a Sub-Group headed by Secretary, Industrial Policy & Promotion to make specific suggestions regarding effecting simplification of procedures relating to private investment.

2. The Sub-Group will comprise the following :–

a	Secretary, Department of Industrial Policy & Promotion	**Chairman**
b	Secretary, Department of Disinvestment	Member
c	Secretary, Ministry of Power (To be represented by Special Secretary)	Member
d	Chief Economic Adviser, Department of Economic Affairs	Member
e	Additional Secretary, Ministry of Statistics & Programme Implementation	Member

3. The Sub-Group may invite specifically any other Department depending on requirement.

4. The Sub-Group will submit its report by the end of January 2002.

Sd/-

(Umesh Kumar)
Director
Tel. No. 3016951.

To

1. All members of the Committee
2. Principal Secretary to the PMO
3. Shri C.K. Mishra, Director, Cabinet Secretariat, Rashtrapati Bhavan.
4. JS (MSS)

Sd/-

(Umesh Kumar)

ANNEX – III

EXECUTIVE SUMMARY OF MCKINSEY'S REPORT

The Government of India (including the central PSUs) invests over Rs. 130,000 crores a year in projects and schemes spanning infrastructure, industry and social development. The potential impact of these investments on stimulating the economy and promoting development is tremendous. However, the effectiveness of these investments is less than desired, as poor project formulation, delays in approval and no clear pinpointing of responsibility mar the process. Therefore, a need was felt at the highest level to recast the government's investment approvals and regulations framework to ensure that the scarce resources are deployed most effectively. A Committee of Secretaries, chaired by Shri V. N. Kaul, was set up with this objective.

McKinsey & Company has been working with the Committee of Secretaries, in association with the Prime Minister's Office and the Cabinet Secretariat over the last 12 weeks, to identify issues affecting the government investment approvals mechanism and to make recommendations on how these could be resolved. In this effort, we focused on the upstream process, i.e., from the conceptualisation of projects to the investment approval. We conducted the project in three phases of roughly 4 weeks each, i.e., Phase 1: Identifying the bottlenecks in the approvals process; Phase 2: Defining the broad solution space; and Phase 3: Detailing the changes needed in the approvals mechanism.

The team's objective was to bring three diverse perspectives to bear-the collective experience of the government, leanings from other governments, and relevant practices from the private sector. We interacted extensively with all relevant ministries and agencies in the government to understand the issues, and examined existing data, reports and studies related to investment approvals. We also obtained the perspectives of members of the Committee of Secretaries, special advisors to the government and independent experts. Second, we developed an in-depth understanding of how investment decision are taken in countries such as the UK, Singapore, New Zealand, Norway and the US, which have undertaken comprehensive administrative reforms. Finally, we drew in the experiences of large private sector corporations, particularly around how the best companies appraise and manage projects, how they incentivise their organizations for performance, how they manage and use knowledge effectively, and what good governance and review practices they employ.

The remainder of this executive summary outlines our key findings on bottlenecks in the approvals process, our recommendations and what it will take to implement the required changes.

Bottlenecks in the Approvals Process

The diagnostic revealed several recent efforts to streamline investment approvals. These include setting deadlines for various stages of the appraisal and approval process; creating the Ministry of Programme Implementation to monitor projects; installing performance reviews at the ministry level; creating empowered bodies for telecom and highways; delegating additional financial powers to Navratnas, Miniratnas and Ministries; and setting up task forces to streamline procedures for public, private and foreign investment.

Despite the improvements resulting from these efforts, the upstream approvals process for government schemes and projects continues to be characterised by delays across the board and poor quality project formulation and appraisal. This is because the root causes of delays and poor quality decisions lie deeper. The underlying causes we have identified can be categorised into three types-process-related issues, organisational constraints and regulatory issues. The diagnostic clearly revealed that while the approval process is a constraint, the real issues lie deeper- in the basic organization structure and performance management systems adopted by the government.

> **The process-related issues** include an overly centralized process with too many projects going through the EFC/PIB and CCEA, responsibility fragmented across 5-8 agencies for a single project and inadequate use of information technology (even basic facilities like e-mail). In addition, there is an absence of professional project management techniques across every stage of the project,

from formulation through appraisal, approval implementation and commissioning.

On the organisational front, government decision-making is plagued by a weak performance culture given that target-setting and performance evaluation for individuals and at the ministry level is indifferent. In addition, there is a lack of critical skills in financial and project appraisal, and IT. Finally, the use of knowledge in decision-making is inadequate.

Finally, on the regulatory front, the fear of audit has created a 'play-it-safe' culture resulting in delayed or sub-optimal decision-making.

It is also clear that several other governments and the private sector have made rapid strides in improving their investment approval and execution mechanisms. These have been contrasted without situation and, where relevant, lessons have been drawn.

The detailed findings from the diagnostic are presented in Chapter 1.

Recommendations

To address the issues outlined above, we have six broad recommendations, outlined below. These are explained in greater detail in Chapter 2.

1. **Increase delegation to ministries and ensure greater accountability.** This would include: (a) creating empowered and accountable Commissions for 3-5 high-priority sectors with large project investments (on the lines of the Telecom Commission. NHAI and Space Commission); (b) for other ministries, increasing delegation to Rs. 200 crore with the approval of the Finance Minister; (c) creating cross-ministry project facilitation teams for critical projects above Rs. 500 crores; and (d) instituting clear target-setting and review mechanisms within ministries.
2. **Create a nodal project appraisal and review unit,** recognising the need for specialised project management skills and the difficulty associated with creating these skills across all ministries. In addition to appraisal, this

nodal agency would undertake stage-gate reviews of large projects with the objective of facilitating and de-bottlenecking. The agency should consist of a small operating core supported by a large network of external experts, through which it will conduct reviews and on-site assessments. The agency should be located at the Planning Commission, and should be formed by merging and strengthening the PAMD and the MoPI.

3. **Create a high-level task force to improve knowledge management and use of information technology** with the objectives of (a) creating knowledge banks of experts, analytical techniques, project experiences and sector trends, to help formulate projects and improve the quality of appraisal and review; and (b) increasing the use of basic information technology such as e-mail, virtual team rooms, public calendars, etc., in communicating information and in coordination. This should be a top-down initiative including external industry experts, and operating through decentralised working teams in areas such as e-governance, knowledge management, IT training and hardware/software up gradation.

4. **Upgrade skills through a combination of internal up skilling and outsourcing expertise.** This would include (a) strengthening financial and project appraisal skills in the project appraisal and review unit, Ministry of Finance and among Ministry Financial Advisors, by creating a core-financial cadre, enforcing qualification guidelines, instituting mandatory training programmes, and secondments from outside the government; (b) outsourcing specialist technical skills for appraisal and review; (c) building familiarity and usage amongst; (c) servants with basic IT tools through regular mandatory training and (d) establishing mechanisms for bringing in external best practices into the government on a regular basis.

5. **Modify the role of audit agencies for greater effectiveness.** This would involve : (a) clarifying the roles of the audit and vigilance agencies to avoid overlap; (b) implementing the concept of independent referral boards comprising carefully chosen individuals with sector

expertise and impeccable integrity to provide advice before investigations proceed for prosecution; (c) creating/ strengthening the audit teams for key sectors, especially those that are technically complex, such as telecom and petroleum; (d) limiting the total timeframe within which an investigation needs to be closed; and (e) undertaking a set of initiatives at PSUs to ensure better expenditure decisions and interface with the audit agencies.

6. **Strengthen the performance management system for the civil services** by (a) ensuring clarity of objectives and targets for all officers (directors and above); (b) modifying the evaluation process from a confidential, one-way system to a development and target-oriented one-introducing mandatory annual performance feedback discussions, defining guidelines to moderate performance ratings, and redesigning the ACR form to provide description of performance at various rating levels; (c) linking performance with consequences, by instituting interviews and peer and upward feedback for key promotions (to JS, AS, Secretary), ensuring consistent non-performers are weeded out, and introducing 10 per cent variable compensation; and (d) undertaking more formal career management and succession planning for all officers of the rank of JS and above, by strengthening the Civil Services Board and ensuring coordination across cadres through a cell in the Cabinet Secretariat.

In addition to making recommendations at the overall level, we have also applied these suggestions to three ministers – Petroleum & Natural Gas, Power and Rural Development – with the aim of testing them and making them as specific as possible. These detailed recommendations are laid out in the Appendices.

Implementation

For each of the six reform themes outlined above, we have defined specific actions that need to be taken for change to occur. Overall, it is essential that this effort be approached with the mindset of a long-term change programme, including a visible, high-powered implementation agency and consultations with stakeholders, rather than a specific set of near-term decisions implemented solely at the discretion of individual ministries.

The recommendations should be implemented in three phases: 0-6 months, 6-12 months and 12-24 months. The individual recommendations have been sequenced as below:

1. Phase 1 (0-6 months) includes the changes the government can implement in the near term, such as increasing the delegation limits of ministries (with FM approval) to Rs. 200 crores, creating the nodal agency for project appraisal and review, instituting facilitation teams for large projects and undertaking targeted skill building and training. Implementing these changes will lead to a reduction in delays in the approvals process within a couple of months.

2. Phase 2 (6-12 months) includes reforms that need further detailing and will take longer to implement, but will build the foundation for long-term health. Initiatives that would be undertaken in this phase include the creation of Commissions in Power and selected other sectors, the introduction of expert reviews by the nodal agency, implementation of skill building strategies and the creation and use of knowledge databases.

3. Phase 3 (12-24 months) encompasses reforms that will result in fundamental changes in the way the government functions. These reforms include long-term capability building, new systems of managing performance and careers within the civil services, changes in the functioning of the audit agencies and a revamp of the government budgeting processes.

Implementation responsibility should lie with a high-powered group of Secretaries with strong involvement of the Cabinet Secretariat and the Prime Minister's Office. Led by a senior secretary or even the Cabinet secretary himself, this body should be supported by a small, handpicked programme office with an independent budget, to oversee the various working groups and task forces required.

A detailed discussion on the sequencing of individual recommendations and the nature of implementation responsibility is provided in Chapter 3.

***

The Government stands at the threshold of major change. The need for change has been recognised, and a willingness to do things differently has begun to percolate through the various ministries and agencies. Decisive, top-down action at this time could significantly change the speed, quality and effectiveness of public investments.

ANNEX – IV

LIST OF REFERENCES

S.No.	*Subject*	*Agency*
1	First draft of the report of the Sub-Group on Simplification of procedures of projects in Private Sector	Sub-Group under the Convenorship of Secretary (IPP), Department of Industrial Policy and Promotion with Secretary Ministry of Disinvestment, Advisor to Finance Minister, Special Secretary, Ministry of Power and Additional Secretary, Ministry of Statistics and Programme Implementation as other members
2	Interim Report of 'Study on System of Clearances required for various types of projects in Public and Private Sector.'	The study was conducted by Ministry of Statistics and Programme Implementation (Project Monitoring Division) with the assistance of Advance Design and Engineering Limited, New Delhi.
3	Report on 'Strengthening Investment Approval Mechanism'	Study commissioned with M/s. McKinsey & Company by Ministry of Petroleum and Natural Gas on the recommendation of the COS.
4	Comments of the Ministry of Power with specific recommendations.	Ministry of Power's comments have been received in response to the draft recommendations made to the Sub-Group under the convenorship Secretary (IPP).
5	Comments on the draft report of the Sub-Group on simplification of procedures in private sector.	Adviser to the Finance Minister Department of Economic Affairs.
6	Base Paper on clearance of projects-a note on procedures and approach.	Ministry of Environment and Forests.
7	Base Paper on simplification of procedures of private investment.	Department of Industrial Policy & Promotion

(Contd...)

(...Contd...)

8	Report on simplification of procedures governing industries.	Administrative Staff College of India, Hyderabad submitted to Department of Industrial Policy & Promotion.
9	Study by NCAER (July, 99) on Foreign Direct Investment in India- Problems and prospects.	Department of IPP
10	Comments on various Ministries on the note circulated by Ministry of Environment on clearance of projects.	Ministry of Environment and Forest.
11	Comments of Ministry of Shipping on procedures and evolving procedures for speedy clearances.	Ministry of Shipping
12	Base Paper on simplification of procedures for investment approval and implementation	Department of Telecommunication, Economic Research Unit.
13	A note for COS regarding clearance of projects. Investment/expenditure and guidelines for appraisal and approval informing fresh financial limits of Plan Scheme/Project.	Department of Expenditure, Plan Finance (O.M No. 1(3)/PF. II/2001 dated 18th February.)
14	Synthesis study carried out on 13 specific projects	Prime Minister's Office.
15	Studies in progress	It has been informed by the Ministry of Environment and Forest that a special study is in progress on Environmental clearance by M/s. McKinsey & Company
16	World Bank Procedures on Project Approval	World Bank
17	Project Approval Procedures	Planning Commission of India
18	Study on 'Competitiveness in Indian Manufacturing' Suggestions from Public Enterprises	CII-World Bank
19.	Environment Clearance related issues.	GAIL
20.	Suggestions about land acquisitions	HPC, IOC, BPC

ANNEX – V

TIME LIMITS FOR APPRAISAL OF PROJECTS/SCHEMES

(i)	Circulation of the Feasibility Report by the Ministries after receiving it from the PSEs to various appraisal agencies (Any examination within the Ministry could be done simultaneously while the Reports are examined by the Appraisal Agencies).	1 week
(ii)	Pre-PIB meeting to be held thereafter.	6 weeks
(iii)	Issue of minutes of the Pre-PIB meeting by Financial Adviser of the concerned Ministry.	1 week
(iv)	Circulation of the PIB Memo.	4 weeks
(v)	Appraisal Note of the Project Appraisal Division of the Planning Commission (in case further clarifications are required to be furnished by the Ministries to the PAMD, they should do it within the stipulated date so that the time limit is adhered to)	4 weeks
(vi)	Submission of PIB Note to the PIB Secretariat in the Department of Expenditure after the receipt of the PAMD Note.	1 week
(vii)	PIB Meeting to consider the proposal thereafter.	2 weeks
(viii)	Issue of the minutes of PIB	1 week

Note: Same time limits are to be followed for EFC cases (except state of Pre-PIB consideration).

ANNEX – VI

F. No. 1(3)/PF II/2001
Government of India
Ministry of Finance
Department of Expenditure
(Plan Finance-II Division)

New Delhi, the 18th February, 2002

OFFICE MEMORANDUM

Subject : Public Investment Expenditure-Guidelines for Appraisal and Approval.

A need has been felt to prioritise the projects/schemes and take up only such projects/schemes, which are financially and economically viable and have higher returns. There is also a need to avoid thin spreading of resources and multiplicity of schemes with similar objectives. Therefore, it is necessary to strengthen decision-making process for investments. At the same time, the process should be simple and quick so that the challenges of the completive economic environment can be met effectively. These considerations will require optimum level of delegation in the system for appraisal and approval of the proposals. Accordingly, the following guidelines/financial limits for appraisal and approval of public investment/expenditure are being prescribed.

2. Appraisal of Plan Schemes Projects :-

	Financial limits of Plan scheme/project	*Appraisal Forum*
(a)	Up to Rs. 5.00 crores	Ministry/Department concerned, in normal course.
(b)	Above Rs. 5.00 crores but less than Rs. 25 crores	Standing Finance Committee of the Department concerned under the Chairmanship of Secretary with Financial Adviser and Joint Secretary/ Director of the concerned

(Contd...)

(...Contd...)

		Division as members with provision for inviting representatives of the Planning Commission, D/o Expenditure and any other Department that Secretary or Financial Adviser may suggest.
(c)	Rs. 25 crores and above but less than Rs. 100 crores	Departmental Expenditure Finance Committee (EFC). Departmental EFC will be chaired by Secretary of the Administrative Department. It will include the Financial Adviser, as the Member Secretary, and the representatives of the Planning Commission and D/o. Expendi ture as members.
(d)	Rs. 100 crores and above but less than Rs. 200 crores	Main Expenditure Finance Committee (EFC). Main EFC will consist of Secretary (Expenditure) who will chair the meeting, Secretary (Planning Commission) and Secretary of the Administrative Department. FA will be the Secretary of this EFC.
(e)	Rs. 200 crores and beyond	Public Investment Board (PIB)/ Main EFC chaired by Secretary (Expenditure). Projects/schemes where financial returns are quantifiable will be considered by PIB, others by the EFC.

(i) It is clarified that SFC/EFC/PIB will be the appraisal forum for any scheme/project. Their recommendations will require approval of competent authority as indicated in para 3 below.

(ii) In respect of Scientific Ministries/Departments, the appraisal forum (EFC) will continue to be chaired by the concerned Administrative Secretary irrespective of the outlay.

(iii) Navratna and Miniratna PSU's have enhanced powers for taking investment decisions as per guidelines issued by the Department of Public Enterprises. This delegation will be continued.

(iv) For schemes/projects involving setting up of new Autonomous Organizations, EFC will be chaired by Secretary (Expenditure) irrespective of their outlays or nature of the Ministry/Department.

(v) Specific approval of Department of Expenditure for creation of new posts in relaxation of standing economy orders will be necessary irrespective of the recommendations of EFC/PIB.

(vi) At present all projects being posed to PIB are considered in the pre-PIB meeting. Pre-PIB process in respect of projects with outlay up to Rs. 500 crores has been dispensed with and the proposals will be considered by PIB directly.

3. *Authority for Approval*

(a) Original Cost Estimates

Project/scheme Outlay	*Approval Authority*
Less than Rs. 50 crores	Minister in-charge of Administrative Ministry.
Rs. 50 crores and above but less than Rs. 100 crores	Minister of Administrative Ministry and the Finance Minister
Rs.100 crores and above	Cabinet/CCEA
Proposals for new autonomous organizations irrespective of outlay	Cabinet/CCEA

(b) Revised Cost Estimates:

(b) (1) RCE cases less than Rs. 100 crores:

(i) RCE cases with outlay of less than Rs. 100 crores arising due to change in statutory levies, exchange rate variations and price escalation within the approved project time cycle and the cases involving further cost increase up to

20 per cent can be approved by the authority as per para 3(a) above in consultation with the Planning Commission.

(ii) RCE cases involving increase of more than 20 per cent after excluding the increase due to change in statutory levies, exchange rate variations and price escalation within the approved project time cycle will require appraisal at the forum as per para 2 above and approval as per para 3(a) above.

(b) (2) RCE cases of Rs. 100 crores and above:

(i) Revised Cost Estimates (RCE), which arises entirely due to change in statutory levies, exchange rate variations and price escalation within the originally approved project time cycle will be approved by the administrative Ministry/Department concerned in consultation with the Planning Commission.

(ii) The first RCE, which is up to 10 per cent of the originally approved cost estimates (after excluding the increase within the originally approved project time cycle due to three factors mentioned in (i) above) will be approved by the Administrative Ministry in consultation with the Planning Commission.

(iii) First RCE, which exceeds 10 per cent but are up to 20 per cent of the originally approved cost estimates (after excluding increase within originally approved project time cycle due to three factors mentioned in (i) above) shall be appraised by the Planning Commission and will be approved by the Administrative Minister and the Finance Minister.

(iv) First RCE which exceeds 20 per cent of the originally approved cost estimates (after excluding increase within originally approved project time cycle due to three factors mentioned (i) above) due to reasons such as time overrun, change in scope, under-estimation, etc., shall be posed to EFC/PIB for appraisal and thereafter to CCEA for approval.

(v) Second or subsequent RCE then 5 per cent of the latest approved cost (first or previous RCE) (after excluding increase due to changes in statutory levies, exchanged rate variation and price escalation within the existing approved project time cycle) will be appraised by the Planning Commission and decided with the approval of Administrative Minister.

(vi) Second or subsequent RCE involving increase of 5 per cent or more of the latest approved cost (first or previous RCE) (after excluding increase due to changes in statutory levies, exchanged rate variation and price escalation within the approved project time cycle) will require appraised by EFC/PIB and approval of the CCEA.

(b) (3): Criterion for appraisal forum and level of authority for approval of RCE will be cost overrun and not time overrun.

(b) (4): The existing procedure prescribes that RCE cases should be decided by the same authority, which had approved the original proposal notwithstanding any subsequent delegation of powers. This applies to RCE cases of the Ministries as well as Navratna and Miniratna CPSUs also even though they have powers, subject to certain conditions, to decide new investments. It is now decided that powers for deciding RCE cases are delegated to the authorities as per powers for fresh approvals.

(b) (5): Where the revised/firmed up cost estimates of scheme/ project exceeds the limit of competent authority who approved the original cost of the scheme, the approval of higher competent authority will be obtained.

(b) (6): While processing the RCE cases the contents of Planning Commission's D.O. No. O-14015/2/98-PAMD dated 19.8.1998 regarding consideration of cost & time overruns and fixation of responsibility by the Standing Committee may be kept in mind.

4. Expenditure on Pre-investment Activities etc.

(a) The delegation of powers for sanctioning pre-investment activity like preparation of Detailed Feasibility/Project Reports will be as follows :

Expenditure/Financial Limit	*Appraisal/approval authority*
Up to Rs. 2.00 crores for preparation of DFR and pre-investment activities (including detailed study for preparation of Feasibility Report but excluding land acquisition/infrastructure facilities) subject to availability of budget/plan funds.	Secretary, Ministry/ Department concerned.
Proposals of PSU up to Rs. 10 crores for preparation of DFR and pre-investment activities excluding land acquisition/infrastructure facilities, if not funded from Budget and PSU is profit making.	Ministry/ Department concerned.
All other cases	Appraisal by Committee of PIB (CPIB), and approval by the authority as per para 3(a) above.

(b) For projects of Ministries of Coal and Road Transport & Highways expenditure on pre-investment activities beyond Rs. 20 crores only will require consideration by Committee of PIB.

(c) The delegation of powers of Ministry of Power to sanction estimates for pre-construction works and for development of infrastructure facilities in respect of Hydro Electric Project will be governed by the Ministry of Power letter No. 16/31/2000-D.O. (NHPC) dated 8.6.2001.

5. *Costing of the Project/Scheme :-*

(a) The cost of the proposal will be inclusive of all components under which expenditure is required to be incurred (like revenue, capital and loans etc.). At present, the costing of the project is done at constant prices. It has now been decided to make it obligatory for the Department to compute the project cost both on constant prices and completion cost basis so that IRR/ERR can be calculated for both scenarios.

(b) The completion cost may be worked out by taking into account the average rate of inflation in the following manner:-

(i) Labour components of the project cost may be updated using the average (of 12 months) of consumer price index for industrial workers.

(ii) For all other components of cost, except labour, the average (of 12 months) of wholesale price index for all commodities may be used.

6. The delegation of financial powers contained in this OM will be exercised only where necessary/requisite funds are available in the Annual Plan and the Five Year Plan outlay as per phasing of the project/scheme. The powers will further continue to be governed by procedural and other instructions issued by Government from time to time like general economy instructions etc. This order supersedes this Department's OM No. 1(5)-PF II/96 dated 6.8.1997. This order will not supersede any specific relaxation granted to a Ministry/Department by the Cabinet/CCEA.

This order will be effective from the date of issue.

This has the approval of the Finance Minister.

Sd/-

(R. N. Choubey)
Joint Secretary (PF II)

Secretaries of all Ministries/Departments
FA's of all the Ministries/Departments

Copy to

1. Adviser, PAMD, Planning Commission
2. Cabinet Secretariat (Shri N. S. Sisodia, Addl Secy.)
3. Prime Minister's Office

ANNEX-VII

PRESENT PROJECT CYCLE

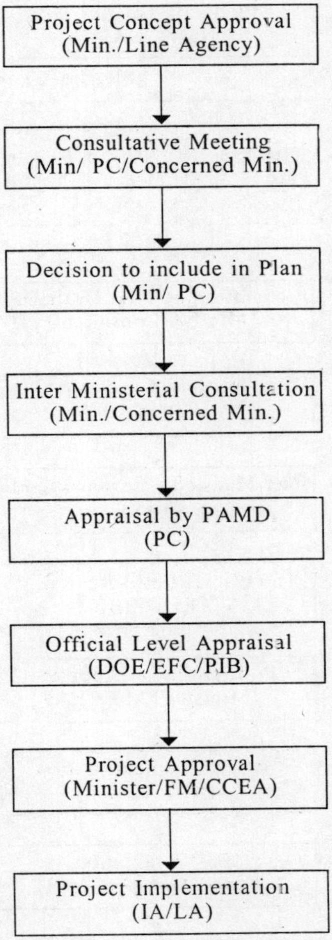

ANNEX – VIII

RECOMMENDED PROJECT CYCLE

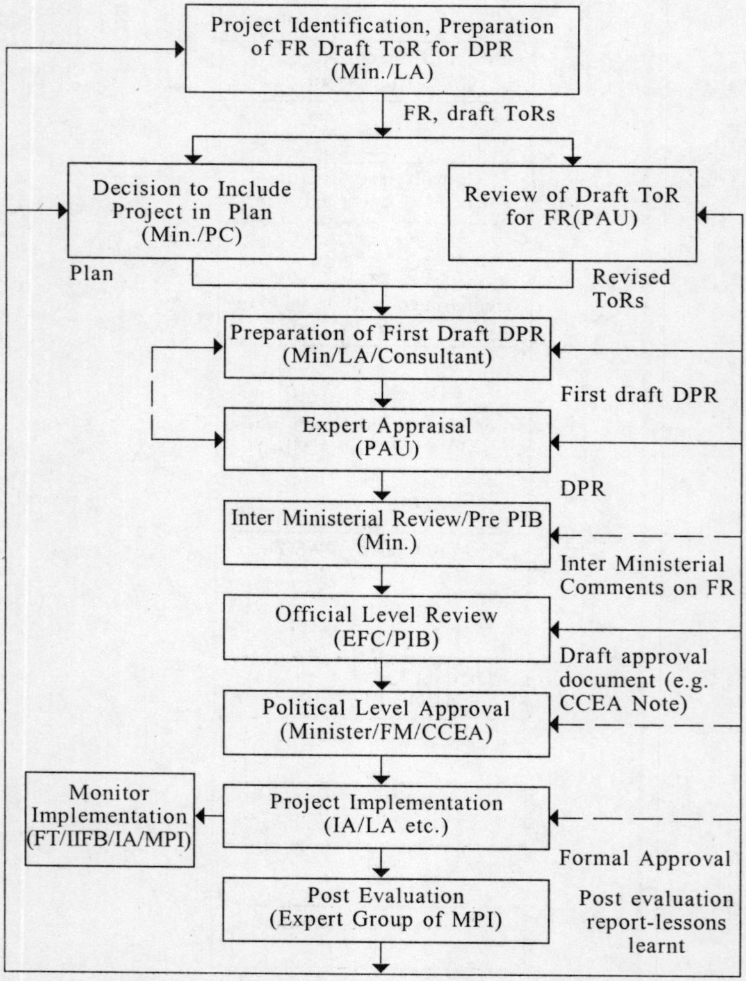

ANNEX – IX

TIME FRAME FOR APPRAISAL OF PROJECTS/ SCHEMES UNDER RECOMMENDED PROJECT CYCLE

(i)	Circulation of the draft Detailed Project Report (DPR) to PAU	1 week
(ii)	Appraisal of draft DPR by the PAU	4 weeks
(iii)	Revision of the DPR based on appraisal by PAU	3 weeks
(iv)	Send copy of DPR to the concerned Ministries for comments	2 weeks
(v)	Submission of PIB Note to the PIB Secretariat in the Department of Expenditure.	1 week
(vi)	PIB Meeting to consider the proposal thereafter	4 weeks
(vii)	Issue of the minutes of PIB	1 week

ANNEX – X

DOWNSTREAM APPROVAL REQUIREMENTS

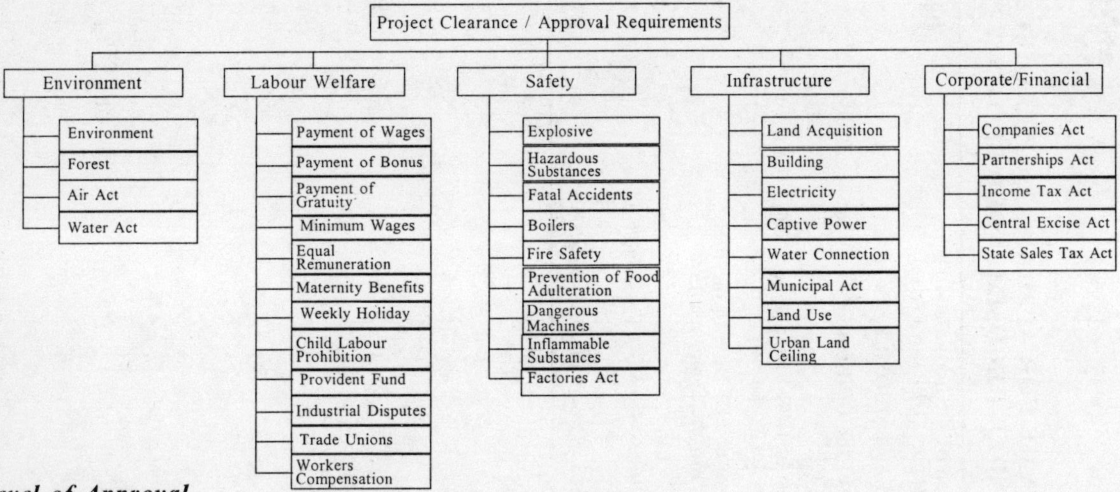

Level of Approval

Environmental:	From Central and State Government
Labour welfare:	From State Government
Safety:	Explosives from Central Government, others from State Government
Infrastructure:	From State Government and Local bodies
Corporate & Financial :	From Central Government, State Sales Tax from State Government

Report on Reforming Investment Approval and Implementation Procedures

Part – II

Downstream Issues — Implementation and Operation

(November 2002)

Contents

Part – II

Downstream Issues – Implementation and Operation, November 2002

LIST OF ANNEXES

Foreword

THE Committee, set up by the Cabinet Secretariat to examine extant procedures for investment approvals and implementation of projects and suggest measures to simplify and expedite the process of both public and private projects, presented Part-I of its report, containing recommendations on the upstream issues, i.e., from the stage of conceptualization of project till investment approval, in May 2002.

A Sub-Group of the Committee specifically looked into various issues relating to investment in schemes and projects in the private sector. The Sub-Group in a number of interactive sessions deliberated at length the issues. The Sub-Group also had the benefit of some of the previous reports and studies on this subject. A synthesis study was also commissioned with A. T. KEARNEY on the factors impeding the implementation of projects.

Part-II of the report contains recommendations on the downstream issues i.e. from the stage of investment approval to the implementation of projects and their operational phase.

The Committee acknowledges the invaluable contribution of Shri S. Prabhakaran and Dr. Rakesh Mohan, who during their tenure as Members of the Sub-Group, contributed significantly to its deliberations and in concretizing many of the recommendations.

New Delhi
November 2002

Sd/-

Pradip Baijal

V. Govindarajan
(Convenor)

N.S. Sisodia

K.K. Jaswal

R. Pooranlingam

Dr. Prodipto Ghosh

Executive Summary

PART-II of Committee's report covers recommendations on downstream issues from the stage of investment approval till implementation of project and its operation. Part-I of the report, containing recommendations on the upstream issues, i.e., from the stage of conceptualization of project to investment approval, was presented on 20.5.2002.

2. Various studies have shown that complexities in the approvals required for primary resources like land, power, etc., multiplicity of approvals, disproportionate level of details sought with applications are among the major difficulties in the implementation of projects. Many approvals also do not seem to serve any public interest. Recent studies have shown that, while handling of approvals at Central level has registered a marked improvement, state level handling of approvals and reducing ground level hassles have emerged as important issues.

Re-engineering of Regulatory Processes

3. Re-engineering of regulatory processes prescribed under various legislations, regulations, etc., is necessary to simplify the procedures for grant of approvals, reduce delays & ground level hassles and simplify the regulation of projects during their operational phase. Re-engineering groups may be set up in the Ministries for detailed examination of each approval requirement under different Acts, Rules and Regulations and re-engineering of the regulatory process. As many approvals as are possible should be placed on self-regulation, i.e., under automatic approval upon filing of necessary documents. Draft Terms of Reference for the re-engineering groups are at Annex-X.

4. The re-engineering groups may be set up, to begin with, in the Ministries of Labour, Environment & Forests, Power, Agriculture, Petroleum & Natural Gas and Department of Industrial Policy & Promotion. These groups would re-engineer the regulatory processes under the Acts, Rules, Regulations, etc., administered by the Ministry, prescribe time limits for grant of non-statutory approvals, develop appropriate trigger mechanism to automatically raise the matter to next higher level in cases of delays, review requirements of multiple approvals, indicate interse priority among various reform measures and examine extant laws with the objective of their consolidation and rationalization. The groups would also recommend a generic structure for the re-engineering of processes at the state level, to be fine-tuned for State specific requirements.

5. The re-engineering groups would complete re-engineering of the regulatory processes within a period of six months, and review updation and consolidation of extant laws within a period of one year. A Committee of Secretaries would review the progress of these groups. The Ministries would present the position on the progress of re-engineering groups in their monthly report to CCER.

Approval for Primary Resources

6. Simplification in procedures relating to approval for primary resources, viz., land, electricity, water, building plans, etc., is necessary. The process of land acquisition takes an inordinately long time due to delays in publication in official gazette. In the absence of a clear rehabilitation policy, acquisition of land gets delayed due to issues of resettlement of displaced persons. Similarly, delays in approval for changes in land use, building plans, etc., from the local authority also delay implementation of projects. Authority to approve building plans may be conferred upon architects registered under the Architects Act, 1972. A comprehensive legislation may be enacted to dispense with the requirement of publication of notices in the official gazette, under various legislations – both Central and State.

Environmental & Forest Clearances

7. Environmental clearance perhaps takes the longest time and causes maximum delays to projects. Cumbersome procedures for environmental clearance and public hearing, submission of

incomplete information, poor quality of EIA/EMP, disproportionate details required with applications, delays in the meetings of the Expert Committees and site visit, etc., are the major reasons behind delays.

8. MOEF has taken several measures to reduce delays in the grant of environmental, forest and coastal zone regulation clearances. The investment limit as well as the list of projects requiring environmental clearance should be made co-terminus with Plan period necessitating review every five years and be also linked with the Consumer Price Index for automatic adjustment with price index. Besides taking up various activities in parallel, MOEF may also examine the document requirement at the stage of receipt of application. Delays in site visits need to be curtailed.

9. Empowered Committees, with representation of all concerned including States, may be set up for expediting decision on environment and forest clearances. Expert agencies may be authorized for initial scrutiny of applications. Diversion of forestland for pre-construction activities may be permitted after the non-forest land identified for compensatory afforestation has been transferred to the forest department and funds for raising compensatory afforestation deposited.

Power Sector Projects

10. Inability of the State Electricity Boards to support payment security mechanism due to their poor financial position is the major roadblock for projects in power sector. Besides delays in finalisation of various agreements, viz., Power Purchase Agreement, Fuel Supply Agreement, Fuel Transportation Agreement, etc., techno-economic clearance from CEA also contributes to delays. Regular meetings of all concerned responsible for various linkages would help reduce delays. The proposed Electricity Bill 2002 will address many of the concerns of existing legislations for speedy implementation of power projects.

Re-engineering or Regulatory Processes at State Level

11. Re-engineering of the regulatory processes on lines similar to re-engineering proposed at Central level would be necessary.

State Governments may consider setting up re-engineering groups to take up re-engineering of regulatory processes in a time bound manner. The progress may be reviewed at the highest level.

Single Window and Composite Application Forms

12. Empowering of the Single Window System at the state level along with re-engineering of regulatory processes would have maximum impact on reducing delays in getting the required approvals and implementing projects. States may consider various alternatives viz., enactment of legislation, amendment to the Rules of Business, etc., for empowering specially constituted bodies to operationalise and empower the 'Single Window System'.

13. Single Composite Application Forms (SCAF) to facilitate issue of all approvals from a single point need to be introduced for large and medium projects, to begin with. An agency at the state level may be responsible for development, implementation and follow up of clearances under SCAF.

Prescribing and Adhering to Time Limits

14. The time frame prescribed for grant of various approvals needs to be followed up and adhered to. Industrial Investment Facilitation Board (IIFB) would follow the grant of various statutory approvals with the concerned Administrative Ministries/ Agencies. At State Level Single Window Mechanism or any other designated agency would undertake similar follow up. Appropriate trigger mechanisms would need to be developed to take the matter to the next higher level, whenever the prescribed time frames are not adhered to.

Regulatory Environment During Operation of Projects

15. The projects even after completion are also subjected to many regulatory requirements in terms of periodic inspections, returns, licenses, etc., Simplification in these aspects is also required.

Inspections & Clearances

16. By clubbing duties of different inspecting authorities from different departments, multiplicity of inspecting authorities can

be reduced. A Committee under Secretary (Industry) of the State Government may decide on the inspection schedule of projects, under both Central and State legislations.

17. Frequency and requirement of clearances and permissions under different Acts, Regulations, etc., need to be reviewed and brought in line with advancement in technologies and experience gained by the industry. Authority for some inspections can also be outsourced to accredited certifying agencies. Internal disciplinary mechanisms of the professional associations, to act against complaints of malpractices, would need to be strengthened.

Registers and Returns

18. The requirement of maintaining separate registers and forms for related subjects under different Acts imposes a heavy burden on projects as well as regulatory authorities and needs to be reviewed. A time limit of, say, 4 weeks may be prescribed within which concerned authorities may respond to these forms for any further clarification. The Labour Laws (Exemption From Furnishing Returns and maintenance of Registers by Certain Establishments) Act, 1988, permitting maintenance of common registers may be made applicable to enterprises, employing up to 500 persons.

Incentivising the States

19. Since the States stand to benefit immensely from regulatory reforms, which will catalyse greater investment flows, there would be greater inclination among the States to undertake such reforms, which unlike other sectoral reforms, are not perceived to have huge political implications. The Government of India may provide technical assistance to the States for re-engineering their regulatory processes. Institution of awards, etc., may be considered to recognise the achievements of States.

20. Assistance under different reform-linked incentive schemes in various sectors may be dovetailed for the purpose of monetary incentive for re-engineering the regulatory processes in the States with clearly earmarked provisions for identified infrastructure components/projects, as may be determined by the State Governments concerned. Additional budgetary provisions may also be considered for augmenting the funds available as incentive to

the States. Institutional arrangements would be necessary to ensure that these funds are properly utilised under appropriately designed projects. The Government may also consider issuing directive to the financial institutions to link lending to States for infrastructure projects with progress on regulatory reforms.

Facilitation & Dispute Resolution Mechanism

21. Industrial Investment Facilitation Board (IIFB), recommended by the Committee in Part-I of its report for being set up as the central facilitation body, would follow up grant of approval for projects with investment of Rs.100 crores and above. Besides, any investor facing difficulties in obtaining approvals from the Ministries/Agencies may also approach IIFB irrespective of the investment limit.

22. Facilitation Teams (FTs), in the Administrative Ministries and States should be set up to facilitate implementation of both public and private projects. Regular interaction with investors would help remove impediments in the implementation of projects.

23. In view of the delays in settlement of disputes through regular proceedings, resolution of disputes through alternative dispute resolution mechanisms needs to be encouraged.

Lack of Information and Transparency

24. Greater transparency in approval administration, easy availability of information on procedural and documentation requirements, time frame and authority responsible for various approvals, status of pending applications along with reasons for delay beyond prescribed time would help reduce delays. A net enabled system could be developed for this purpose.

25. Forms for all types of approvals/clearances along with procedural and documentary requirements should be available in a downloadable format on the websites of concerned departments/ agencies or State Level Investment Promotion Agency. Necessary systems may be put in position for electronic submission of these applications.

26. In order to curb the tendency of abuse of power by implementation machinery at the field level resulting in delays in

grant of approvals, disciplinary proceedings against public servants, both at central and state level, should invariably be initiated in such cases and concluded expeditiously. Stringent action should be taken in cases of proven abuse of power.

Sensitisation and Awareness Generation

27. Sensitizing people about the best practices in India and elsewhere, initiatives taken in Central Ministries and States, etc., through seminars, workshops, meetings, etc., would be necessary. A separate exercise would need to be undertaken to design the components of documentation and dissemination needs, assess resource availability & requirement and implementation methodology, which can be taken up as a project by Industry Associations.

28. Periodic publication of information on performance of States on 8 to 10 critical parameters and ranking states on these parameters would generate healthy competition among States and incentivise them for undertaking further reforms. Government may also encourage Industry Associations, Rating Agencies, etc., to take up this exercise of rating of States on regulatory reforms and simplification of procedures.

Greater Use of IT

29. A time bound action plan for greater use of IT in approval administration would be necessary. National Institute of Smart Governance, being set up, can provide the necessary technical support. In view of the growing use of computers in day-to-day transactions, computerized forms may be accepted for maintaining registers and filing of returns.

Capacity Building

30. Capacity of personnel engaged in approval, implementation, facilitation, monitoring and evaluation of projects would need to be strengthened through orientation trainings on modern project management techniques, use of IT, monitoring & evaluation techniques, etc. Assistance of multilateral financial institutions may be availed of for this purpose. Ministries/Departments of Government of India and the State Governments will also require

support for the actual process of re-engineering of their regulatory processes. An inventory of the global best practices would need to be prepared. Multilateral financial institutions may be approached for technical assistance. Reputed training and research institutions, both in the public and in the private sector, may also be associated in the training of staff and the re-engineering of regulatory processes at the state level.

1

Introduction

CABINET Secretariat, vide its order dated 24.09.2001, set up a Committee with Shri V.N. Kaul, Secretary, Petroleum and Natural Gas as convenor, to examine extant procedures for investment approvals and implementation of projects and to suggest measures to simplify and expedite the process for both public and private investment. Following the appointment of Shri V.N. Kaul as Comptroller & Auditor General of India, Shri V. Govindarajan, Secretary DIPP was designated convenor of the Committee vide cabinet Secretariat order dated 19.3.2002. Copies of the orders are at Annex-I and I-A respectively.

1.2 A sub-group was also setup with Shri V.Govindarajan, Secretary DIPP, as convenor, to look into various issues relating to investment in schemes and projects in private sector; including those related to infrastructure and also downstream issues. A copy of the order is at Annex-II

1.3 Meetings of the Sub-Group were held on 7.12.2001, 11.03.2002, 28.05.2002, 2.07.2002 and 23.07.2002 to discuss various issues. The Sub-group, during its deliberations, also considered several case studies, reports and material on similar subjects as well as material prepared by other Ministries. The sub-group also referred to the base papers prepared by various Ministries/Organisations. A list of references is at Annex-III.

1.4 The Committee presented Part-I of its report to the Cabinet Secretary on 20.05.2002 containing its recommendations on the upstream issues, i.e., from the stage of conceptualization of project to investment approval. Part-II of the report covers recommendations on the downstream issues, from the stage of investment approval till implementation of project and its operation.

2

Existing Procedures for Approval and Operation

THE Industrial Policy Reforms, initiated in 1991, have substantially liberalized the industrial licensing requirements, removed restrictions on investment & expansion, facilitated import of foreign technology and inflow of Foreign Direct Investment (FDI). Industrial licensing is now virtually abolished except for a few industries, still reserved for public sector, and six other industries where it is still considered necessary on strategic/ environmental safety considerations. In tune with the liberalised Licensing Policy, the Locational Policy has also been significantly simplified. Zoning and land use regulations as well as Environmental legislations, however, continue to regulate industrial locations.

2.2 Industrial undertakings exempt from industrial license including existing units undertaking substantial expansion are required to only file Industrial Entrepreneur Memoranda (IEM) for the purpose of monitoring industrial trends in the economy. In respect of manufacture of items retained under compulsory licensing, reserved for exclusive manufacture by small-scale industries and for locations not conforming to the locational policy, industrial undertakings are required to apply for industrial license. Approvals are normally available within 4-6 weeks of filing the application.

2.3 Simultaneous with the dismantling of the elaborate and complex industrial licensing regime, simplified policies and procedures allowing Foreign Direct Investment have also come in force in virtually all sectors except those of strategic concern. FDI for a large number of activities is now permitted through automatic route under powers delegated to RBI For remaining activities Government approval is granted on the recommendation of Foreign Investment Promotion Board (FIPB). In almost 95-98 percent cases, decision is communicated by FIPB within 4-6 weeks of filing the application.

2.4 Under FIPB route, projects involving foreign investment with estimated project cost of up to Rs. 600 crores are approved at the level of Commerce and Industry Minister. Cases beyond Rs. 600 crores, are considered by the Cabinet Committee on Economic Affairs (CCEA). There is no restriction in terms of investment limit under the automatic route.

Stages a Typical Project Has to Pass Through

2.5 A project after approval from concerned authorities of the Central and State Governments, as the case may be, has to typically pass through the following stages during its implementation:

Sl. No.	*Type of Clearance*	*Authority*	*Act under which required*
Central Level Clearances			
1.	Registration as a Company	Registrar of Companies	The Companies Act, 1956
2.	Clearance from Coastal Regulation Zone	MOEF	The Environment (Protection) Act. 1986
3.	Environment Clearance	MOEF	The Environment (Protection) Act, 1986
4.	Forest Clearance for diversion of forest land	State Forest Department/MOEF	The Forest (Conservation) Act, 1980
5.	Explosive License	Controller of Explosives	The Explosives Act, 1884
6.	Certificate of commencement of business	Registrar of Companies	The Companies Act, 1956
7.	Rehabilitation and Resettlement Plan	State Government/ MOEF	
8.	Permission for Import of goods	Director General Foreign Trade	Exim Policy

(Contd...)

(...Contd...)

Sl. No.	*Type of Clearance*	*Authority*	*Act under which required*
9.	Pollution Clearance	State Pollution Control Board (SPCB)/Central Pollution Control Board (CPCB)	The Water (Prevention and Control of Pollution) Act 1974 & The Air (Prevention and Control of Pollution) Act, 1981
State Level Clearances			
1.	*Allotment of Land*		
a.	Allotment of land/shed in industrial areas	Concerned Industrial Development Authority	
b.	Allotment of Government Land	District Collector/ Revenue Department	State Land Revenue Act
c.	Acquisition of land	District Collector/ State Government	The Land Acquisition Act, 1894
2.	*Change in land use*		
a.	Conversion of Land use to Non agriculture purposes	District Collector/ Revenue Department	State Land Revenue Act
b.	Change in land use in urban areas	Town Planning Department	State Urban Improvement/ Municipal Act
3.	*Approval of building plan*		
a.	Approval of building plans in Industrial areas	Concerned Industrial Development Authority	
b.	Approval of building plans in other areas	Local Authorities#	Municipal Byelaws
4.	'No Objection' from Fire Department	Fire Services Department #	
5.	Release of power connection	State Electricity Board or its successor entities	
6.	Consent for setting up captive power plant	State Electricity Board or its successor entities	The Electricity (Supply) Act, 1948

(Contd...)

(...Contd...)

Sl. No.	*Type of Clearance*	*Authority*	*Act under which required*
7.	*Release of water connection*		
a.	Release of water connection in Industrial Areas	Industrial Development Authority	
b.	Release of water connection in other areas	State Water Supply Department	
8.	Site Clearance Certificate - required in case of identified highly polluting industries	State Government	The Factories Act, 1948
9.	Boiler Certification	Chief Inspector of Boilers	The Indian Boilers Act, 1923
10.	Registration as a Factory	Chief Inspector of Factories	The Factories Act, 1948
11.	Sales Tax Registration	Sales Tax Department	State Sales Tax Act
12.	Registration Under the Trade Union Act, 1926	Labour Department of State Government	The Trade Unions Act, 1926
13.	Registration under the Provident Funds Act, 1925	Labour Department of State Government	The Provident Funds Act, 1925
14.	Registration under Shops and Establishments Act, 1988	Labour Department of State Government	The Shops and Establishments Act, 1988
15.	Registration under Industrial Disputes Act, 1947	Labour Department of State Government	The Industrial Disputes Act, 1947
16.	Registration under Minimum Wages Act	Labour Department of State Government	The Minimum Wages Act, 1948
17.	Registration under the State Employees Insurance Act 1948	Labour Department of State Government	The State Employees Insurance Act, 1948

Pertains to Local bodies

2.6 Besides the above general clearances required for most projects, sector specific projects require additional clearances. An illustrative list of specific clearances required for projects in the power sector is as under:

Sl. No.	*Type of Clearance*	*Authority*	*Act under which required*
a.	**Statutory Clearances-Central Government**		
1.	Techno-economic clearance	Central Electricity Authority	Sections 29 & 30 of the Electricity (Supply) Act, 1948
2.	Pollution Clearance (Water and Air)	State Pollution Control Board/ Central Pollution Control Board	The Water (Prevention and Control of Pollution) Act 1974 and the Air (Prevention and Control of Pollution) Act, 1981
3.	Forest Clearance	State Government & MOEF	The Forest (Conservation) Act, 1980
4.	Civil Aviation Clearance	National Airports Authority of India	The Indian Aircraft Act, 1934
5.	Defence clearance	Ministry of Defence	
6.	Stage-I Site Clearance from MOEF in case of Mega and Pithead projects	MOEF	The Environment (Protection) Act, 1986
b.	**Non-Statutory Clearances - Central Government**		
1.	Fuel Supply Agreement	Ministry of Coal/ Ministry of Petroleum & Natural Gas	
2.	Fuel Transportation Agreement	Ministry of Railways/ Ministry of Petroleum & Natural Gas/ Ministry of Coal	
3.	Rehabilitation and Resettlement of displaced persons due to land acquisition	State Government/ MOEF	
4.	Water Availability	State Government/ Ministry of Water resources in case of hydel projects	
5.	Long Term Coal Linkage	Ministry of Coal (Standing Linkage Committee)	
6.	Gas Linkage	Ministry of Petroleum & Natural Gas	

(Contd...)

(...Contd...)

Sl. No.	*Type of Clearance*	*Authority*	*Act under which required*
c.	**Non-Statutory Clearances - State Government**		
1.	State Electricity Board clearance	SEB/State Government	Section 44 of The Electricity (Supply) Act, 1948
2.	Power Purchase Agreement	Between developer and SEB	
d.	**Other Institutions**		
1.	Financial Closure	Financial Institutions	

2.7 In addition to a large number of clearances, the power projects are also required to obtain many approvals/licenses periodically from many agencies during operation of the project. An illustrative list of periodic approvals/licenses to be obtained for operating a power plant is as under:

Sl. No.	*Regulatory Process*	*Frequency*	*Regulatory Body*
a	**Central Government**		
1	Coal Linkage Allocation (short term)	3 months	Ministry of Coal
2	Gas Linkage Allocation (short term)	As per need	Ministry of Petroleum & Natural Gas
b	**State Government**		
1	Air and water consent order	Yearly	State Pollution Control Board
2	Boiler Certification under Indian Boiler Regulation	Yearly	Boiler Inspector
3	Inspection under Factories Act	6 months	Factory Inspector
4	License to store petroleum products	3 years	District Supply Officer
5	Calibration and stamping of weights and measures	5 years	Meteorological Department
6	Boiler License Renewal	Yearly	Under the Indian Boilers Act
7	Approval of plans for construction/extension under Factories Act	As per need	Factories Inspector

Industrial Legislation

2.8 Administration of industries and other sectors of economy have been allocated to the Union and State Governments under the Union and State Lists under the Constitution of India. A number of legislations related to land revenue, land ceiling, local government, State taxation, etc., are also applicable to the industrial and other projects. In addition, many related subjects like trade unions, industrial disputes, social security, factories, labour welfare, etc., fall in the Concurrent List. A large number of Acts and Rules, therefore, regulate various aspects of economic activities, and departments responsible for the administration of these Acts are responsible for various clearances to be issued under the respective Acts. An illustrative list of Acts- both Central and State, regulating the industry in general is at Annex-IV.

2.9 While the requirement of obtaining licenses which was the major bottlenecks of pre-liberalization era is no longer a major constraint, most of the problems now relate to 'ease of doing business' and removing such problems would benefit both Indian and foreign companies. While many of the regulations and procedures are necessary, and will have to be continued, poor administrative mechanisms have emerged as key problem.

2.10 It can be concluded that while overall policy have been liberalised, reforms in institutional mechanism and procedural simplification to translate policy liberalisation into ease of doing business have generally lagged behind. Main bottlenecks relate to multiplicity of laws on the same subject, multiple approvals still required after approval of the project, innumerable returns to be filed and registers to be maintained and multiplicity of inspections. A great deal of this lies within the State domain, and therefore any attempt to remove the bottlenecks would necessarily require complete involvement of State Governments.

Institutional Arrangements for Various Approvals and Facilitation

2.11 Following institutional mechanisms exist for approval of industrial and FDI projects at the level of Government of India Level:

i. Foreign Investment Promotion Board (FIPB) for approving foreign investment proposals not falling under the automatic route.

ii. Project Approval Board (PAB) for approving foreign technology transfer proposals not falling under the automatic route.

iii. Licensing Committee (LC) for considering and recommending proposals for grant of industrial license.

2.12 In addition, concerned Ministries/Departments issue various approvals as per the allocation of business and various Acts being administered by them.

2.13 At the State level, State Investment Promotion Agency and, at the district level, District Industries Centres, generally look after projects. Concerned departments of the State Government handle sectoral projects.

2.14 At the Central Government level, Foreign Investment Implementation Authority (FIIA) has been established in the Department of Industrial Policy & Promotion, to assist foreign investors in resolution of their operational difficulties and in getting necessary approvals. Apart from the Ministries of Government of India, senior officials from States and representatives of apex Industrial organizations and investors also participate in the meetings of FIIA. Besides, Fast Track Committees (FTCs) have been set up in 30 Ministries/Departments for close monitoring of projects with estimated investment of Rs. 100 crores and above and for resolution of issues hampering implementation.

3

Some Previous Reports & Studies

MAIN findings/recommendations of some of the previous reports/studies as well as case studies commissioned to identify specific impediments to early implementation of projects are summarized below:

Case Studies Conducted by PMO

3.2 PMO commissioned 13 case studies, in the private and public sector, to identify various procedural, institutional, regulatory and implementation bottlenecks that cause delays in approval, commissioning and operation of such projects. These case studies covered the following categories of projects:

i. Infrastructure including power, road, refineries and telecommunications.

ii. Knowledge intensive projects such as manufacture of drugs.

iii. Service sector projects in banking, food and beverages, etc.

iv. Small and medium scale projects in the fields of textiles, garments and auto ancillaries.

3.3 Findings of 5 case studies were integrated by A.T. KEARNEY into a synthesis study, which has identified the following four key issues for projects in power sector:

i. Primary resources, such as land, require clearance from multiple agencies.

ii. Multiple clearances need to be obtained from the same agency, e.g., CEA in case of power projects.

iii. Environmental clearances require disproportionate level of details

iv. Certain clearances do not appear to serve any specific purpose or public interest.

3.4 The analysis of the clearances has shown that environmental and forest clearances, land acquisition formalities and techno-economic clearances take up most time and effort and, therefore, require urgent intervention. A copy of the presentation by A.T. KEARNEY is at Annex-V.

Case Studies of Projects in the Power Sector

3.5 Despite liberalisation, investment in power sector has been slow to come by primarily because of some fundamental issues affecting this sector. Case studies of projects in the power sector have highlighted following key impediments to speedy implementation of projects:

i. Poor financial position of the State Electricity Boards, presently the sole agency for purchasing power. Inability to provide payment security leads to delays in financial closure of projects.

ii. Delays in obtaining various clearances like fuel linkages, power purchase agreement, etc., due to differences in perceptions of participants.

iii. Statutory process of clearance of schemes.

3.6 A new power plant requires a number of approvals and linkages before it can be commissioned. An illustrative list of major approvals required before commissioning power plants is at paragraph 2.6.

Studies by Ministry of Statistics and Programme Implementation

3.7 The Ministry of Statistics and Programme Implementation had commissioned a study on 'Systems of Clearances Required for Various Types of Projects in Public and Private Sector' with Advance Coal Management & Marketing Private Ltd. and Advance Design and Engineering Ltd.

3.8 This study has found the following, in order of severity, as major impediments to implementation of projects:

i. Environmental clearance
ii. Land acquisition
iii. Forest clearance
iv. CEA clearance
v. Site clearance

Study by NCAER on 'Compilation of Industrial Policies and Procedures Governing FDI Projects'

3.9 The study by NCAER, in 1998, on 'Compilation of Industrial Policies and Procedures Governing FDI Projects' has also listed specific approvals required for projects in some of the major infrastructure sectors and issues hampering implementation. The report has focused on the steps to environmental clearance, land, building design approval, electricity & water connections and labour related aspects.

3.10 Responses received from managers of 120 MNCs in 1999 on 32 parameters relating to investment decisions and their implementation were used by NCAER to create an index that assigned negative ratings in respect of responses which said 'below satisfactory', positive values to responses which said 'above satisfactory' and zero to 'satisfactory'.

3.11 Out of the 32 factors studied only in 10, ratings of satisfactory or above were reported. In the remaining 22 factors, the ratings were below satisfactory. Non-ethical practices, transparency and regulatory framework have emerged as areas where the ratings are low. Similarly power condition and transport have received unsatisfactory ranking signifying areas where immediate improvements are required.

Study by Administrative Staff College of India (ASCI)

3.12 The study by Administrative Staff College of India (ASCI) has listed 36 permissions typically required for setting up industrial projects and has suggested simplification in various Acts, procedures for registration, inspections and maintenance of records and registers. The study has listed 27 inspectors for inspection of an industrial undertaking (Annex-VI), Inspection registers and returns to be maintained by the industry (Annex-VII) and 42 returns/forms to be completed by a medium size company (Annex-VIII) where simplifications are warranted.

3.13 The study has recommended that legal banking is needed to bring about procedural simplification, reduce delays in various approvals and reduce number of registers and returns. It has suggested enactment of a special legislation to achieve these objectives and, simultaneously, bring in necessary changes on other legislations governing the industrial projects.

Direct Feedback from Investors

3.14 Direct feedback from foreign investors to Foreign Investment Implementation Authority has shown that 50 per cent of references relate to implementation issues including delays in grant of approvals and clearances, 20 per cent issues relate to changes in policies/Acts, etc., while another 20 per cent seek some relaxations in the existing conditions with 10 per cent miscellaneous.

Study by Centre for Monitoring Indian Economy

3.15 Department of Industrial Policy & Promotion, in May 2001, commissioned a study with the Centre for Monitoring Indian Economy (CMIE) to identify reasons for slow progress in the implementation of investment projects. This study, based on responses from promoters of 304 projects comprising 165 from private sector, 78 from Government sector and 61 involving FDI, conducted during the period May-October 2001, has revealed that about 19 per cent of the respondents consider Governmental clearance to be a problem in project implementation.

3.16 The study had further shown that getting clearances from local authorities is a greater problem than from the Central or State Governments. The finding of this study is summarised below:

Clearance By	*Seriously problematic*	*Mildly Problematic*
Central Government	2.3%	15.3%
State Government	3.9%	14.8%
Local Government	2.6%	18.2%

FICCI-FDI Survey 2002

3.17 A survey of 385 foreign companies, conducted by Federation of Indian Chambers of Commerce & Industry (FICCI) in March 2002, has shown that handling of approvals at Central level has registered to marked improvement over the previous year with 93 per cent respondents rating it from good to average against only 61 per cent last year. Infrastructure, particularly in telecom, has also shown improvement compared to last year. 70 per cent of respondents have reported the ease of bringing in funds as 'good to average' and 69 per cent respondents have expressed that repatriation of funds can be carried out rather easily.

3.18 The survey has shown that regulatory framework and ground level hassles are becoming more of an impediment. 43 per cent of the respondents have described tax regime and 35 per cent of respondents have described labour laws a serious problem. 52 per cent of the respondents rated regulatory framework as bad. In contrast to the high ratings for handling of approvals at central level, 38 per cent of the respondents found state level handling of approvals bad while 74 per cent respondents reported ground level hassles to be high. 76 per cent respondents have expressed the view that reducing ground level hassles is imperative for future FDI inflows.

4

Review of Extant Procedures for Clearances

THE policy reforms initiated during the last decade have liberalized the economy by deregulation, removing restrictions in terms of licensing and by introduction of competition, etc. However, simplification of the rules and regulations governing different sectors of the economy and of procedures for various approvals and clearances has generally lagged behind. As a result, the economy continues to be regulated under a plethora of laws. While several initiatives have been taken at the Central and State level towards simplification of procedures, such measures have largely concentrated on simplification of procedures, delegation of greater authorities at field level, etc., within the gamut of the prevailing laws and have generally not looked at the very need for many of these permissions and simplification or consolidation of laws. As a result, the benefits of liberalization of the economy have not been fully reaped since cumbersome procedures continue to hamper investment.

4.2 Among the most commonly noted bottlenecks in implementation of projects are:

i. Multiplicity of laws governing same or similar set of issues.

ii. Requirement of a large number of approvals/permissions.

iii. Separate clearances/approvals required from different authorities on same or similar issues.

iv. Too many points of contact between investor and authorities.

v. Lack of transparency in the administration of clearances and approvals.

vi. Large number of returns and amount of information to be provided to many departments/agencies.

vii. Little communication and information-sharing among related departments.

Consolidation of Regulatory Framework

4.3 Besides the requirement of clearances/approvals for implementation of projects, many inspection and reporting requirements during the operation of projects, viz., an elaborate and complex system of records and registers to be maintained, inspections by a number of regulatory bodies, periodic renewal of approvals/licenses, etc., also regulate the operational phase of projects. The operating environment suffers from actual lack of transparency and information on steps to be taken for various approvals. These regulatory constrains have a decided bearing on the ease of doing business and, thereby, influence investment decisions.

4.4 Simplification in the regulatory environment would necessarily require changes in the regulatory processes. An illustrative list of Acts, both Central and State, regulating the projects is at Annex-IV. Many of the enactments regulating projects were enacted long back, in many cases over 50 years ago. While the economic environment has undergone a near total transformation, the regulatory framework under these legislations has not changed much. In fact, with growing concerns over environmental, safety and other issues, the regulatory framework has evolved to cover such vital aspects also. At present, in many cases multiple legislations regulate some issues, viz., labour welfare and safety. This not only makes their enforcement very cost-ineffective but also makes compliance difficult as the requirements prescribed under each legislation have to be separately complied with.

4.5 The extant laws need to be consolidated and updated by weeding out legislations that have outlived their utility, bringing others in line with the present day technological, environmental, competitive and social requirements. This will also make administration as well as compliance effective.

Re-engineering of the Regulatory Processes

4.6 In order to simplify the procedures for grant of approvals, reduce delays and simplify regulation of projects during their operational phase, re-engineering of the regulatory processes prescribed under various legislations, regulations, etc., is an immediate necessity. Unless the procedures prescribed under extant laws are simplified to meet the requirements of the present economic, technological and competitive environment, delays in the grant of approvals are unlikely to come down significantly. Re-engineering of the regulatory processes is also necessary to reduce ground level hassles, make administration and compliance easy as well as amenable to IT tools and to minimise interface between project promoters and official machinery.

4.7 Re-engineering of the regulatory processes would require detailed interaction with the Ministries/States administering these legislations and is too elaborate an exercise to be undertaken by the Committee at this stage. Re-engineering groups may be formed in the Ministries administering Act regulating implementation and operation of projects. The re-engineering groups may review and complete the illustrative list of Acts given at Annex-IV and approval requirement, at the Central and States level, at Annex-IX pertaining to their Ministry/Department. To begin with, such re-engineering groups could be formed in the Ministries of Labour, Environment & Forests, Power, Agriculture, Petroleum & Natural Gas and the Department of Industrial Policy & Promotion.

4.8 These groups, under the Chairmanship of Secretary of the concerned Department/Ministry, may include other officers and representatives of the attached and sub-ordinate offices responsible for grant of various approvals. Representatives of the State Governments and other Ministries may be associated as considered necessary. Industry Associations, being important stakeholders, may also be associated. Assistance of public management specialists may also be taken, as considered necessary, to bring in professional inputs and international experience in best practices. In addition, considering the vast experience, intimate knowledge of extant processes and expertise available in-house in existing implementing machinery, their close interaction with outside experts would be useful. While a panel of experts for reference may be prepared for greater coherence of views, the choice of experts may be left with concerned Ministries to suit their requirements.

4.9 Re-engineering groups would recommend re-engineering of the regulatory processes and systems, which are to be retained for administration by the Government, to embody the following principles:

i. Clear and non-discretionary decision rules to realize the public interest to be protected as provided by law, and no extraneous objectives:

ii. Minimising and standardising requirements of information and documentation specific to the applicant (i.e., dispensing with the need to bring information which is either already available to the public or available to the regulator from other public agencies) to support just the decision rules and no more;

iii. No queue jumping without specific and documented supervisory level authorisation;

iv. Reducing stages and levels of review;

v. Defined time limits for each stage of processing, as well as the process overall, with a preliminary stage for confirmation that all required information/documentation has been provided, to which the regulator will not revert;

vi. Standardised response, including furnishing of reasons in the event of refusal, to enable the applicant to represent meaningfully against such refusal;

vii. Real-time monitoring of each stage of the process by supervisory authorities; and

viii. One stage of official review for redressal of grievances.

4.10 Re-engineering groups would examine each approval/ permission requirement under different legislations, rules and regulations, for their re-engineering in the following order:

i. Category A: where any violation may result in minor third-party impacts, which are easily remediable/compensable. In such cases, self regulation may be the norm with legal penalties if violation is detected ('blinking traffic lights' model).

ii. Category B: where violation may result in some significant third-party impacts, but not involving proximate danger to life or serious injury, and still remediable/compensable. In such cases, professional outsourcing may be preferred to direct case-by-case regulation by a Government agency. The professional providers of such services may be formally designated by their respective professional agencies (e.g. engineers, architects, etc.), and the basis of their certification sufficiently documented to enable determination of professional malpractice (by the regulatory agency, which may move the concerned professional association for de-registration)('stop-go traffic lights' model).

iii. Category C: where violation may result in high risks of serious third-party impacts or long-term damage to key natural resources or cultural assets. Only in such cases would prior case-by-case regulation be advisable by a public agency ('policeman regulating traffic' model).

The Committee felt that as many approvals as are possible should be placed on self-regulation, i.e., automatic permission upon filing of necessary documents.

4.11 The re-engineering groups should also prescribe time limits for grant of non-statutory approvals and develop systems for ensuring grant of approvals within this time limit. These groups should develop appropriate trigger mechanisms to automatically raise the matter to the next higher level in case the concerned authorities fail to decide the matter within prescribed time limits. The re-engineering groups would also indicate interse priority among various regulatory reforms being proposed by the group so that reforms aiming at maximum simplification are undertaken first. They would also examine the extant laws being administered by their Ministry with the objective of consolidation of laws, weeding out laws that have outlived their utility and to generally bring them in alignment with the present technological, economic and competitive environment.

4.12 Simplification of procedures, including quality of appraisal, followed by commercial banks and financial institutions is also important for timely flow of investment into projects. Lack of institutional capacity in the banks and financial institutions to meet the requirements of project financing also needs to be suitably addressed. These issues are too detailed for the Committee to look into at this stage. The re-engineering group to be set in the Ministry of Finance may consider such issues for taking further appropriate action.

4.13 A large number of approval/permissions are administered at the State level and it would not be possible to suggest changes in the prevailing processes specific to each state. The re-engineering groups may indicate the best practices adopted in different states and elsewhere and suggest a generic structure of the re-engineering of the regulatory processes. State specific fine-tuning of specific institutional and statutory/regulatory features of each state may be undertaken in consultation with concerned states.

4.14 The re-engineering groups should finalise their recommendations within a period of six months for the re-engineering of the regulatory processes and, within a period of one year, for review, updation and consolidation of legislations. IIFB, recommended for being set up by the Committee in Part-I of its report, would co-ordinate re-engineering of regulatory processes with the re-engineering groups set up in different Ministry/ Departments. A Committee of Secretaries under Cabinet Secretary, with Secretaries to Government of India in the Ministries/ Departments of Labour, Environment & Forests, Power, Agriculture, Petroleum & Natural Gas, Industrial Policy & Promotion, Information Technology, Revenue and Additional Secretary in the PMO as members, would review on a monthly basis the progress of re-engineering groups and act as a trigger in case of any delay in the re-engineering processes. A position report on re-engineering of regulatory processes will be included as one of the items in the monthly report of the concerned Ministry to the Cabinet Committee on Economic Reforms (CCER). Draft Terms of Reference for the re-engineering groups are at Annex-X.

Capacity Building for Re-engineering of Regulatory Processes

4.15 Various Ministries/Departments of Government of India as well as the State Governments would require technical assistance for capacity building of the personnel associated with the re-engineering of the regulatory processes and administration of approvals. In addition, the Ministries/Department of Government of India and the State Governments will also require support for the actual re-engineering of their regulatory processes. An inventory of the global best practices would need to be prepared. Multilateral financial institutions may be approached for necessary technical assistance. Reputed training and research institutions, both in the public and private sector, may also be associated in the training of staff and the re-engineering of regulatory processes at the state level. A concept paper on the technical assistance requirements is at Annex-XI.

Review of Procedures for Some of the Main Approvals for Projects

4.16 While each sector would have its specific set of approvals and difficulties in obtaining these approvals, there are many approvals, which are required by a large number of projects. Approvals related to land acquisition, possession of land, approval of building plans, release of electricity and water connection, environmental clearance, etc., are instances of such approvals, which affect many projects. Some issues affecting a majority of projects are dealt with in the following paragraphs:

Approval of Location of Projects, Building Plans and Changes in Land Use

4.17 Multiplicity of approvals pertaining to land development, utilization, as well as restrictions in availability of utilities, etc., influence the location of investment and many agencies have to be approached for these clearances. In general, the following clearances are required in respect of location of a project:

i. Restrictions in respect of land use and zoning.

ii. Approval of building plans from local self-government institutions or industrial development organization.

iii. Approval from factories, town planning, labour, fire services departments, wherever applicable.

iv. Restrictions, if any, in respect of power load in specific areas.

Land Acquisition

4.18 Under the existing provisions, the process for land acquisition is very long drawn and cumbersome. Starting from identification of land, the process can take nearly 18 months to 2 years. Case studies by NTPC have shown that, even under the best case scenario, physical possession of land was expected only 18 months after identification of the requirement. A flow chart showing the stages involved in land acquisition and the time taken at each stage is at Annex-XII. Among the major reasons identified to be causing delays in land acquisition are:

i. Proposals are routed through various agencies in the State Government, viz., Power department in case of Power projects, Revenue and Law Departments in State Government.

ii. Delays in publication of notifications in the official Gazette.

iii. Disputes pertaining to quantum of compensation.

4.19 Delays in land acquisition could be reduced by following measures:

i. Need for publication in official gazette may be dispensed with in view of their limited circulation and considerable delays in their publication. Instead, publication in a vernacular newspaper having adequate circulation in the area should be deemed sufficient. A comprehensive legislation to dispense with the requirement of publication of notice in official gazette under different legislations may be considered.

ii. The State Government may appoint a nodal officer for follow up of clearances required from concerned departments.

iii. There is no clear cut policy on Relief & Rehabilitation leading to problems being faced at the time of implementation of R&R plan with project-affected persons insisting on employment. The National Rehabilitation Policy is under preparation by the Ministry of Rural Development. A clear R&R Policy would reduce delays on this account during implementation of projects. The Ministry of Rural Development may also consider setting time limits for implementation of rehabilitation measures by concerned project authorities.

Land Availability and Utilisation

4.20 Land being a necessary element in most projects, complexities in the procedures related to allotment of Government land, purchase of private land and getting its land use changed impact project implementation. While land availability in industrial and other specially developed areas developed by the State level agencies has been considerably streamlined, getting land outside such areas is still a very complex process. Although agricultural land can be purchased from Government agencies or private parties, its conversion to appropriate land use is still required. Proposals for conversion of land to non-agriculture purposes have to pass through many levels. In case of land situated in urban areas involving changes in the master plan, a public notice inviting objections is often necessary, which considerably delays the process. In many cases clearances under the Urban Land Ceiling (Regulations) Act is also needed. The requirement for such approvals would need to be reviewed during the re-engineering of the regulatory processes.

Approval of Building Plans

4.21 Approval of building plans by local authorities is another area where considerable delays are experienced highlighting the need to simplify the process. Powers to approve building plans can be given to architects registered under the Architects Act, 1972, who could certify the building plans as being in conformity with applicable building byelaws. Alternatively, specific time limits need to be fixed and adhered to for approval of building plans by the local authorities and, in case the local bodies do not issue permission within the prescribed period, the approval would be deemed to have been given. In both types of cases, the owner should be held responsible for any deviations from the building byelaws.

Release of Electricity and Water Connection

4.22 Delay in release of electricity and water connection also delays implementation of projects. The process for release of these connections, particularly for electricity, is cumbersome and the applicant is required to visit a large number of offices. State Electricity Boards, fearing an adverse impact on their revenues, are often reluctant to accord permissions to industries for setting up captive power plants. Since the release of connection also depends on the capacity of the existing system, a high degree of discretion vests with concerned official. Similar problems are encountered in case the sanctioned load is to be revised. Problems also exist in case of water connections, but are less acute.

4.23 Applications for release of new connection or for changes in the existing connections could be received at a single point in the SEB or its successor entities and technical constraints, if any, need to be resolved in a fixed time. Regular review of progress of release of electricity and water connections, at least for medium and large projects, and progress of augmentation works at the level of the State Investment Promotion Agency, Single Window Agency or any other designated agency, would help in reducing delays. Many states have taken initiatives to introduce single composite application form, which also include application form for electricity connection. The proposed Electricity Bill, 2002 also seeks to prescribe time limits for release of electricity connections.

Environmental Clearance

4.24 Many developmental projects are required to obtain clearance under the following legislations/notifications:

i. The Environment (Protection) Act, 1986

ii. The Water (Prevention and Control of Pollution) Act, 1974

iii. The Air (Prevention and Control of Pollution) Act, 1981

iv. Forest (Conservation) Act, 1980

v. Wildlife (Protection) Act, 1972

vi. EIA Notification, 1994

vii. CRZ Notification, 1991

4.25 Depending upon the nature of the project, environmental and pollution control clearances are required from Central/State Government/agencies. MOEF has, in its notification of 27.1.94, listed 29 categories of projects where environmental clearance is necessary from the MOEF. One more item was added to the list in January 2000. Broadly, environmental clearance is mandatory where the investment is above Rs. 100 crores, in the sectors of petroleum refineries, fertilizers, hydrocarbon exploration, primary metallurgical industries, cement and paper. In the sectors of highly polluting industries/hazardous industries, generally all proposals require environmental clearance. Environmental Impact Assessment (EIA) is mandatory for the 30 identified categories of industries covered under the notification of 1994 and its subsequent amendment. Public hearing has been made mandatory since April 1997 for greater involvement of stakeholders and local population and to maintain transparency in decision-making.

4.26 As per the provisions of the Environmental Impact Assessment (EIA) Notification of 1994, site-specific projects require two stage clearances. Stage-I (site clearance) is required for five categories of projects, namely river valley projects, pit-head thermal power projects, mining projects, ports and harbours. After obtaining site clearance, project authorities are permitted to undertake survey and investigations, prepare feasibility reports and collect environmental data, etc. Based on this information, Environmental Impact Assessment Report has to be prepared by the promoters of seeking final environmental clearance from MOEF.

4.27 After getting the EIA report, application for environmental clearance is submitted by the project authorities to the MOEF. The application is to be accompanied by a feasibility report, Environmental Impact Assessment Report (EIA), Environmental Management Plan (EMP) and details of public hearing. The applicant is also required to obtain a 'No Objection Certificate' from the State Pollution Control Board (SPCB), which is issued only after completing the public hearing. The projects are then evaluated and assessed by an Expert Committee constituted for various developmental sectors. In case of projects located in critically polluted or ecologically sensitive areas, site visits are undertaken by a Sub-Group for ground verification. The recommendations of the Expert Committee are considered in the MOEF and final environmental clearance is issued.

4.28 A flow chart showing the steps involved in environment clearance and time taken for each stage is at Annex-XIII. While a time limit of 90 days is stipulated for completing appraisal, various studies/reports, etc., have shown in that environmental clearance perhaps takes the longest and causes maximum delays in implementation of projects. In case of power projects, the entire process of environment clearance including preparation of the EIA and EMP could take up to 28 months. Inadequate information on critical aspects of EIA reports also delays appraisal. MOEF also accepts Rapid EIA for all projects except river valley projects for which a comprehensive EIA is insisted upon. To improve the quality of EIAs, MOEF should consider setting up a data centre, which could serve as a one-stop source for obtaining reliable and validated data for preparing EIAs.

4.29 Some of the main causes behind delays in environmental clearances have been identified by project promoters as:

i. Cumbersome procedure for environmental clearance and public hearing.

ii. Submission of incomplete information and poor quality of EIA/EMP necessitating additional information.

iii. Reopening of technical issues at every stage and raising of fresh issues during the course of grant of environmental clearance.

iv. Delays in the meetings of the Expert Committee and site visit, if considered necessary, before clearance.

4.30 MOEF has taken several policy initiatives to reduce delays in the grant of environmental and coastal zone regulation clearances. Some of the steps taken are given below:

i. The EIA Notification was amended in 1997 to delegate powers to state governments for environmental clearance of certain categories of thermal power projects such as co-generation plants, coal-based power plants up to 250 MW. Gas/naphtha based projects up to 500 MW, coal based power plants with CFBC technology up to 500 MW, etc.

ii. Amendment has been made in 1997 to exempt improvement and widening/strengthening of highways with marginal land acquisition (20 m width on either side) along existing alignments provided they do not pass through ecologically sensitive areas.

iii. Construction of roads for defence purposes in border areas has been exempted from the purview of EIA Notification.

iv. The Notification has been amended to dispense with the requirement of public hearing in respect of following categories of projects:

   a. Small-scale industrial undertakings located in industrial areas/estates.

   b. Widening and strengthening of highways.

   c. Mining projects of major minerals (lease up to 25 ha.)

   d. Units to be located in EPZ/SEZ.

   e. Modernization of existing irrigation projects.

v. Manufacture of drugs based genetically engineered micro-organisms, etc., has been exempted from the purview of EIA Notification by a recent amendment.

vi. In order to expedite public hearing process, the EIA Notification has been amended to prescribe a time limit of 60 days for completing the public hearing by the State Pollution Control Boards/Pollution Control Committees.

4.31 Similarly, a number of amendments have been carried out to streamline the original CRZ Notification of 1991 and simplified procedures and policies have been incorporated for expeditious clearance from CRZ angle. These include provisions for taking up developmental activities such as exploration and extraction of oil/gas, setting up of LNG facilities, construction of pipelines, conveyor systems and transmission lines and projects relating to atomic energy sector in CRZ areas.

4.32 MOEF has, by way of an amendment in the EIA notification, further streamlined the procedures as follows:

i. Enhancing the investment threshold from the previous limit of Rs. 50 crores to Rs. 100 crores for new projects.

ii. Exemption of modernization projects in the river-valley sector with investment up to Rs. 100 crores or command area less than 10,000 ha. from the purview of environmental clearance.

iii. Simplification of project documentation with regard to pipeline transport projects, etc.

4.33 MOEF has also amended the CRZ Notification 1991 on 21.5.2002 permitting non-polluting industries in the field of information technology and other service industries, desalination plants, beach resorts and related recreational facilities in the CRZ area of the notified Special Economic Zone (SEZ). In addition, the Ministry has also dispensed with 'No Development Zone (NDZ)' in CRZ-III of SEZ and existing ports, and permitted salt harvesting by solar evaporation of seawater in inter-tidal areas.

4.34 Suggestions to reduce delays in environmental clearances:

i. The investment limit for certain categories of projects requiring environmental clearance has, during deliberations by the Committee, been enhanced by MOEF from Rs. 50 crores to Rs. 100 crores. The investment limit as well as the list of projects requiring environmental clearance should be made co-terminus with Plan period necessitating a review every five years. It is also desirable to link this limit with CPI for automatic adjustment with inflation in future.

ii. Instead of the present procedure under which various stages of environmental clearance are undertaken seriatim, MOEF should evolve a procedure to take up activities in parallel.

iii. MOEF should also examine if all the documents referred to in the explanatory memorandum attached to the EIA Notification, 1994 need to be insisted upon at the time of receipt of application itself.

iv. Site visits, if necessary, must be carried out within a month of submission of application. In case the site visit is not carried out within the prescribed period, it may be deemed that such visits are not required and the next stage of approval process may be taken up.

v. Expert Committee may raise all issues at the first meeting itself and Members not present may send their comments to the Committee in writing. In case any Member does not give his or her comments within the prescribed period, it should be presumed that he or she has no comments to offer and the next stage of approval process taken up.

vi. Once first stage site clearance has been given, final clearance to be issued after commissioning of all necessary plant & machinery may be accorded as deemed approval if it is not granted within the prescribed time, unless the competent authority for valid reasons to be recorded extends this time limit.

Forest Clearance

4.35 Clearances from Forest authorities are requested for projects requiring diversion of forest land for non-forestry purposes. The MOEF gives clearance for diversion of forestland. Proposal for diversion of forestland has to be submitted to the Forest department in the district. After detailed site survey by the field staff, a compensatory afforestation plan is prepared and sent to the State Forest department. After departmental approval, this proposal requires approval of the State government before being sent to the MOEF.

4.36 In the MOEF, the proposal is scrutinised and a site inspection report from field offices is taken before an Expert Committee considers the case. A site visit by the Expert Committee may be required. Recommendations of the Expert Committee are processed by the MOEF for according the forest clearance. A flow chart showing the steps to forest clearance and the time taken at each stage is at Annex-XIV. It may be seen that the entire process of forest clearance may take up to 13 months.

4.37 The issues causing delays in forest clearance have been identified as:

i. Two stage Forest clearance where first an 'In Principle' clearance is issued and once conditions mentioned therein are fulfilled and compliance report is received by MOEF, formal forest clearance is issued.

ii. There is considerable delay in identification of non-forest lands for compensatory afforestation.

4.38 MOEF has taken several steps to reduce delays in forest clearance. These include:

i. MOEF has delegated powers to decide on proposals for diversion of forestland up to 5 ha. to its 6 Regional Offices located at Bhopal, Bhubaneshwar, Bangalore, Lucknow, Chandigarh and Shillong.

ii. It has prescribed a simplified format for submission of proposals involving forest areas up to 2 ha., provided no felling of trees is involved.

iii. For hill areas and districts having more than 50 per cent forest cover, it has permitted compensatory afforestation to be raised over an extent of double the degraded forest instead of normal stipulation of raising it over equivalent non-forest land provided the forest land required does not exceed 20 ha.

iv. State Governments have been given general permission to allow execution of projects regarding laying of underground pipelines for drinking water supply, electricity cables, telephone lines and optical fiber cables along roads which do not involve any felling of trees.

v. The area limit for mandatory site inspections has been raised from 40 ha. to 100 ha.

vi. Proposals for diversion of forest land up to 5 ha. are entertained even if the Nodal Officer submits these instead of the State Government, thereby reducing the number of layers.

vii. The major user agencies have been persuaded to create a forest bank for compensatory afforestation purposes so that final approval for the project can be issued by the Ministry at first instance itself instead of the in-principle (first stage) approval after setting off the compensatory afforestation area from the land bank.

4.39 From the procedure prescribed for forest clearance, it is seen that the proposal initiated at the district level in the State and recommended by the State Government is again examined by the Regional Director of MOEF before being forwarded to the MOEF. These proposals, therefore, pass through various levels in concerned departments and are repeatedly scrutinised at the field, department and Government level in State as well as Central Government. It would be useful to set up an Empowered Committee for Forest Clearance where all concerned departments/agencies of the State and Central Government can be represented and cases decided expeditiously.

4.40 MOEF may consider permitting diversion of forestland for pre-construction activities based on the 'in-principle' clearance after the non-forest land identified for compensatory afforestation has been transferred to the forest department and funds for raising compensatory afforestation deposited by the user agency. Forestland required for main project components can be approved later based on final clearance.

4.41 For cases requiring environmental and forest clearances detailed information is required to be submitted at the time of filing application. Under the existing arrangements, MOEF has prescribed a checklist for documentation and conducts preliminary scrutiny of the proposals on receipt. The Expert Committee at the time of consideration of proposals may also require additional information. This process consumes considerable time and effort.

4.42 Considering the requirement of voluminous information to be submitted for obtaining these approvals, it is recommended that expert agencies may be authorised for initial scrutiny of applications for environmental and forest clearances for completeness of essential information before these are submitted to the concerned authorities for approval. The time limits prescribed for the grant of approvals may be reckoned from the date of filing of applications with concerned authorities.

Impediments to Specific Clearances Required by Projects in Specific Sectors

4.43 Besides the clearances mentioned earlier normally required by a large number of projects, sector-specific projects, particularly in the infrastructure sectors, need additional clearances. The Sub-Group has examined the difficulties in getting specific clearances/ approvals in the power and road sectors. Main difficulties and suggestions for reducing delays in getting these clearances/ approvals are dealt with below:

Power Sector

4.44 Under section 29 of the Electricity (Supply) Act, 1948, every scheme involving capital expenditure exceeding such sum as may be fixed from time to time, requires concurrence of the Central Electricity Authority (CEA). This clearance, popularly called the tech-economic clearance, applies to both generation and transmission schemes. In respect of captive generation, clearance from the State Electricity Board is required under section 44 of the Act. If the capacity of the captive generating plant exceeds 25 MW, SEB is also required to consult CEA.

4.45 Some of the major impediments to speedy implementation of power projects in the private sector are:

i. Poor financial position of the State Electricity Boards, who are presently the sole buyer of electricity, and the inability of States to push forward power sector reforms. As a result, SEBs do not have adequate payment capacities for power to be purchased from private power producers. Financial institutions insist on adequate payment security arrangement to be put in place to ensure regular payment by SEBs. Inability of SEBs to provide escrow cover and other payment security guarantees acceptable to the financial institutions, delays financial closure and the projects get stalled.

ii. Delays in finalisation of various agreements such as Power Purchase Agreement, Fuel Supply Agreement, Fuel Transportation Agreement, etc., acceptable to all concerned parties and financial institutions.

iii. The process of getting techno-economic clearance from the CEA is a time-consuming one. Several references are made to the CEA.

4.46 The common issues involved in the main clearances and suggestions for reducing such delays are covered below:

a. Delay in clearance for water requirement

Procedure and Issues:

i. Application indicating consumptive requirement of water, source and drawal points is submitted to State Government.

ii. Necessary approval is to be obtained from State Government and Central Water Commission. Permission for Ministry of Water Resources (MOWR) is needed in cases of water sources involving inter-state issues.

iii. Lack of consensus on water sharing between States delays projects.

Suggestions for reducing delays:

i. MOWR may accord clearances within 6 months by convening meetings of all concerned states.

b. Notifications under section 29 of the Electricity (Supply) Act, 1948

Procedure and Issues:

i. Details of the power project are published in the official gazette and newspapers giving 2 months' time for filing objections. Corrigendum is also to be published in case of even minor changes in key features.

ii. Delays in publication in the official gazette, need for fresh publication in case of changes in key features and 2 months' time allowed for filing objections also delay the grant of approval under section 29. This process can take about 8-9 months before the scheme get finalized for consideration to CEA.

Suggestions for reducing the delay:

i. In view of larger reach of newspapers today, publication in vernacular newspapers having adequate circulation in the area should suffice and the need for publication in the official gazette may be dispensed with. The Committee has made a recommendation to this effect at paragraph 4.19.

ii. The time for filing objections may be reduced to 1 month.

iii. Fresh publication may be necessary only in case of major changes in nature and scope of the project (over 20 per cent in cost terms excluding standard updation in cost due to exchange rate variation, changes in the tax/duty structure, etc.)

iv. Since public hearing is mandatory for NOC from State Pollution Control Board, the requirement of section 29 may altogether be dispensed with.

c. Coal Linkages

Procedure and Issues:

i. Project authorities approach MOP/CEA with project details for recommending to SCL (Long Term), Ministry of Coal for grant of long-term linkage.

ii. MOC considers the request and gives 'in principle' clearance.

iii. Coal linkage is granted by SLC in its meetings that are held only once or twice a year, leading to delays in coal linkages.

Suggestions for reducing delays:

i. SLC should meet more frequently and a Joint Committee comprising representatives from MOP, MOC, CIL and Power Utilities needs to be formed to identify new mining blocks for new power stations.

d. Ash utilization conditions by MOEF

Procedure and Issues:

i. As per the present norm, 100 per cent utilization is required by the ninth year while there is no tie up for ash utilization at the DPR stage.

Suggestion for reducing delays:

i. The time frame should be extended to the life of the project as reckoned at the appraisal stage, subject to a maximum of 25 years.

ii. For stations having dry ash storage facilities like construction of ash mound with adequate safeguards as prescribed, the ash stored at the ash mound can be considered as ash utilized, as it does not pose any environmental hazard.

4.47 Besides the above, clearance from Coastal Zone Regulations may also be required. It has been proposed by the Ministry of Power that clearances from CRZ aspects should be given, on case to case basis, based on the investigations carried out by identified agencies as per defined norms and should not be linked to drawing up of the total coast line. The competent authorities should give clearance within one month of submission of the report.

4.48 Government of India has been assisting the states in the resolution of these issues. Model PPA and Fuel Supply Agreements have been drafted with the help of international consultants. Poor financial health of the power utilities in the public sector has emerged as the major reason behind slow pace of implementation of power projects in private sector. Reforms in the power sector, therefore, assume paramount importance and unless the financial health of the sector is restored, private investment will be difficult to come by. Government of India has been supporting the states in the reform and restructuring of the State Electricity Boards. Memoranda of Agreements (MOA) have been signed with many states on time-bound implementation of the reform programme and financial institutions have been extending credit to the SEB's/ Successor Companies based on agreed roadmaps.

4.49 The proposed Electricity Bill, 2002 will address many of the concerns of existing legislation in speedy implementation of power projects and will replace the existing Indian Electricity Act, 1910 and the Electricity (Supply) Act, 1948. Under the proposed legislation, techno-economic clearance from CEA under section 29 of the Electricity (Supply) Act. 1948 will no longer be required in respect of non-hydro generation projects. The requirements of clearance by CEA is proposed to be continued in case of hydro projects because of the issues involving inter-State rivers, dam safety and design, etc., besides the need for comprehensive and optimum development of hydro potential of rivers. The Electricity Bill, 2002 also proposes to do away with any clearance from the SEB before setting up captive power plants.

4.50 Under the proposed Electricity Bill, 2002, a time limit of 90 days has been prescribed for grant of license. The existing provision of approval of the Central Transmission Utility/State Transmission Utility before obtaining a transmission license is also proposed to be done away with.

Road Projects

4.51 Road projects generally require extensive land acquisition, relocation of displaced persons, removal of construction on acquired lands and shifting of utilities managed by various departments/agencies. This requires very close coordination between a large number of agencies of the Central and State Government. Some of the issues hampering progress of projects in road sector are:

i. Delay in land acquisition as lands, which have to be acquired alongside existing alignments, are often under use/occupation. This requires removal of a large number of structures, relocation and rehabilitation of a large number of persons and removal of encroachments from Government lands.

ii. Often utilities like electricity and telecom poles, pipelines, cables, etc., are located alongside existing road alignment that need to be shifted before work can start. Shifting/relocation of utilities requires clearance from various departments, which also have to relocate these utilities. Besides involvement of a number of Governmental agencies in relocation of utilities, non-availability of information on exact location of underground installations also causes delays in completion of such works. Each agency is required to plan and implement relocation of such utility. Often these do not get synchronized with project progress, leading to delays in implementation project.

4.52 A task force under Secretary to State Government in charge of Public Works Department may be set up for coordination among concerned agencies, both State and Central, for shifting of utilities so that the work for shifting all utilities could be taken up simultaneously by the concerned agencies in a well coordinated manner.

Multiplicity of Clearances

4.53 There are many activities where clearances from many Government departments/agencies and other authorities have to be obtained. For instance, to set up a captive power plant, even after taking permission from the State Electricity Board, separate clearances/permissions/licenses have to be obtained from local authorities, police, public works department, District Collector, Controller of Explosives, etc. Except the clearances required from the safety point of view, other clearances could be made automatic. Even on safety related aspects, clearance from one agency, say District Collector, should suffice. The requirement of multiple clearances for an activity from different agencies or multiple clearances from the same agency may also be reviewed at the time of re-engineering of regulatory processes.

Re-engineering of Regulatory Processes at State Level and Single Window Clearance

4.54 Re-engineering of the regulatory processes at the state level on lines similar to the re-engineering proposed at Central level would be necessary to examine the approval requirements under extant laws, prescribe time limits, develop appropriate trigger mechanisms to automatically raise the matter to the next higher level in cases of delay in decision making, review extant laws and indicate inter-se priority among proposed regulatory reforms. The State Governments may consider setting up groups to take up re-engineering of regulatory processes at the state level in a time-bound manner. The progress may be reviewed at the highest level.

4.55 After investment approval in case of public projects and financial closure in case of private projects, the project needs to obtain necessary approvals/permissions from the concerned departments of the Government of India/State Government before the commencement of operation/during operation. Such cases for approvals/permissions are examined in various departments of the Central/State Government with respect to their functions. Most approvals/permissions for implementing the project after investment approvals pertain to the state level agencies.

4.56 In the absence of adequate networking among departments/ agencies, necessary linkages among various departments/agencies do not get established and the processes of approvals in different departments become stand-alone processes with findings of examination of any issue by one department not being made available to other departments. Examination of applications in different departments, in isolation of examination already carried out by other departments, leads to delays and, at times, conflict of opinion among departments. The concept of Single Window system was conceived to overcome the inordinately long time taken in obtaining all approvals/licenses, etc., from concerned Government departments/agencies. It was expected that, with Single Window system, all approvals will be issued at one place or at least one single agency will follow up the issue of necessary approvals.

4.57 Although specialised investment promotion agencies have been set up by most States, in view of the control over approval mechanism by respective line departments, these investment promotion agencies have not been able to effectively address the needs of the Single Window system. Powers to accord approvals are vested in various departments/agencies under their respective statutes and notifications. Existing legal framework does not support the Single Window concept, as it does not empower any department, body or agency with overriding powers to accord all requisite clearance under the Acts administered by different departments. Under such circumstances, the success of the Single Window system depends to a large extent on the leadership of the State.

4.58 Many States have attempted to overcome this difficulty through suitable institutional changes. Andhra Pradesh has, in June 2002, promulgated the Andhra Pradesh Industrial Single Window Clearance Ordinance, 2002 to provide legal backing to the single window clearance system. Earlier, a special legislation, 'The Andhra Pradesh Infrastructure Development Enabling Act, 2001,' was enacted which empowers the 'Infrastructure Authority' established under the Act to monitor the grant of approvals by different departments and grant such approvals in case the concerned departments failed to grant the approvals within prescribed time. In Rajasthan, Rules of Business have been amended and specially empowered bodies set up to accord approvals for subjects under different departments. In Chattisgarh state, 'The Chattisgarh Audyogik Nivesh Protsahan Adhiniyam, 2002' has been enacted. State level initiatives are covered in greater detail in Chapter 5 of the report.

4.59 The Committee recommends that an empowered Single Window system at the state level is vital to reduce delays in various approvals. This, along with re-engineering of the regulatory processes, would have maximum impact on reducing delays in getting required approvals and implementing the projects. The single window agency at the state level should be empowered to lay down time frames for approvals, review the grant of approvals by concerned agencies/departments, local bodies, etc., accord approvals in case concerned departments/agencies do not grant these approvals in a predetermined time frame, and also give appropriate directions to the concerned agencies/departments. The states may consider various alternatives such as enactment of legislation, amendment in the Rules of Business, etc., to operationalise and empower the single window system. Model legislation on the lines of 'The Andhra Pradesh Infrastructure Development Enabling Act, 2001', 'The Andhra Pradesh Industrial Single Window Clearance Ordinance, 2002' or 'The Chattisgarh Audyogik Nivesh Protsahan Adhiniyam, 2002' could be considered for expediting clearances.

4.60 While such legislations are limited to subjects in the State list, many infrastructure project-related issues would fall under the Union/Concurrent list. Under these circumstances, the effectiveness of States' initiatives would be limited and would need to be reinforced with similar initiatives at Central level. The 'Industrial Investment Facilitation Board (IIFB)', recommended by the Committee in Part-I of its report for being set up as the central facilitation body, would follow up the grant of approvals for projects with investment of Rs. 100 crores and above. Besides, any investor facing difficulties in obtaining approvals from the Ministries/Agencies may also approach IIFB irrespective of the investment limit. IIFB would also prescribe time limits for grant of various non-statutory approvals in consultations with the concerned Ministries. FIIA would continue to look after specific difficulties being faced by foreign investors.

Single Composite Application Form (SCAF)

4.61 Industrial projects and projects in other sectors are governed by numerous Acts and regulations, each requiring specified forms to be filled, returns to be filed and registers to be maintained. The information required in many of these forms is similar with a lot of repetition and overlap. Different departments/ agencies have to be approached for these clearances. Composite application forms aim at consolidating the applications required for basic clearances/approvals in one set. Attempts towards introduction of composite application by consolidation of all applicable forms in their present form without a serious attempt towards reduction, if not elimination, of redundant forms and avoiding repetition of information in different forms cannot result in simplification of procedures.

4.62 Many states have developed single composite application forms (SCAF) for clearances generally required by large and medium projects. State level investment promotion or facilitation agencies, that receive these composite application forms, are responsible for obtaining necessary clearances from concerned departments. At the District level, the respective District Industry Centres (DICs) are generally responsible for obtaining such clearances. A high-powered committee monitors progress of grant of approvals under these composite applications. State level initiatives in introducing single composite application forms are covered at length in Chapter 5.

4.63 These initiatives for single window clearances are welcome steps to facilitate issue of all approvals from a single point and need to be extended to all types of projects. A lot of work also needs to be done for simplification of forms prescribed for different approvals. Different approvals from the same department can be combined into a single approval. State Level Investment Promotion Agency or any other designated agency may be assigned the specific responsibility for development, implementation and follow up clearances from concerned departments/agencies under Single Composite Application Forms, for large and medium projects to begin with.

4.64 Similarly, greater use of information technology tools by the State and Central Government departments and their networking could allow information sharing among concerned departments, avoid the need for providing separate information to different departments and permit simultaneous processing of cases in different departments/agencies and thereby cutting down time taken in granting such approvals. Under such arrangements, the process of verification/examination carried out at one place need not be repeated elsewhere and information on examination by other departments/agencies would be readily available.

Incentivising the States

4.65 Several States have already undertaken measures to simplify their regulatory procedures and the need for reforming the regulatory framework is well recognized and accepted at the state level. Reforms in regulatory processes, unlike other sectoral reforms, are not perceived to have huge political implications, and states are more likely to undertake such measures. Since the States stand to benefit immensely from such reforms, which will catalyse greater investment flows, there would be greater inclination among states to undertake such reforms and, therefore, non-monetary incentives in the form of technical support, sensitization about practices elsewhere, performance of the states, institution of awards, etc., may be effective.

4.66 Many progressive states are quite sensitive to investor perceptions. Documentation and dissemination of information on best practices in India and other developing economies would sensitise people and exert pressure on the regulatory system to deliver better services and, thereby, create pressure for undertaking regulatory reforms. The Committee felt that simplification in the regulatory processes would be a one-time as well as an ongoing exercise. The States would need to be supported during the exercise of re-engineering of the regulatory processes. The Government of India may provide technical assistance to the states for re-engineering of their regulatory processes for which assistance of multilateral financial institutions may be availed. A concept paper on technical assistance is at Annex-XI.

4.67 The State Governments and the Central Government are already implementing a number of schemes and projects focusing on infrastructure augmentation for industries in the states. Government of India is also providing reform-linked assistance under Accelerated Power Development and Reform Programme (APDRP) and Urban Reform Incentive Fund (URIF). In addition, an amount of Rs. 2500 crores has been provided in the Union Budget for 2002-03 for ushering in policy reforms in sectors which are constraining growth and development. The proposed monetary incentive scheme may be dovetailed with various incentive schemes and clearly earmarked for identified infrastructure components/projects, as may be determined by the State Governments concerned. Additional budgetary provisions may also be considered for augmenting the funds available as incentive to the states. Institutional arrangements would be necessary to ensure that the funds are properly utilised on appropriately designed projects. The Government may also consider issuing directive to the financial Institutions to link lending to states for their infrastructure projects with the progress of regulatory reforms. This would further incentivise the states for undertaking regulatory reforms and to simplify procedures for approval and implementation of projects.

Prescribing and Enforcing Time Limits for Approvals

4.68 IIFB would, in consultation with the concerned Administrative Ministries, prescribe time limits for the grant of various non-statutory approvals and follow up the grant of various statutory approvals with the concerned Administrative Ministries/ Agencies. Cases of delay in approvals by the Ministries/ Departments of Government of India will be followed up by IIFB with the concerned for their expeditious resolution. As the representative of the concerned States would also be co-opted in IIFB, cases involving delays at the level of State Departments would be followed up in IIFB. Besides, the State Level Single Window Mechanism or Investment Promotion Agencies would follow up the grant of approvals by the departments/agencies of State Government. Re-engineering of the regulatory processes would also enable many approvals to be replaced by either deemed approvals or automatic approval upon fulfilling the requirements. Individual Ministries/Departments, both at Central and State level, should develop appropriate trigger mechanisms to take the matter to the next higher level whenever the prescribed time frames are not adhered to.

4.69 The recommendations to empower the State Level Single Window system also include recommendation to suitably empower such bodies to decide on cases of approvals, in case the concerned departments fail to decide within the prescribed time limits. This would ensure that the cases for approvals are not delayed.

Regulatory Environment During Operation of Projects

4.70 A study conducted jointly by CII and the World Bank in January 2002 on 'Competitiveness in Indian Manufacturing' based on firm level survey has shown that nearly 16 per cent of management's time in India is spent in dealing with regulatory authorities. The average number of visit by regulatory authorities in a year for the 10 surveyed states was 11.5 with states having better investment climate having lesser number of visits.

4.71 As stated earlier at paragraphs 3.17 & 3.18, a survey of 385 foreign investors conducted by FICCI in March 2002, has shown that 74 per cent of respondents have reported ground level hassles to be high and 76 per cent respondents have observed that reducing ground level hassles is imperative for enhancing FDI inflows. 38 per cent respondents have rated state level handling of approvals 'bad' in contrast to 93 per cent respondents reporting handling of approvals at central level from 'good to average'

4.72 Removing the ground level hassles by making the system of reporting meaningful, less bureaucratic and by minimizing interaction between project and regulatory agencies will simplify the operating environment for the projects. Some of the issues related to interface of the regulatory machinery with the project are briefly covered below:

Inspections

4.73 Multiplicity of inspecting authorities from different departments creates operational difficulties for the projects during their operation. A study by ASCI has listed at least 27 different kinds of inspections for industrial undertakings by various agencies. Most of these inspections will be applicable to other projects as well. An illustrative list of inspectors of various departments is at Annex-VI.

4.74 The number as well as frequency of inspections needs to be reduced. Besides clubbing duties of different inspecting authorities to reduce the number of inspectors, annual inspections could also be carried out at one time by all concerned departments as a team after giving advance notice. Some inspections can still be carried out as surprise inspections by special teams of concerned departments. A Committee under the Secretary (Industry) of the

State Government may decide on the inspection schedule of projects under both Central and State legislations.

4.75 Numerous Acts regulating the operation of enterprises, prescribe periodic renewal of approvals/licenses, etc. This requires frequent interaction with concerned regulatory agencies. With advancement in technologies and experience gained by the industry, it should be possible to revise the frequency of these clearances and permissions. Requirement of permission under the Factories Act before taking up construction, external and internal inspection, etc., needs to be reviewed. The period for renewal of license for factories may be increased to three years from the present limit of one year. The Ministry of Labour has already initiated the process of carrying out comprehensive amendments to the Factories Act, 1948. The re-engineering groups, during the re-engineering of regulatory processes, may also look into the inspection requirements. Periodic inspections may be necessary only for Category-C issues where the frequency of inspections would vary across regulatory issues.

4.76 At present a lot of time is spent on inspections by various departments. Besides clubbing these inspections into a few combined inspections, the authority for conducting inspections can also be given to accredited external certifying agencies with responsibility assigned to them for ensuring various statutory compliances by the units inspected. Along with outsourcing of approval, authority for inspection & pre-examination, etc., internal disciplinary systems of professional associations to act against complaints of malpractices would need to be strengthened. Induction of outside experts could be considered.

Registers and Returns

4.77 An enterprise during its operation has to maintain a large number of registers and file many returns. An illustrative list of registers and returns to be maintained under Central Acts is at Annex-VII. A medium size company is required to maintain 42 different types of returns/forms. (Annex-VIII). Multiplicity of Acts and the procedural requirements under each Act require a large number of registers to be maintained even for identical objectives. For example, separate attendance and payment registers have to be maintained under the following Acts:

i. The Factories Act, 1948

ii. The Minimum Wages Act, 1948

iii. The Contract Labour (Regulation and Abolition) Act, 1970

iv. The Payment of Wages Act, 1936

v. The Payment of Gratuity Act, 1972

vi. The Employees' State Insurance Act, 1948

vii. The Provident Funds Act, 1925

4.78 The stipulation of maintaining separate registers under each Act for related subjects imposes a heavy burden on the project as well as the regulatory authorities and needs to be reviewed. Instead of maintaining different registers, a single register or electronically maintained database may be sufficient. The Labour Laws (Exemption From Furnishing Returns and Maintenance of Registers by Certain Establishments) Act, 1988, permits maintenance of common registers but is presently applicable to only small-scale enterprises, employing up to 19 persons. This restriction and punishments prescribed under this Act for violation being more stringent than what individual laws impose has restricted its use. It is recommended that this law be made applicable to larger number of industries by increasing the limit of persons employed to 500.

4.79 Besides reducing the number of forms to be submitted by a unit, there should be a time limit, of say 4 weeks, within which the concerned authorities may respond to these forms for any clarification required. After this period, the form submitted by the unit should be deemed to have been accepted and approved. As a growing number of industries and business undertakings are now using computers for their day-to-day transactions, computerized records may be accepted for maintaining registers and filing of returns.

4.80 Re-engineering groups during re-examination of regulatory issues suggested at paragraph 4.10, may also look at consolidation of reporting, record keeping and inspection requirements under extant laws to minimize the points of contact between project promoters and regulatory authorities, allow electronic reporting and record keeping and bring together provisions dealing with same subject. Mandatory reporting requirement may be needed only for Category-C issues, and documentation, but not reporting, for Category-B issues. In general, Category-A issues may be exempt from documentation/reporting.

Facilitation Mechanisms

4.81 Facilitation Teams (FTs), recommended by the Committee in Part-I of the report for being set up in the Administrative Ministries, would facilitate implementation of projects, both public and private, involving investment of Rs.100 crores and above. The FTs would also include representatives from departments responsible for according various clearances as well as concerned State Governments.

4.82 At the State level also facilitation mechanisms are needed since a large number of approvals/clearances required for implementation of projects pertain to the departments/organizations of the State Government. Besides regular review and follow up of grant of approvals, Single Window Agency or State Investment Promotion Agency may interact at least once every three months with the investors on the factors impeding implementation of projects, scope for further simplification of procedures and facilitate resolution of difficulties being encountered by them in the implementation of their projects.

Settlement of Legal Disputes

4.83 Many investors have identified time-consuming legal processes and delays in settlement of legal disputes as an impediment to implementation of their projects. As disposal of cases gets delayed in regular judicial proceedings, recourse to alternate dispute redressal remedies is becoming increasingly important. International Centre for Alternative Dispute Resolution (ICADR) has been established as a society under the aegis of the Ministry of Law and Justice, to promote alternative dispute resolution facilities. (www.ICADR.org). ICADR, besides appointing arbitrators/conciliators, also keeps track of the proceedings for their early conclusion. Almost all commercial, civil and labour disputes, in respect of which parties are entitled to conclude a settlement, can be settled by alternate dispute resolution procedures. This remedy is also available to foreign companies under the provisions of the Arbitration and Conciliation Act, 1996, provided there is an agreement between the parties to refer their disputes to arbitration, conciliation or mediation. Even when the parties have not included the arbitration/conciliation clauses in their original agreements for referring their disputes to ICADR, they can enter into a separate agreement for settling their dispute through arbitration/conciliation and reference to ICADR.

4.84 ICADR has been receiving on an average, only 2-3 cases every month for appointment of arbitrators. While alternative dispute resolution offers expeditious resolution of disputes, yet the small number of cases referred for arbitration suggests limited knowledge and awareness about this mechanism. It would be useful to give wide publicity to the alternate dispute resolution mechanism. All Ministries of Government of India and State Governments could encourage investors to include appropriate provisions in agreements to refer their disputes for resolution by alternative methods. Concerned departments can also provide information about ICADR on their websites.

4.85 Apart from ICADR, state level initiatives have also been taken to reduce delays in settlement of disputes and to provide an alternative system of dispute resolution. Under the 'Andhra Pradesh Infrastructure Development Enabling Act, 2001', a Conciliation Board, comprising 3 Members with a retired High Court Judge as its Chairperson, has been established to assist the Government agency or Local authority and any developer to reach an amicable settlement of their disputes. The Board is empowered to call upon the party to dispute to file its reply. Conciliation proceedings will need to be completed in 3 months. This time limit can be extended by 90 days on the request of both parties.

Lack of Information and Transparency

4.86 Lack of transparency in the system of grant of approvals and difficulties in obtaining necessary information on the procedural and documentary requirements for various approvals, latest orders and instructions, also cause delays. Sometimes even the forms or specific information to be provided for getting approval are not readily available. It is recommended that every department must clearly spell out its policy framework for investment, approvals required from both Central and State

Governments, agencies responsible for grant of each approval, their contact address, procedural requirements for each approval, prescribed time frame, etc. Information on the applicable Acts and Rules should also be widely disseminated.

4.87 A net-enabled information system should be developed to provide this information. To begin with, such net-enabled information system could be developed by each department of the Central and State Governments as a distinct part of their website. This could subsequently be interconnected across departments to provide all related information at one point.

4.88 Forms for all types of approvals/clearances along with information on the procedural requirement and list of documents to be attached must be available on the websites of concerned departments/agencies or State Level Investment Promotion Agency in a downloadable format. This may be completed with the next six months. Any deficiency in the particulars furnished in the application must be conveyed to the applicant within a specific time frame, of say 7 days, and an acknowledgment on receiving complete application must be issued. Necessary systems may be put in position, within one year, for electronic submission of these applications. Status of pending applications should be made public at regular intervals and must also be available on the department's website along with reasons for delay in approval beyond prescribed time. This may be done within three months' time.

4.89 Periodic publication of information on the performance of states on 8-10 critical parameters and ranking states on these parameters would generate healthy competition among states and incentivise them for undertaking further reforms. The SIA newsletter of the Department of Industrial Policy & Promotion containing details of state wise IEMs is now available on the website of the department. While some Ministries/Departments are making public information on the performance of states in various parameters, it needs to be done on a broader scale and on a regular basis. In view of the wide disparities in the present level of regulatory reforms in the states, it may be useful to categorise the states based on their existing levels of reforms and rank them accordingly within their categories to generate competition among similarly placed states. Administrative Staff College of India may also study the procedures prevalent in states and supplement this with feedback from investors on the quality of decision making.

Sensitisation and Awareness Building

4.90 Sensitizing people about the best practices elsewhere, initiatives taken in Central Ministries and States, etc., would be a highly effective method of creating awareness about regulatory reforms. Towards this objective, documentation of the best practices in India and other developing economies, and their dissemination through seminars, workshops, meetings, etc., would be necessary. Industry associations, States, etc., may be associated for documentation. The sensitization exercise needs to be taken deeper to the level of citizens who would exert pressure on the system to deliver better services and thereby create the pressure for undertaking regulatory reforms. A separate exercise would need to be undertaken to design the components of the documentation and dissemination needs, assess resource availability & requirement and implementation methodology, which can be taken up as a project by the Industry Associations. While each department would be undertaking this exercise in relation to the programmes under their jurisdiction, States would need to be actively associated. PMO is also considering a sensitization programme for the reform programmes and their impact on the lives of citizen. Regulatory reforms could also be considered for inclusion in such a programme.

4.91 It is felt that mere simplification of procedures would not suffice, as the attitude of implementation machinery at the field level is also crucial for reducing hassles and harassment. Abuse of power resulting in delays in grant of various approvals needs to be curbed. It is, therefore, necessary that disciplinary proceedings are invariably initiated in such cases against public servants, both at central and state level, and are concluded expeditiously. Stringent action should be taken in cases of proven abuse of power.

Greater Use of IT in Approval Administration

4.92 Greater use of IT tools in the administration of various approvals would not only reduce delays and bring in more efficiency but would also increase transparency. Some Ministries/ Departments have taken initiatives in this direction by providing information requirements for various approvals, status of pending case, etc. It is necessary that these individual initiatives be integrated through an inter-Ministry as well as intra-Ministry effort. This would require rewriting of office procedures making these amenable to IT tools, standardization of data requirements, inter-linked processing across Ministries, eventually allowing on-line filing of applications & returns and processing of applications.

4.93 In the course of re-engineering of the regulatory processes, it must be ensured that the outcomes are amenable to e-governance. A major Centrally Sponsored Scheme (CSS) is under preparation for the 10th Five Year Plan, jointly by the Department of Administrative Reforms and Department of IT, and a technical support institution, the 'National Institute of Smart Governance', is being set up at Hyderabad. The re-engineered processes may accordingly be implemented from the scratch by IT systems.

4.94 It would be necessary to have a time bound action plan for greater use of IT in approval administration. Generally speaking, The Ministries/Departments should be able to place information on the website on the status of pending applications, procedural and documentary requirements with various applications with in three months. Application forms for various approvals could be made available in downloadable form on the websites within six months. Interconnecting Ministries and allowing on-line filing of applications and returns should be possible with one year while connecting the States with the central system should take place within two years.

Skill Upgradation and Attitudinal Changes in Administrative Machinery

4.95 Liberalisation in the policy framework needs to be supported by simplification of procedures and a re-orientation of the machinery handling such issues. Functioning of the offices of various departments/agencies need to be brought in line with the present day technologies and practices. These offices need to drastically reduce their paperwork and instead move towards paperless working. Regular training of the staff at cutting edge level is necessary to bring about and sustain this attitudinal change.

4.96 The Committee in Part-I of its report has furnished recommendations on the capacity building needs. Training of the officials of line agencies & members of the Facilitation Teams on modern project management techniques, use of IT, etc., would benefit project implementation. The functionaries in various Government departments/agencies responsible for according various clearances/approvals must be imparted training on modern management practices, greater use of IT in grant of approvals as well as post commissioning regulatory requirements. The extant procedures must be revised to reflect the present business and technological environment.

5

State Level Initiatives

MANY states have launched initiatives to simplify the procedures, reduce delays in approval administration and facilitating implementation of projects. The steps taken in some of the states are briefly covered below:

Andhra Pradesh

5.2 A special Act, the 'Andhra Pradesh Infrastructure Development Enabling Act, 2001' has been enacted laying down a strong legal framework for reducing delays in obtaining various approvals and clearances. The Act empowers the 'Infrastructure Authority', established under the Act, to grant all clearances and permissions for any project in case concerned departments do not grant these clearances in the prescribed time frame.

5.3 The Act also authorizes the 'Infrastructure Authority' to prescribe time limits for according clearance for projects by departments and also to periodically review the status of clearances. It also empowers the 'Infrastructure Authority' to give directions to any Government agency or local authority or other authority or developer or any other person with regard to implementation of any project, which are binding upon such agency/authority or developer.

Andhra Pradesh Industrial Single Window Clearance Ordinance, 2002

5.4 The Andhra Pradesh Industrial Single Window Clearance Ordinance promulgated on 22.6.2002 provides for District and State level Single Window Clearance Committees, Empowered Committees and State Board. Single Window Clearance

Committees would receive applications for all clearances for setting up industrial units, review and monitor the processing of applications and forward the orders of the competent authorities to the applicant. These Committee would also inform the applicant the date on which the application was received by the competent authority and the date on which the application may be deemed to have been approved in the case of deemed approval.

5.5 The Empowered Committee besides reviewing the disposal of applications by the District and State level Committees, would also examine the orders passed by these Committees and pass appropriate orders. The orders of the Empowered Committee will be binding on the District and State Committees. Similarly, the State Board may examine any orders passed by the Empowered Committee and pass appropriate orders.

5.6 The ordinance empowers the State Government to prescribe a combined application form which all departments or authorities are mandated to accept. The ordinance also empowers the State Government to prescribe the time limits for processing and disposal of applications. The competent authorities can ask for additional information only once before the expiry of time period for disposal of such applications. The State Government may also notify the clearance in respect of which failure of the competent authority to pass final order on the application within the prescribed period shall result in deemed approval.

Tamil Nadu

5.7 In Tamil Nadu, a High Powered State Level Investment Promotion Board and a Project Approval Authority have been established to accord composite clearances to the projects. The composite application form covers the following clearances:

i. Local body clearance.

ii. Environmental clearance from TNPCB under the Air & Water Acts.

iii. Land allotment by SIPCOT/TIDCO/SIDCO.

iv. Reclassification of land use.

v. Water supply.

vi. Power connection (Temporary/permanent)

vii. Registration under The Factories Act, 1948.

viii. Registration under The Indian Boilers Act, 1923.

5.8 Investors have to file the composite application form with the Documentation and Clearance Centre (DCC) in the GUIDANCE Bureau. Follow up of these applications with concerned departments for speedy clearance is the responsibility of the GUIDANCE. The Project Approval Authority under the Chairmanship of Chief Secretary reviews the status of these applications.

5.9 In many other States similar initiatives have been taken. In Andhra Pradesh also a Centralized Documentation and Clearance Centre (CDCC) has been established in the Commissionerate of Industries to assist the entrepreneurs of large and medium projects in obtaining all clearances through a single consolidated application. A district cell of the CDCC looks after the cases of SSI.

Rajasthan

5.10 The Government of Rajasthan introduced the Single Window system in March 2000, with the setting up of Empowered Committees and introduction of Single Composite Application Forms (SCAF) for clearances/approvals/services needed for setting up of large and medium industries. The Bureau for Investment Promotion (BIP), which is the State Level Investment Promotion Agency, receives all composite application for projects valued at over Rs. 3 crores, projects promoted by NRIs, 100 per cent EOUs and FDI projects irrespective of value. Projects valued at less than Rs. 3 crores are received in the respective DICs.

5.11 SCAF includes forms for the following approvals/ clearances:

i. General information about the project.

ii. Information for provisional registration of Industry.

iii. Information about allotment/acquisition of land in other than State Industrial Development Agency's institutional areas.

iv. Information about allotment/acquisition of land in State Industrial Development Agency's institutional areas.

v. Information required by State Pollution Control Board for consent to establish under Air & Water Acts.

vi. Information required for site clearance by the Environment Department.

vii. Information required for application for electricity connection.

viii. Information required for application to Inspectorates of Factories & Boilers.

ix. Information required for conversion of agriculture land.

5.12 Escort officers are nominated in BIP for each large project. Applications under SCAF are received in the BIP/DIC, as the case may be, and are forwarded to the nodal officers in the respective department who are required to indicate any lacuna in application to the nominated escort officer in BIP/DIC within 7 days. After completion of all formalities by the applicant, BIP/DIC accepts the application after verifying the checklist provided by the respective departments. Applications are sent to respective departments by BIP/DIC and follow up of the approvals/clearances are the responsibility of BIP/DIC. The disposal of these applications is monitored by the Empowered Committees. A total of 246 applications involving a proposed investment of Rs.5,600 crores have been cleared till June 2002, under single window clearance system since March 2000.

Chattisgarh

The Chattisgarh Audyogik Nivesh Protsahan Adhiniyam, 2002

5.13 The Chattisgarh Audyogik Nivesh Protsahan Adhiniyam, 2002 provides for setting up of District Investment Promotion Committee under the District Collector, Divisional Investment Promotion Committee under the Divisional Commissioner and State Investment Promotion Board under the Chief Minister. Notwithstanding anything contained in any law enacted by the legislative assembly of the state and being in force, the District and Divisional Committees are empowered to exercise powers of any local Government and of any authority or agency of the State Government in respect of the following:

i. Identification and allotment of land.

ii. Identification, allocation and facilitation of sources of water and other utilities including electric power.

iii. All approvals in respect of matters relating to the implementation of the projects from the local Governments.

iv. Approvals, if any, relating to matters concerning the welfare of labour and

v. Approvals, if any, relating to the Chattisgarh Environment Control Board (in case of Divisional Committee).

5.14 The State Investment Promotion Board exercises powers in respect of all proposals referred to it by the District and Divisional Committees or brought before it by the investor or suo-moto. The Board also exercises powers for simplification of procedures of the State Government in respect of any matter relating to investment and operation of projects and fixation of minimum wages.

5.15 The members of the District and Divisional Committee are jointly and severely responsible for providing the services contained in the schedule for which specific time limits have also been prescribed.

6

Recommendations

6.1 Central Government Level

I. Policy Related:

IN order to simplify the procedures for grant of approvals, reduce delays and simplify the regulation of projects during their operational phase, re-engineering of the regulatory processes prescribed under various legislations, regulations, etc., is necessary. Simplification of procedures prescribed under extant laws is necessary to reduce delays in the grant of approvals. Re-engineering of the regulatory processes is also necessary to reduce ground level hassles, make administration and compliance easy as well as amenable to IT tools and minimise interface between project promoters and official machinery.

Re-engineering of the Regulatory Processes

i. Simplification of the extant procedures for approvals/ clearances would also require basic changes in the regulatory process prescribed under relevant legislations. Detailed examination of each approval requirement under different Acts, rules and regulations would need to be carried out for re-engineering of the regulatory process in the following order:

   a. Self-regulation, i.e., automatic approval upon filing of necessary documents ('blinking traffic lights' model).

   b. Professional outsourcing with sufficient documentation of certification to enable determination of professional malpractices ('stop-go traffic lights' model).

c. Prior case-by-case regulation by public agency ('policeman regulating traffic' model).

(Paragraph: 4.10)

The Committee felt that as many approvals as are possible should be placed on self-regulation, i.e., under automatic permission upon filing of necessary documents.

ii. Re-engineering of the regulatory processes is too elaborate an exercise to be undertaken by the Committee at this stage since extensive consultations with the concerned Ministries would also be required. It is therefore, recommended that re-engineering groups may be formed, to begin with, in the Ministries of Labour, Environment & Forests, Power, Agriculture, Petroleum & Natural Gas and Department of Industrial Policy & Promotion. These Groups under the chairmanship of the Secretary of the concerned Ministry/ Department could include representative of the attached and sub-ordinate offices responsible for granting various approvals. Representatives of the State Governments and other Ministries may be associated as considered necessary. Industry Associations, being important stakeholders, may also be associated. Assistance of a public management specialist may also be taken, as considered necessary, to bring in professional inputs and data on international experience in best practices. Close interaction with the personnel in the existing implementation machinery would be essential. While a panel of experts may be prepared for reference, the choice may be left to the Ministry to suit their requirements. Suggested Draft TOR for the re-engineering groups is at Annex-X. The functions of the re-engineering groups would be as follows:

a. Re-engineering of the regulatory processes under extant laws on the principle laid down at Paragraphs 4.9 & 4.10.

(Paragraph: 4.10)

b. Prescribe time limits for grant of non-statutory approvals and develop systems for ensuring grant of approvals within this time limit.

(Paragraph: 4.11)

c. Develop appropriate trigger mechanisms to automatically raise the matter to the next higher level in case the concerned authorities fail to decide the matter within prescribed time limit.

(Paragraph: 4.11)

d. To indicate inter-se priority among the regulatory reforms being proposed by the group so that reforms aiming at maximum simplification are undertaken first.

(Paragraph: 4.11)

e. Examine the extant laws being administered by their Ministries with the objective of consolidation of laws, weeding out laws that have outlived their utility and to generally bring them in line with the present technological, economic and competitive environment. Illustrative list of Acts at Annex-IV may be reviewed and compiled for the Ministry by the re-engineering group.

(Paragraph: 4.11)

f. Review requirement of approvals from multiple agencies or multiple approvals from a single agency.

(Paragraph: 4.53)

g. Indicate best practices adopted within the country and elsewhere and suggest a generic structure for re-engineering of the regulatory processes at the State level. State specific fine-tuning may be undertaken in consultation with the States.

(Paragraph: 4.13)

iii. The re-engineering group to be set up in the Ministry of Finance may look into the issues of simplification of procedures adopted by Commercial Banks and Financial institutions and their capacity building needs to meet the requirements of project financing aimed at reducing delays in timely flow of investments to projects.

(Paragraph: 4.12)

iv. The re-engineering groups should complete the re-engineering of the regulatory processes within a period of six months, and review, updation and consolidation of extant laws within a period of one year.

(Paragraph: 4.14)

v. A Committee of Secretaries may review the progress of re-engineering groups on a monthly basis and act as a trigger in case of any delay in the re-engineering process. IIFB would co-ordinate re-engineering of regulatory processes in consultation with the re-engineering groups set up in different Ministries/Departments. The concerned Ministries will include a position report on the re-engineering of regulatory processes as an item in the monthly report of the concerned Ministry to CCER.

(Paragraph: 4.14)

Other Policy Issues

vi. The Government of India may consider institution of awards, rating of States, etc., for recognising the progress made by States in undertaking regulatory reforms.

(Paragraph: 4.65)

vii. Assistance under different reform linked incentive schemes in various sectors may be dovetailed for the purpose of extending monetary incentive for re-engineering of regulatory processes in the States, with clearly earmarked funds for identified infrastructure components/projects, as may be determined by the State Governments concerned. Additional budgetary provisions may also be considered for augmenting the funds available as incentive to the States. Institutional arrangements would be necessary to ensure that the funds are properly utilised under appropriately designed projects. The Government may also consider issuing directive to the financial Institutions to link lending to States for their infrastructure projects with the progress of regulatory reforms.

(Paragraph: 4.67)

viii. A comprehensive legislation may be enacted to dispense with the requirement of publication of notices, under various legislations -both Central and State, in the official gazette. Publication in a vernacular newspaper having adequate circulation in the concerned area should be considered sufficient for this purpose.

(Paragraph: 4.19)

ix. The National Rehabilitation Policy, under preparation by the Ministry of Rural Development, may be finalized quickly to reduce delays on account of rehabilitation issues during implementation of projects. The Ministry of Rural Development may also consider setting time limits for implementation of rehabilitation measures by the concerned project authorities.

(Paragraph: 4.19)

x. Disciplinary proceedings should invariably be initiated against public servants, both at central and state level, for abuse of power resulting in delays in grant of approvals. Stringent action should be taken in cases of proven abuse of power.

(Paragraph: 4.91)

II. Procedural

i. MOEF should consider setting up a data centre, which could serve as a one-stop source for obtaining reliable and validated data for preparing EIAs.

(Paragraph: 4.28)

ii. Instead of the present procedure under which the various stages of clearances in the MOEF are undertaken one after another, MOEF should evolve a procedure to take up activities in parallel. MOEF should also examine if all the documents referred to in the explanatory memorandum attached to the EIA Notification, 1994 need to be insisted upon at the time of receipt of application itself.

(Paragraph: 4.34)

iii. While the Committee was deliberating upon this issue, the investment limit for certain categories of projects requiring environmental clearance has been enhanced by MOEF from Rs. 50 crores to Rs. 100 crores. The investment limit as well as the list of projects requiring environmental clearance should be made co-terminus with Plan period necessitating a review every five years. It is desirable to link this limit with CPI for automatic adjustment for inflation in future.

(Paragraph: 4.34)

iv. In case site visits for environmental and forest clearance are not carried out within the specified time period, it may be deemed that such visits are not required. Similarly, in case the members of the Expert Committee do not give their response within specified time period, it may be presumed that they have no comments to offer and next stage of the approval process may be taken up.

(Paragraph: 4.34)

v. MOEF may consider permitting diversion of forestland for pre-construction activities based on the 'in principle' clearance after the non-forest land identified for compensatory afforestation has been transferred to the forest department and funds for raising compensatory afforestation deposited by the user agency.

(Paragraph: 4.40)

vi. In case of environmental and forest clearances, expert agencies may be authorized to initially scrutinise applications for essential requirements before formally submitting to the department/agency concerned. The department/agency should accept applications only after confirming the availability of essential requirements. The time limits prescribed for clearances should be reckoned from the date of acceptance of application.

(Paragraph: 4.42)

vii. Water clearance and coal linkages need to be expedited for power projects by periodic meetings of all concerned by the respective Ministries.

(Paragraph: 4.46)

viii. The requirement of registers and forms to be maintained under different Acts needs to be reviewed. Instead of the present requirement of maintaining a separate register for the purposes of each Act, even when the subject matters are related, common registers or reports in electronic formats must be introduced. The Labour Laws (Exemption From Furnishing Returns and Maintenance of Registers by Certain Establishments) Act, 1988, permits maintenance of common registers but is applicable to only small-scale enterprises, employing up to 19 persons. Its scope needs to be increased to cover enterprises employing up to 500 persons. This recommendation aims at reducing the enormous paperwork which is required now and most of which just gets filed.

(Paragraph: 4.78)

III Institutional Arrangements

i. The Committee, in Part-I of its report, has recommended setting up of the Industrial Investment Facilitation Board (IIFB), as a central facilitation body, to follow up the grant of approval for projects with investment of Rs. 100 crores and above. Besides, any investor facing difficulties in obtaining approvals from the Ministries/ Agencies may approach IIFB irrespective of investment limits. FIIA would continue to look after specific difficulties being faced by foreign investors.

(Paragraph: 4.60 & 4.68)

ii. Empowered Committees for Forest Clearance may be set up with representation from concerned departments/ agencies for disposal of cases requiring forest clearance.

(Paragraph: 4.39)

iii. Facilitation Teams may be set up in the Administrative Ministries dealing with projects with investments of Rs. 100 crores and above and other priority sector projects.

(Paragraph: 4.81)

iv. While outsourcing approvals, authority for inspection & pre-examination, etc., internal disciplinary systems of the professional associations would need to be strengthened to act against complaints of malpractices. Induction of outside experts could be considered.

(Paragraph: 4.76)

v. Periodic publication of information on the performance of States on 8-10 critical parameters and ranking the States on these parameters would generate healthy competition among the States and incentivise them for initiating further reforms in their regulatory processes. Government may encourage Industry Associations, Rating Agencies, etc., to take up the exercise of periodic publication of information on the relative performance of States in undertaking regulatory reforms and may provide inputs on the rating criteria.

(Paragraph: 4.89)

vi. Industry Associations and States may be encouraged to document and disseminate information on best practices in India and elsewhere, initiatives undertaken by States, etc. A separate exercise would need to be undertaken to design the components of the documentation and dissemination needs, assess resource availability & requirement and implementation methodology, which can be taken up as a project by the Industry Associations.

(Paragraph: 4.90)

IV. Capacity Building

i. Government of India may provide technical assistance to the States for capacity building of personnel and also re-engineering of regulatory processes for which assistance of multilateral financial institutions may be availed. Reputed Training and Research Institutions may be associated in this process. Inventory of the global best practices may also be prepared.

(Paragraph: 4.15)

6.2 Common to Central & State Levels

i. Greater publicity needs to be given on the availability of the alternative dispute resolution mechanism. Investors must be encouraged to refer their disputes for resolution through ICADR. All Ministries of Government of India and State Governments must encourage investors to incorporate suitable provisions in their contract agreements or to enter into arbitration agreements if a need for arbitration were to arise.

(Paragraph: 4.84)

ii. A net-enabled information system should be developed to provide information on investment policies, sector wise approvals required from both Central and State Governments, the agency responsible for approval, its contact address, procedural requirements for the approvals, prescribed time frame, etc. Information on the applicable Acts and Rules should also be available. To begin with, such net-enabled information system could be developed by each department of the Central and State Governments as a part of their website. This could subsequently to interconnected across departments to provide all related information at one point.

(Paragraph: 4.87)

iii. Forms for various permissions/approvals should be made available in downloadable format within the next six months at the website of all departments of the Central and State Governments. Necessary Systems may be put in position for electronic submission of these applications within one year.

(Paragraph: 4.88)

iv. All departments/agencies must be required to make public the status of pending applications. This information should also be available on their websites. This recommendation may be implemented within the next three months. Specific reasons for delays in granting approvals beyond prescribed period must also be indicated.

(Paragraph: 4.88)

v. A time-bound action plan may be prepared for progressively higher use of IT in approval and operational administration of projects starting from information on procedural requirements and status of pending applications, and may be implemented within three months, and progressively extended to applications like electronic acceptance of applications within one year and inter-connecting Ministries and States within two years.

(Paragraph: 4.94)

vi. The functionaries in various departments/agencies responsible for according various clearances/approvals and in the Facilitation Teams must be imparted training on modern management practices and greater use of IT in project approval administration as well as post commissioning regulation.

(Paragraph: 4.96)

6.3 State & Local Self Government Levels

I. Policy Related:

i. Re-engineering of the regulatory processed on lines similar to the re-engineering proposed at Central level would be necessary. The State Governments may consider setting up re-engineering groups to take up re-engineering of regulatory processes in a time bound manner.

(Paragraph: 4.54)

ii. The Committee recommends enactment enactment of a suitable legislation or alternate arrangements such as amendment in the Rules of Business, etc., by the State Governments for empowering specially constituted bodies to operationalise and empower 'single window system' at the State level. The Single Window Agency should be empowered to lay down the time frames for approvals, review the issue of approvals by concerned agencies/ departments, accord approvals in case concerned departments/agencies do not grant these approvals in a predetermined time frame, and also give appropriate directions to the concerned agencies departments/local bodies. Model legislation on the lines of the Andhra Pradesh Infrastructure Development Enabling Act, 2001, Andhra Pradesh Industrial Single Window Clearance Ordinance, 2002 or Chattisgarh Audyogik Nivesh Protsahan Adhiniyam, 2002 could be considered for expediting clearances.

(Paragraph: 4.59)

II. Procedural

i. In order to reduce delays in acquisition of land, the nodal department in the State Government must be entrusted with the responsibility of obtaining various approvals within the State Government.

(Paragraph: 4.19)

ii. The system of approval of building plans from local authorities needs to be streamlined. In case the local authority fails to decide the application within stipulated time, the approvals should be deemed to have been given. In such cases, however, the applicant will still be responsible for adherence to the applicable building byelaws.

(Paragraph: 4.21)

iii. The powers of approval of building plans may also be given to architects registered under the Architects Act, 1972. Based on the certification by the architects, intimation to the local authority should be deemed sufficient.

(Paragraph: 4.21)

iv. The application forms for electricity and water connections, at least for medium and large projects, should be included in the single composite application form (SCAF). Concerned agencies/department must notify areas having any constraint in capacities of systems or availability of water, power, etc. State Level Investment Promotion or any other designated agency should periodically review the disposal of such cases as also progress of augmentation works.

(Paragraph: 4.23)

v. Once first stage site clearance has been issued, final clearance to be issued after commissioning of all necessary machinery and completion of other requirements may be a deemed approval if it is not granted within the prescribed time.

(Paragraph: 4.34)

vi. State Level Investment Promotion Agencies or any other designated agency may be assigned the specific responsibility for development, implementation and follow up of clearances from concerned departments/ agencies under Single Composite Application Forms, for large and medium projects to begin with.

(Paragraph: 4.63)

vii. Multiplicity of inspecting authorities from different departments and frequency of their visits can be reduced by clubbing duties of different inspecting authorities. In order to reduce the number of inspections, a team of inspectors from different departments may be deputed for joint inspection after giving advance notice. A Committee under the Secretary in charge of Industries Department in the State Government can prescribe the schedule for such combined inspections. The powers to carry out regular and routine inspection may also be given to expert agencies.

(Paragraph: 4.74 & 4.76)

viii. A time limit, of say 4 weeks, may be prescribed within which the concerned authorities need to respond to periodical returns submitted to them for any further clarifications. After this time limit, the information given should be deemed to have been accepted and approved.

(Paragraph: 4.79)

III. Institutional Arrangements

i. A task force under the Secretary in charge of department dealing with public works in the State Government may be set up for coordination among the concerned agencies for shifting of utilities so that the work for shifting all utilities could be taken up simultaneously by all concerned agencies in a co-ordinated manner.

(Paragraph: 4.52)

ii. State Level Single Window Agency or State Invest Promotion Agency may interact at least once every three months with the investors on the factors impeding implementation of projects, scope for further simplification of procedures and facilitate resolution of difficulties being experienced by them in implementation of projects.

(Paragraph: 4.82)

6.4 Prescribing and Enforcing Time Limits

i. Individual Ministries/Departments, both at Central and State levels, should develop appropriate trigger mechanisms to take the matter to the next higher level whenever the prescribed time frames are not adhered to.

(Paragraph: 4.11)

ii. The empowered State Level Single Window agency may also monitor the grant of approvals by the Local bodies and district level functionaries and grant of approvals, in case these are not granted by the concerned authorities within the prescribed time limits.

(Paragraph: 4.59)

iii. IIFB at Central level and the empowered Single Window agency at the State level would prescribe the time limits for grant of non-statutory approvals in consultation with concerned Ministries/Departments.

(Paragraph: 4.59 & 4.68)

iv. IIFB would follow up with the concerned Ministries/ Departments at Centre and State level cases of delays in the grant of approvals in case of projects with investment of Rs. 100 crores and above both in public and private sector.

(Paragraph: 4.68)

Annexures

ANNEX – I

No.212/9/2/2001-CA.IV
Government of India/Bharat Sarkar
Cabinet Secretariat/Mantrimandal Sachivalaya
Rashtrapati Bhavan

New Delhi -110004, the 24th September, 2001

OFFICE MEMORANDUM

In pursuance of the deliberations of the meeting held on 4th September, 2001 under the Chairmanship of the Prime Minister, to discuss a fiscal stimulus initiative for the economy, it has been decided to set up a Committee to examine the extant procedures for investment approvals and implementation of projects and suggest measures to simplify and expedite the process for both public and private investment.

2. The Committee will comprise the following:

1. Shri V.N. Kaul, Secretary, Ministry of Petroleum and N.G.-Convenor
2. Shri P.V. Jayakrishnan, Secretary, Ministry of Environment and Forests
3. Shri A.K. Basu, Secretary, Ministry of Power
4. Shri C.M. Vasudev, Secretary, Department of Expenditure
5. Shri Shyamal Ghosh, Secretary, Department of Telecommunication
6. Shri Vinod Vaish, Secretary, Ministry of Labour
7. Shri Pradip Baijal, Secretary, Department of Disinvestment
8. Shri V. Govindarajan, Secretary, Department of IPP
9. Dr. Rakesh Mohan, Adviser to FM and Chief Economic Adviser, DEA

10. Shri K.V. Irniraya Secretary, M/o Statistics & Programme Implementation
11. Dr. Pradipto Ghosh, Additional Secretary, PMO
12. Shri N.S. Sisodia, Additional Secretary, Cabinet Secretariat-Member Secretary

3. While the above Committee will suggest measures to simplify the procedures, a Sub-Group headed by Secretary, IPP will make specific suggestions regarding effecting simplification of procedures relating to private investment. These suggestions would be incorporated in the main report.

4. The Committee will be service by the M/o Statistics and Programme Implementation.

5. The Committee will submit its report by 31st January, 2002.

Sd/-

(C.K. Mishra)
Director
Tel. No. 379-2204

ANNEX – I-A

No.212/9/2/2001-CA.IV
Government of India/Bharat Sarkar
Cabinet Secretariat/Mantrimandal Sachivalaya
Rashtrapati Bhavan

New Delhi, the 19th March, 2002

OFFICE MEMORANDUM

Reference this Secretariat OM of even number dated the 24th September 2001 regarding setting up a Committee to examine the extant procedures for investment approvals and implementation of projects and suggest measures to simplify and expedite the process for both public and private investment.

2. Shri V. Govindarajan, Secretary, D/Industrial Policy & Promotion, will be the Convenor of the said Committee, with immediate effect in place of Shri V.N. Kaul, Secretary, Ministry of Petroleum & Natural Gas, who has been appointed as Comptroller and Auditor General of India.

3. Other terms and conditions of the Committee remain unchanged.

Sd/-
(Ravi Mittal)
Director
Tel. No. 379-2204

To

All members of the Committee.
All Ministries/Departments.

Copy for information to:

a. Shri V.N. Kaul. C&AG of India.
b. Shri Brajesh Mishra, Principal Secretary to the Prime Minister.

Sd./-
(Ravi Mittal)
Director
Tel. No. 379-2204

ANNEX – II

No. 5/5/2001-FIIA
Government of India
Ministry of Commerce & Industry
Department of Industrial Policy & Promotion
Udyog Bhavan, New Delhi.

Dated, the 9th October, 2001.

OFFICE MEMORANDUM

In pursuance of the Cabinet Secretariat's O.M. No. 212/9/2/2001-CA.IV dated 24th Sept. 2001 regarding fiscal stimulus initiative for the economy, it has been decided to set up a Sub-Group headed by Secretary, Industrial Policy & Promotion to make specific suggestions regarding effecting simplification of procedures relating to private investment.

2. The Sub-Group will comprise the following:

a	Secretary, Department of Industrial Policy & Promotion	Chairman
b	Secretary, Department of Disinvestment	Member
c	Secretary, Ministry of Power (To be represented by Special Secretary)	Member
d	Chief Economic Adviser, Department of Economic Affairs	Member
e	Additional Secretary, Ministry of Statistics & Programme Implementation	Member

3. The Sub-Group may invite specifically any other Department depending on requirement.

4. The Sub-Group will submit its report by the end of January 2002.

Sd./-

(Umesh Kumar)
Director
Tel. No. 3016951.

To

1. All members of the Committee
2. Principal Secretary to the PMO
3. Shri C.K. Mishra, Director, Cabinet Secretariat, Rashtrapati Bhavan.
4. JS (MSS)

Sd/-

(Umesh Kumar)

ANNEX – III

LIST OF REFERENCES

Case Studies

a. 13 case studies of specific projects undertaken by PMO to identify specific procedural, institutional, regulatory and implementation bottlenecks that cause delays in the approval, commissioning and operation of projects and the synthesis study by A. T. KEARNEY based on 5 case studies of power sector projects.

b. Case studies of power projects by NTPC.

Reports & Studies

a. Report on 'System of Clearance Required for Various Types of Projects in Public & Private Sector' by Consultants appointed by the Ministry of Statistics and Programme Implementation. (November 2001)

b. 'Foreign Direct Investment in India' carried out by NCEAR (March, 1998)

c. 'Simplification of Procedures Governing Industries' by Administrative Staff College of India (December, 1999.)

d. Study commissioned by the Department of Industrial policy & Promotion with CMIE on the causes behind slow implementation of projects. (April-September 2001)

e. "Simplification and consolidation of registers of records to be maintained by the employers and the returns or notices required to be submitted by them under various Labour Laws" by Ministry of Labour.

f. Report on Administrative Reforms by CII

g. Prime Minister's Council on Trade & Industry; Subject Group on Administrative and Legal Simplifications.

h. Prime Minister's Council on Trade & Industry, "Unshackling Indian Industry"

i. FICCI study on "Impediments to investments- Regulatory and Procedural Bottlenecks"

j. McKinsey report on "Achieving a quantum leap in India's FDI"

k. CII-World Bank Study on 'Competitiveness in Indian Manufacturing' (January 2002)

l. FICCI-FDI Survey (March 2002) of 385 Foreign Companies

Acts and Legislations

a. The Andhra Pradesh Infrastructure Development Enabling Act, 2001

b. Labour Laws (Exemption from Furnishing Returns and Maintaining Registers by Certain Establishments) Act, 1988

c. Andhra Pradesh Industrial Single Window Clearance Ordinance, 2002

d. Chattisgarh Audyogik Nivesh Protsahan Adhiniyam, 2002

Base papers and inputs from Ministries/ Departments/Organisations

a. Base paper on Simplification of procedures for investment approvals and implementation from various Ministries/ Departments.

b. Comments and notes received from IOCL, BPCL, HPCL and GAIL

c. Base paper on the Ministry of Environment and Forest and response on the comments received from various Ministries on the base paper

d. Suggestions by Department of Fertilizer

e. Note from Ministry of Statistics and Programme Implementation on implementation of Central Sector Projects

Other Material

a. Steps taken by State Governments to bring about administrative reforms to cut down delays in grant of various approvals

b. Single composite Application Forms for Industries in Rajasthan

c. Common Application Form for Single Window Clearance in Tamil Nadu

d. Compilation of Application Forms in Uttar Pradesh

e. Information on International Centre for Alternative Dispute Resolution (ICADR)

ANNEX – IV

Illustrative List of Acts Requiring Simplification for Registration and Regulation of Industry

S.No.	Act
I	**Central Acts**
A	***Labour Related Laws***
1	Apprentice Act, 1961
2	Bonded Labour System (Abolition) Act, 1976
3	Child Labour (Prohibition and Regulation) Act, 1986
4	Collection of Statistics Act, 1953
5	Contract Labour (Regulation and Abolition) Act, 1970
6	Dangerous Machines (Regulation) Act, 1983
7	Employees Provident Fund and Miscellaneous Provisions Act 1952
8	Employees State Insurance Act, 1948
9	Employers Liability Act, 1938
10	Employment Exchange (Compulsory Notification of Vacancies) Act, 1959
11	Employment of Children Act, 1938
12	Equal Remuneration Act, 1976
13	Factories Act, 1948
14	Fatal Accidents Act, 1855
15	Industrial Disputes Act, 1947
16	Labour Laws (Exemption from Furnishing Returns) Act, 1988
17	Maternity Benefits Act, 1961
18	Minimum Wages Act, 1948
19	Payment of Bonus Act, 1965
20	Payment of Gratuity Act, 1972
21	Payment of Wages Act, 1948

22 Persons with Disabilities (Equal Opportunities) Protection Act, 1996

23 Trade Unions Act, 1926

24 Weekly Holidays Act, 1942

25 Workers Compensation Act, 1923

B Financial Laws

1 Central Excise Act, 1944

2 Central Sales Tax Act, 1956

3 Income Tax Act, 1961

C Corporate Laws

1 The Companies Act, 1956

2 Indian Partnership Act, 1932

D Environmental Laws

1 Air (Prevention and Control of Pollution) Act, 1981

2 Environment (Protection) Act, 1986

3 Water (Prevention and Control of Pollution) Act, 1974

E Infrastructure Acts

a. Ministry of Power

1 Electricity (Supply) Act, 1948

2 Indian Electricity Act, 1910

b. Ministry of Rural Development

1 Land Acquisition Act, 1894

F Other Regulations

a. Department of Consumer Affairs

1 Essential Commodities Act, 1955

2 Standards of Weights and Measures Act, 1976

b. Department of Industrial Policy & Promotion

1 Explosives Act, 1884

2 Indian Boilers Act, 1923

3 Inflammable Substances Act, 1952

c. *Ministry of Health*

1 Prevention of Food Adulteration Act, 1954

G *Other Central Acts Applicable to Specific Sectors*

1 Beedi and Cigar Workers (Conditions of Employment) Act, 1966

2 Dock Workers (Regulation of Employment) Act, 1948

3 Interstate Migrant (Regulation of Employment & Conditions of Service) Act, 1979

4 Motor Transport Workers Act, 1961

5 Working Journalists and other Newspaper Employees (Conditions of Service and Miscellaneous Provisions) Act, 1955

II State Acts

1 Shops and Establishments Act, 1988

2 State Sales Tax Act

3 Urban Land (Ceiling and Regulation) Act, 1976

4 State Panchayat Raj Act

5 State Municipality Act

6 State Urban Areas (Development) Act

7 State Land Revenue Act

8 State Land Tenancy Act

Synthesis Study
'Barriers to Approvals and Implementation of Investment Projects'
Prime Minister's Office
The Associated Chambers Of Commerce and Industry Of India
(ASSOCHAM)
&
A. T. KEARNEY

Structure of the Study and the stages of research as undertaken by the PMO

Stage 1 Problem Identification	Stage 2 Synthesis	Stage 3 Redesign	Stage 4 Implementation
• Case studies of actual projects at different scales and sectors, covering both public and private investments • Each case study would provide • Flow sheet detailing Clearances & Agencies, Time required, inputs, Person-months and Rents paid • Verbal description of problems faced • Ambiguities and lack of clarity in procedures	• Information provided by stage 1 to be synthesized • Prioritization of downstream regulatory processes by Level of effort and time involved • Typical flow sheet of each process detailing generic problem encountered	• "As Is" flow sheet for each approval step • Separate flow sheet for PSUs and FDI projects • Highlight inefficiencies • Detail documentation requirements • Relate documentation to approval steps • Highlight inefficiencies • Revised flow sheet Authorities responsible • Evaluation/Decisions • Documentation • Time required	• Adoption of redesigned procedures and documentation requirements by public agencies at different levels

Presentation Structure of the synthesis study based on the inputs as received from the various case studies that have been submitted

- The objectives of the preliminary exercise undertaken by the PMO
- Key findings of the Synthesis study
- Prioritization of different clearances

The Prime Minister's Office has undertaken an initiative to rationalize investment procedures to ensure heightened business interest in India-from within and abroad

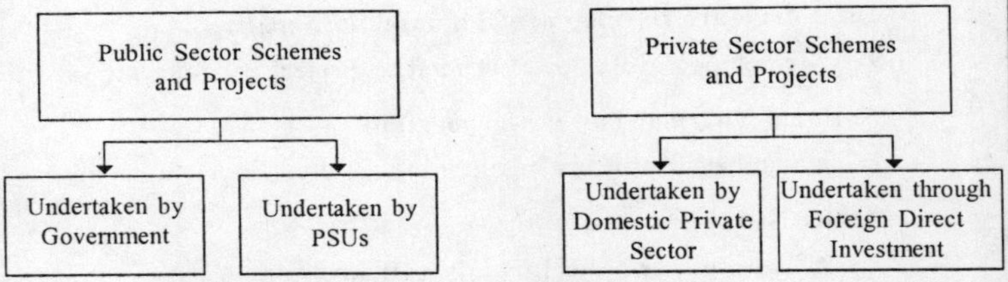

Unclear Regulatory Clearances and Approvals

- Complex and unclear procedures
- Huge documentation requirements
- Lack of clear relationship between procedures and required documentation

Need for revision of procedures and documentation requirements to reduce the time, effort and cost involved in obtaining approvals

A.T.Kearney & ASSOCHAM worked together to synthesize experiences of different agencies & highlight some of the key impediments and action imperatives

STAGE ONE-inputs from the case studies

- Case studies of actual projects at different scales and sectors, covering both public and private investments
- Each case study provided
  - Flow sheet detailing Clearances & Agencies,
  - Time required, inputs, Person-months and Rents paid
  - Verbal description of problems faced
  - Ambiguities and lack of clarity in procedures

STAGE TWO- compilation of the findings from the case studies

- Information provided by stage 1 to be synthesized
- Prioritization of downstream regulatory processes by Level of effort and time involved
- Typical flow sheet of each process detailing generic problems encountered

The synthesis study, for purpose of analysis, has relied on case studies provided by leading agencies

- **Infrastructure Development Finance Corporation**
  - A combined cycle power generation project by a private investor
- **National Thermal Power Corporation**
  - A number of projects highlighting different issues
- **ASSOCHAM**
  - A hydro power project by a private investor
- **Confederation of Indian Industries**
  - A highway project
- **Federation of Indian Chambers of Commerce and Industry**
  - A drug manufacturing plant

The synthesis analysis is based on facts and data provided in the case studies and not conjecture

The analysis of the case studies has revealed the width and variety of downstream clearances required for getting projects off the ground to the implementation stage

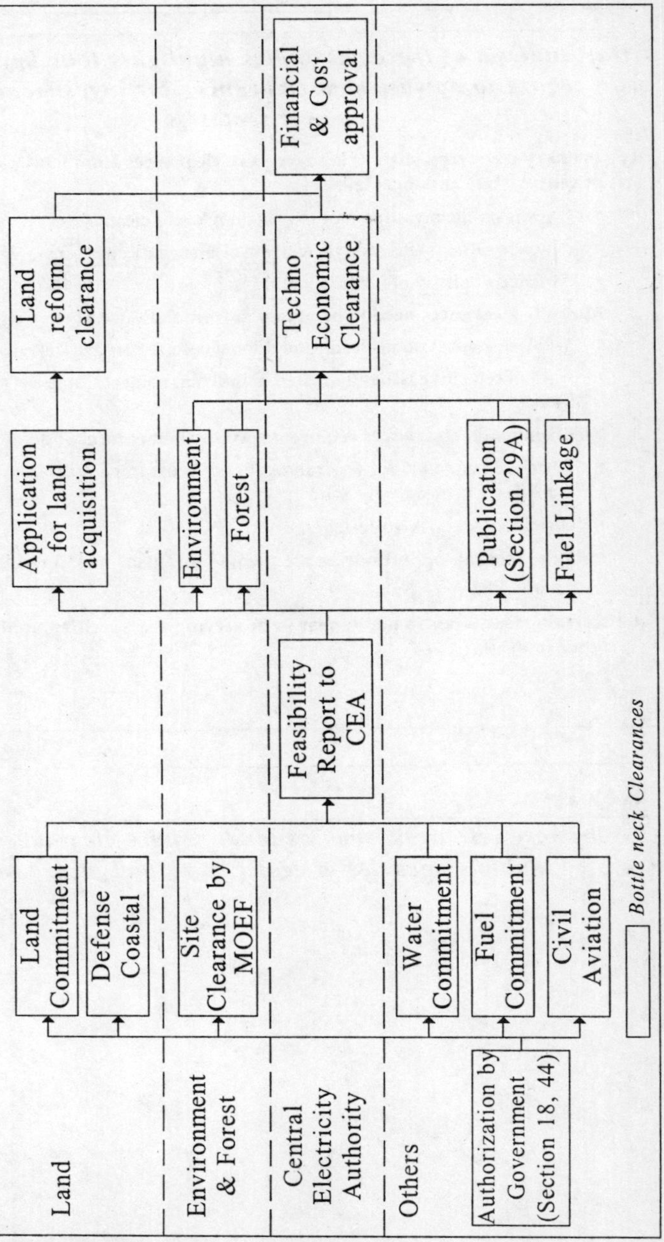

Our analysis of the case studies highlights four key issues with regard to downstream clearances for investments in the power sector

1. **Primary resources, such as land, require clearances from multiple agencies at centre, state and local level**
   - Onus is on the investing party to obtain relevant clearances
   - Absence of facilitative/single window clearance mechanisms
   - Absence of clarity of jurisdiction in instances
2. **Multiple clearances need to be obtained from the same agency e.g. CEA**
   - Multiple contact points lead to additional costs, effort and delays
   - A lot of repetitive issues discussed at different points of time by the same agency
3. **Environmental clearances require disproportionate level of detail**
   - Terms of reference for environment and forest impact assessment studies are difficult to comply with
   - Unrelated data is solicited
   - Rent seeking opportunities are created and deal making skills need to be invoked
4. **Certain clearances do not appear to be serving any specified public or other interest**

Key Issue 1

Primary resources, such as land, require clearances from multiple agencies at center, state and local level

Key Issue 2

Multiple clearances need to be obtained from the same agency e.g. CEA

In Principle Clearance	Techno-Economic Clearance	Financial Package Clearance	Final Cost Approval
• Time frame 6 months appears excessive • Queries raised by various wings like economic, thermal, legal, civil etc • The project cost is usually cut at this stage without clear reasons	• Normal time frame 1-2 years • Clearance on various aspects like technology used, performance parameters, commercial viability etc • SEB/state government approval required before TEC–no conditional processing	• Normal time frame 9 months! • Technical issues are raised again • Forex rate fluctuation leads to restatement of costs with related notification issues • Signed financial documents required which is not practical • No clarity on whether competitively bid projects require this clearance	• Normal time frame 1-2 years • Technical aspects are raised once again

CEA may wish to consider a single window clearance encompassing the financial package and the final cost approval, where relevant

Key Issue 3

Environmental clearances require disproportionate level of detail

Application to District Forest Officer	Forest Valuation & alternate land Identification	State Government Clearance	Central Government Clearance
• A number of documents, certificates, maps to be attached with application form • A number of agencies involved in the approval process like the Village Sarpanch, archeological department, forest officers etc	• A very detailed study required on evaluation for loss of forest. Details like species wise and girth wise abstract of trees • Detailed afforestation scheme prepared	• Post clearance from the District Forest Officer, clearances are required from five to six level state government officials • Any query raised at one of the level flows down all the way to the DFO and then flows up. The multiple level of clearances take a very long time	• After the state government clearance, the file is sent to the regional Ministry of Forest official • The final clearance is given by the Ministry of Forest in Delhi

A reality check on the terms of reference and rationalization of touch points for environment related clearances can facilitate the investment process

Key Issue 4

Certain clearances do not appear to be serving any specified public or other interest

Detailed Flow Sheet of the Land Ceiling Clearance

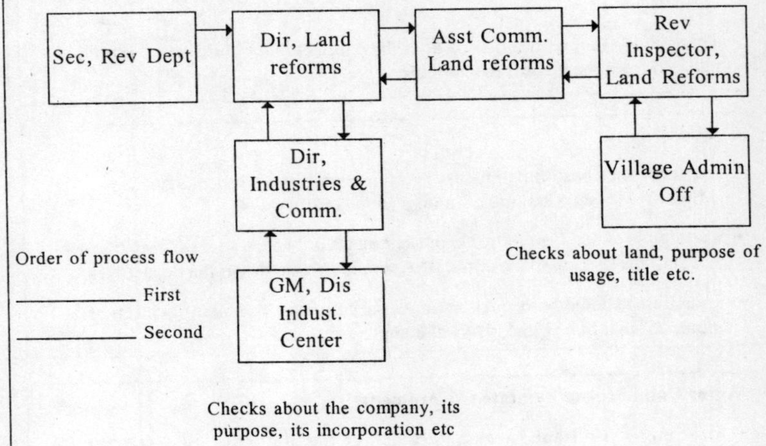

The relevance of the clearance may need to be examined/ made automatic -especially where the land is accorded by the state government

Additionally, there is scope to simplify procedures of certain clearances to reduce lead times

- **Section 29 Compliance**
  - Requirement of publication in state gazette must be dispensed with. These publications have very limited circulation, but are potential cause of delays
  - There should be clear guidelines as to when a corrigendum notification is required. At present CEA insists on a corrigendum notification even for small changes
  - Time allowed for representation after the publication of notification should be reduced from the present two months

- **Coal linkage**
  - Is a very time consuming process involving many government agencies (Ministry of Coal, Coal India limited, Ministry of Power)
  - Standing Linkage Committee at present meets only once in six months, hence delaying the prcesses. The committee should meet as when the need arises.
  - Time frame should be stipulated for all the activities from identification of source to final mine block by Coal company

- **Water Commitment by State Government**
  - Any inter-state issue inordinately delays the allocation of water for power projects.
  - In case of a dispute, Ministry of Water Resources should take the lead of calling regular meeting of all concerned state representatives where in the focus should be to give special permission to the concerned project

The analysis of the case studies reveals that Forest Clearances, Land Acquisition Formalities and Techno Economic Clearances consume the most time and effort

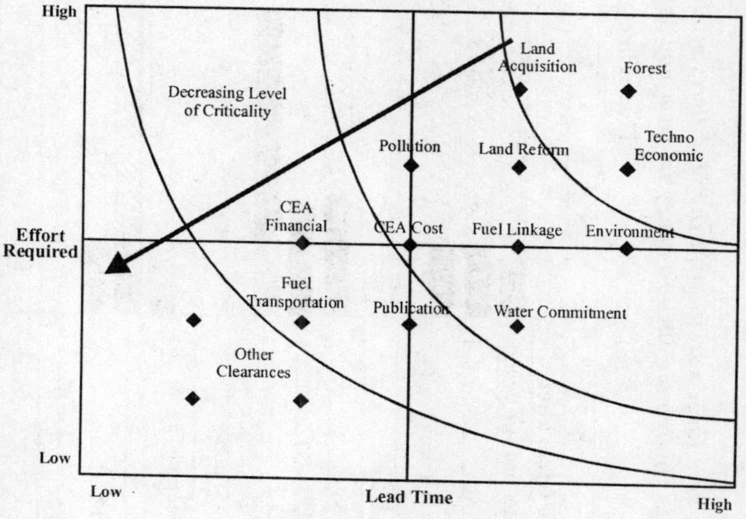

There also appears to be very large variation in the lead times of clearances for different projects, indicating inconsistency in form and spirit

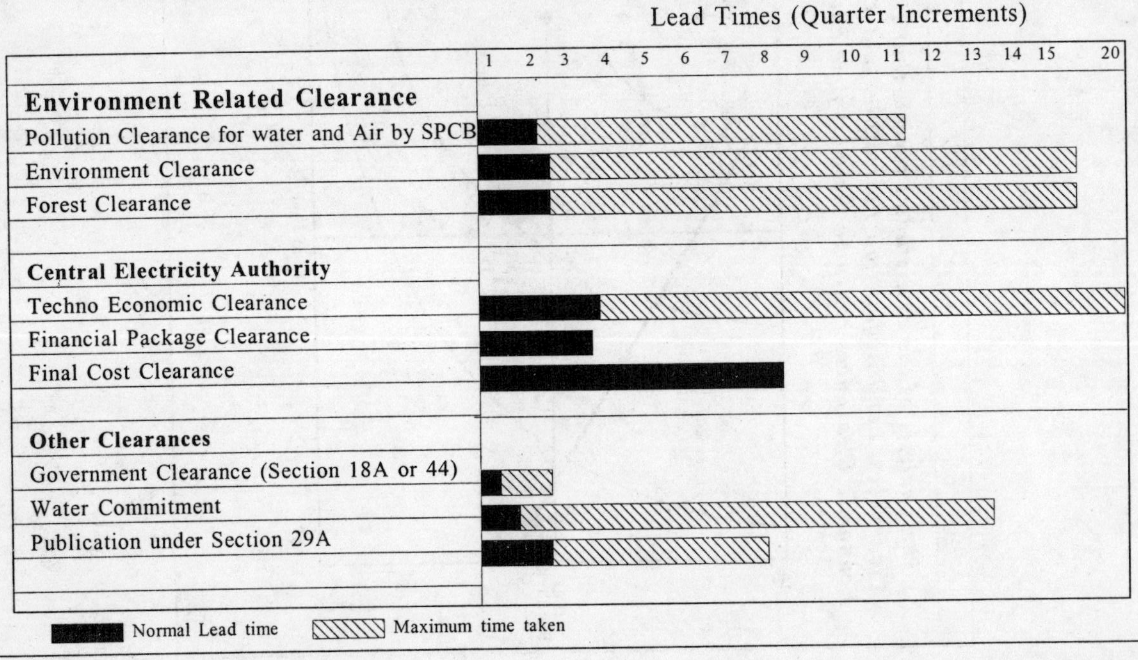

There also appears to be very large variation in the lead times of clearances for different projects, indicating inconsistency in form and spirit (2)

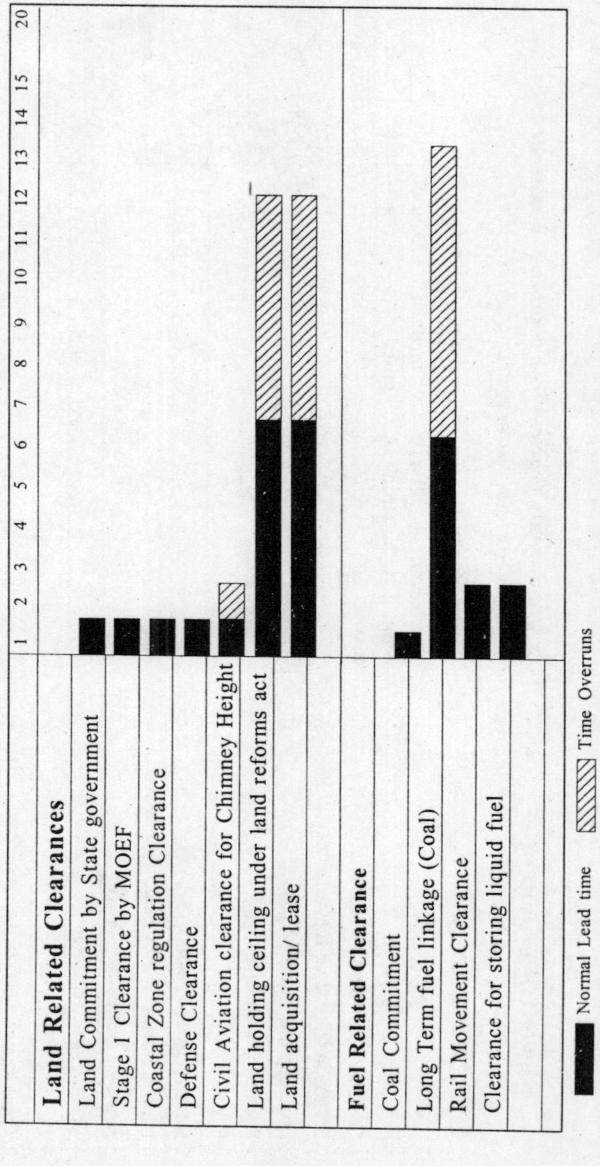

An analysis of prioritized clearances again reveals that environmental and land acquisition clearances appear to be areas requiring intervention/redesign (1)

Clearances	Maximum Duration	Effort Required	Clarity of procedures	Overall Priority
Environment related Clearance				
Pollution Clearance for water and air by SPCB	3	4	2	3
Environment Clearance	5	3	3	4
Forest Clearance	5	5	2	5
Land related Clearances				
Land Commitment by State government	1	1	2	1
Stage 1 Clearance by MOEF	1	1	2	1
Coastal Zone regulation clearance	1	2	2	2
Defence Clearance	1	1	5	2
Civil Aviation clearance for Chimney Height	2	1	1	2
Land holding ceiling under land reforms act	4	4	5	4
Land acquisition/lease	4	5	5	5

Maximum Duration
1- Very fast
5- Very slow

Effort Required
1- Very low
5- Very high

Clarity of procedures
1- Very clear
5- Very ambiguous

Overall Priority
1- Not important
5- Very important

An analysis of prioritized clearances again reveals that environmental and land acquisition clearances are perceived to areas requiring intervention/redesign (2)

Clearances	Maximum Duration	Effort Required	Clarity of procedures	Overall Priority
Central Electricity Authority				
Techno Economic clearance	5	4	2	4
Financial Package clearance	2	3	3	3
Final Cost Clearance	3	3	3	3
Fuel related Clearance				
Coal Commitment	1	1	1	1
Long Term fuel linkage (Coal)	4	3	4	4
Rail Movement Clearance	2	2	2	2
Clearance for storing liquid fuel	2	2	3	2
Other Clearances				
Government clearance (Section 18A or 44)	2	1	1	2
Water Commitment	4	2	3	3
Publication under Section 29 A	3	2	2	3

Maximum Duration
1- Very fast
5- Very slow

Effort Required
1- Very low
5- Very high

Clarity of procedures
1- Very clear
5- Very ambiguous

Overall Priority
1- Not important
5- Very important

Action Items

Comprehensive and concerted action on the four key issues, in the next phase, will facilitate investments and provide learnings for rationalizing clearances

1. **Reduce Clearances, From Multiple Agencies at Center, State and Local Level, for Primary Resources, Such as Land** ✓
2. **Reduce Multiple Clearances From the Same Agency/ministry - CEA** ✓
3. **Rationalize the Information Requirements in Environmental Clearances** ✓
4. **Dispense With Certain Clearances That Do Not Appear to Be Serving Any Specified Public or Other Interest** ✓

ANNEX – VI

Illustrative List of Inspectors Under Different Legislations

S.No.	Inspector
A	**Labour Laws Related**
1	Employees State Insurance Fund Inspector
2	Factories Inspector
3	Labour Inspector
4	Provident Fund Inspector
B	**Other Act Related**
1	Apprenticeship Advisor
2	Chief Inspector of Boilers
3	Controller of Weights and Measures Inspector
4	Electricity Inspector
5	Fire Inspector
6	Food Inspector
7	Hazardous waste Inspector
8	Mines Inspector
9	Municipality Inspector (For units located in Municipal Areas)
10	Professional Tax Assessor
11	Public Health Inspector
12	Shops and Establishment Act Inspector
13	State Sales Tax Inspector
C	**Other Inspectors**
1	Small Scale Industry Inspector (if SME)
2	State Excise Inspector (If involved in the production of State Excisable products)
D	**Central Government Inspector**
1	Air Inspector
2	Central Excise Inspector
3	Customs Inspector
4	Income Tax Inspector
5	Export Inspection Council Inspector for Export Units
6	Banks Inspector (For mortgaged stock etc.)
7	SIDBI Inspection Team (For credit from SIDBI)
8	Water Inspector

ANNEX – VII

Inspection, Register Maintenance and Returns to be Maintained Under Central Acts

S. No.	Name of the Act	Inspection Section	Register Section	Returns to be filed Section
1	Air (Prevention and Control of Pollution) Act, 1981	24-26		Rule 14 of Environment Protection Act
2	Apprenticeship Act, 1961	29	29	29
3	Child Labour (Prohibition and regulation) Act, 1986	17	11 and Rule 16	
4	Contract Labour (Regulation and Abolition) Act, 1970	28	29	Rule 82
5	Dangerous Machines (Regulation) Act, 1983	27-30	18	State Rules
6	Employees Provident Fund and Miscellaneous Provisions Act, 1952	13		EPF Scheme Para 33, 35, 36, 55
7	Employee State Insurance Act, 1948	45	44	44
8	Employment Exchange (Compulsory Notification of Vacancies) Act, 1959	6		5
9	Environmental Protection Act, 1986	10	20	20, Rule 14
10	Equal Remuneration Act	9	8, Rule 6	
11	Factories Act	7,9		
12	Indian Boilers Act, 1923	5,17		
13	Maternity Benefits Act, 1961	15-17	20	
14	Minimum Wages Act, 1948	Rule 26-B/19	18/ Rule 26	Rule 21
15	Motor Transport Workers Act, 1961	4-6	AP Rules 17,28,30, 33-38	AP Rules 39

(Contd...)

(...Contd...)

S. No.	*Name of the Act*	*Inspection Section*	*Register Section*	*Returns to be filed Section*
16	Payment of Bonus Act, 1965	27	26 & Rule 4	Rule 5
17	Payment of Gratuity Act, 1972	7-A, 7-B	AP Rules 6	AP Rules 5
18	Payment of Wages Act, 1948	14, 14A	13A	
19	Prevention of Food Adulteration Act, 1954	9-11		
20	Standard of Weights and Measures Act, 1976	29		
21	Water (Prevention and Control of Pollution) Act, 1974	20,23		Rule 14 of Environment Protection Act

ANNEX – VIII

Returns/Forms to be Maintained by a Medium Size Company

S.No.	*Department*	*Nature of Returns*	*Responsibility (Dept.)*
A.	**Inspector of Factories**		
1.	Form No. 20	Annual Return	
2.	Form No. K.L.&M	Annual Return	
3.	Form No. 21	Half Yearly Return	
4.	Form No. 2	Annual Return	
5.	Form No. 17	Notice of Accident	
6.	Form No. IV	Annual Return	
B.	**Labour Department**		**Personnel**
7.	Form No. V	Annual Return	
8.	Form No. D	Annual Return	
9.	Form No. III	Annual Return	
10.	Form No. XXV	Annual Return	
11.	Form No I&IV	Annual Return	
12.	Form No. D	Annual Return	
C.	**Employment Exchange**		**Personnel**
13.	Form No. ER-I	Quarterly	
14.	Form No. ER-II	Bi- Annual Return	
D.	**Provident Fund Office**		
15.	Form No. 12A, 5 & 10 & 3	Monthly Return	
16.	Form No. 3A & 6A	Annual Return	
E.	**ESI Department**		**Personnel**
17.	Form No. 6	Half- yearly return	
18.	Form No. 2	Monthly	
F.	**Apprentice Advisor**		**Personnel**
19.	Form No. APP-2	Half-yearly	
20.	Form No. 1A	Yearly	
21.	Form No. APP4	Yearly	
G.	**Pollution Control Board**		**Personnel**
22.	Concept Air & Water	Yearly Return	
23.	Environment Statement	Yearly Return	

(Contd...)

(...Contd...)

S.No.	*Department*	*Nature of Returns*	*Responsibility (Dept.)*
24.	Water Consumption	Yearly Return	
H.	**National Sample Survey**		**Personnel**
25.	Statistical Date	Annual	
I.	**Commercial Tax Office**		**Accounts**
26.	Entry Tax Form No. 3	Monthly	
27.	Entry Tax Form No. 5	Monthly	
28.	Sales Tax Form No. 3	Monthly	
29.	Sales Tax Form No. 4	Monthly.	
J.	**Income Tax Office**		**Accounts**
30.	TDS Salary Form No. 24	Yearly	
31.	TDS Salary Form No. 18	Yearly	
32.	TDS Form No. 21	Yearly	
33.	TDS Form No. 26c	Yearly	
34.	TDS Form No. 16K	Yearly	
35.	TDS Form No. 26K	Yearly	
36.	TDS Form No. 26J	Yearly	
37.	TDS Form No. 27A	Yearly	
38.	Com. Income Tax Form No. 1	Yearly	
K.	**Central Excise**		**FGS**
39.	Form No. RT-12	Monthly	
L.	**Director Statistics**		**Costing**
40.	Production Return	Monthly	
M.	**Labour Department**		**Administration**
41.	Form No. G	Annual Return	
42.	Form No.AA	Renewal of License	

ANNEX – IX

Downstream Approval Requirements

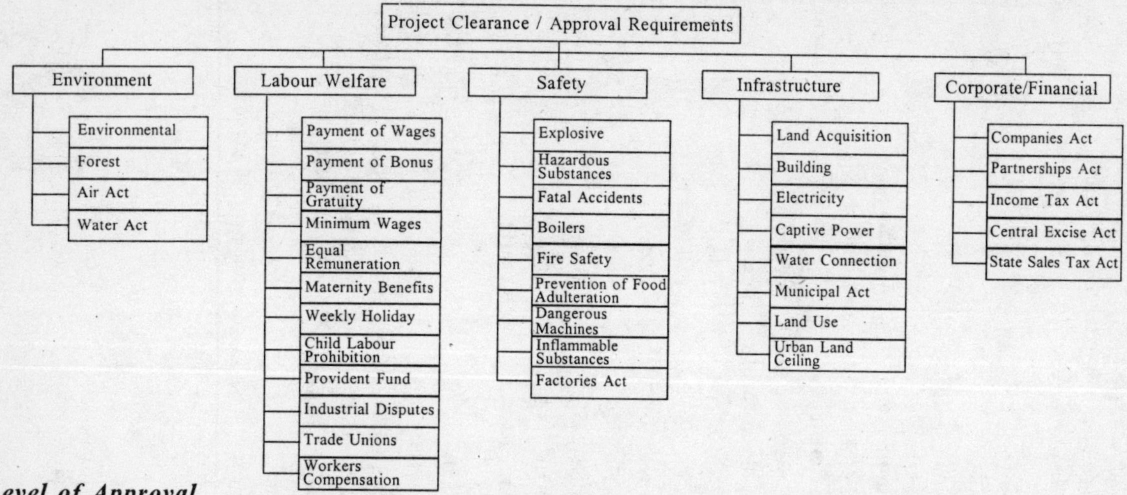

Level of Approval

Environmental: From Central and State Government
Labour welfare: From State Government
Safety: Explosives from Central Government, others from State Government
Infrastructure: From State Government and Local bodies
Corporate & Financial: From Central Government, State Sales Tax from State Government

ANNEX – X

Draft Terms of Reference for the Re-engineering Groups to be set up in Administrative Ministries

Objective

In order to simplify the procedures for grant of approvals and reduce delays, re-engineering of the regulatory processes prescribed under various legislations, regulations, etc., is necessary. Unless the procedures prescribed under extant laws are simplified to meet the requirements of the present economic, technological and competitive environment, delays in the grant of approvals are unlikely to reduce significantly. Re-engineering of the regulatory processes prescribed under different legislations, regulations, etc., is necessary to reduce ground level hassles, make administration and compliance easy as well as amenable to IT tools and minimise interface between project promoters and official machinery.

Composition

2. Re-engineering groups would be formed in the Ministries administering Acts regulating the implementation and operation of projects. An illustrative list of such central Acts is available at Annex-IV. To begin with such re-engineering groups would be formed in the Ministries of Labour, Environment & Forests, Power, Agriculture, Petroleum & Natural Gas and Development of Industrial Policy & Promotion.

3. These groups, under the Chairmanship of Secretary of the Department, would include other officers and representatives of the attached and sub-ordinate offices responsible for granting such approvals. Representatives of the State Governments and other Ministries may be associated as considered necessary. Industrial Associations, being important stakeholders, may also be associated. Assistance of public management specialist may be taken, as considered necessary, to bring in professional inputs and international experience in best practices.

Functions of the Re-engineering Groups

4. The Regulatory processes and systems, which are to be retained for administration by the Government, are to be re-engineered to embody the principles of:

i. Clear and non-discretionary decision rules to realize just the public interest to be protected as provided by law, and no extraneous objectives;

ii. Minimising and standardizing requirements of information and documentation specific to the applicant (i.e. not bring information which is either publicly available or available to the regulator from other public agencies) to support just the decision rules and no more;

iii. No queue jumping without specific and documented supervisory level authorization;

iv. Reducing stages and levels of review;

v. Defined time lines for each stage of processing, as well as the process overall, with a preliminary stage for confirmation that all required information/documentation has been provided, to which the regulator will not revert;

vi. Standardised response, including furnishing of reasons in the event of refusal to enable the applicant to represent meaningfully against the refusal;

vii. Real time monitoring of each stage of the process by supervisory authorities; and

viii. One stage of official review for redressal of grievances

5. The re-engineering groups would undertake the following:

i. Examine approval/permission requirement under each legislation, regulation, etc., for their re-engineering in the following order:

   a. Category A: where any violation may result in minor third-party impacts, which are easily remediable/compensable. In such cases, self regulation may be the norm, with legal penalties if violation is detected ('blinking traffic lights' model).

b. Category B: where violation may result in some significant third party impacts, but not involving proximate danger to life or serious injury, and still remediable/compensable. In such cases professional outsourcing may be preferred to direct case-by-case regulation by a Government agency. The professional providers of such services may be formally designated by their respective professional agencies (e.g. engineers, architects, etc.), and the basis of their certification sufficiently documented to enable determination of professional malpractice (by the regulatory agency, which may move the concerned professional association for de-registration) ('stop-go traffic lights' model).

c. Category C: where violation may result in high risks of serious third-party impacts or long-term damage to key natural resources or cultural assets. Only in such cases would prior case-by-case regulation be advisable by a public agency ('policeman regulating traffic' model).

While doing so, as many approvals as are possible should be placed self-regulation i.e. under automatic permission upon filing of necessary documents.

ii. Prescribe time limits for the grant of non-statutory approvals and develop systems for ensuring grant of approvals within this time limit. The re-engineering groups should also develop appropriate trigger mechanisms to automatically raise the matter to the next higher level in case the concerned authorities fail to decide the matter within the prescribed time limits.

iii. The re-engineering groups would also examine the extant laws being administered by their Ministry with the objective of consolidation of laws, weeding out laws that have outlived their utility and to generally bring them in line with the present technological, economic and competitive environment.

iv. The re-engineering groups would also indicate the inter-se priority among the various regulatory reforms being proposed by the group such that reforms aiming at maximum simplification are undertaken first.

v. A large number of approvals/permissions are administered at the State level and it would not be possible to suggest specific changes in the processes prevailing in each state. The re-engineering groups may indicate the best practices adopted in different states and elsewhere and suggest a generic structure of the re-engineering of the regulatory processes. State specific fine-tuning to the specific institutional and statutory/regulatory features of each State may be undertaken in consultation with concerned States.

vi. The groups may finalise their recommendations within a period of six months for the re-engineering of the regulatory processes and within one year for the consolidation of legislations.

Review of Progress

6. A Committee of Secretaries under Cabinet Secretary, with Secretaries to Government of India in the Ministries/Departments of Labour, Environment & Forests, Power, Agriculture, Petroleum & Natural Gas, Industrial Policy & Promotion, Revenue, Information Technology and Additional secretary in the PMO as members, would review on a monthly basis the progress of the re-engineering groups and act as trigger in case of any delay in the re-engineering processes.

7. IIFB would co-ordinate the re-engineering of regulatory processes with the re-engineering groups set up in different Ministries/Departments.

8. A position report on the re-engineering of regulatory processes will be included as one of the items in the monthly report of the concerned Ministry to the CCER.

ANNEX – XI

Concept Paper for the Proposed Technical Assistance for Undertaking Re-engineering of the Regulatory Processes

Objective

Personnel working in various Ministries/Departments as well as in the State Governments would require training, skill upgradation and support for undertaking re-engineering of regulatory processes and to be able to play an effective role in the facilitation process. Re-engineering groups to be formed in various Ministries/ Departments of the Government of India would, besides undertaking re-engineering of the regulatory processes prescribed under the Acts, Rules and Regulations, being administered by their Ministry/ Department, also play an important role in guiding and advising re-engineering processes at the State level. Technical assistance of multilateral capabilities within the Ministries/Department as well as State Governments to facilitate the re-engineering process.

Technical Assistance-Capacity Building & Re-engineering of Regulatory Processes

2. The Ministries/Departments of the Government of India and the State Governments would require technical assistance for capacity building of the personnel engaged with the policy formulation as well as implementation of various regulatory processes. In addition, the Ministries/States will also require technical support for the actual re-engineering of regulatory processes and to ensure that the re-engineered processes embody the requirements of IT mode. As a precursor to this, an inventory of global best practices will also need to be prepared. One of the Multilateral Financial Institutions (MFIs) can be approached for funding assistance for such study.

3. The report has, in paragraph 4.7, recommended that re-engineering groups may be established in 6 Ministries/Departments to begin with. These re-engineering groups, besides re-engineering the regulatory processes prescribed in the Acts, Rules and regulations being administered by their respective Ministries/ Departments, would also collect details and list out best practices adopted in various States and elsewhere and suggest a generic structure for the re-engineering of the regulatory processes at the

State level. Similar re-engineering groups may also be set up at the State level for undertaking re-engineering of the regulatory processes at that level.

Association of Training and Research Institutions

4. Since a large number of approvals/permissions, etc., are administered at the State level, a greater focus on capacity building at the State level would be required. Ministries/Departments of the Government of India and the State Governments may avail the services of training and research institutions for the capacity building needs. An illustrative list of such institutes is given below:

S. No.	*Name of the Institute*	*Place*
	State Sector	
1	Administrative Staff College of India	Hyderabad
2	Lal Bahadur Shastri National Academy of Administration	Mussoorie
3	National Productivity Council of India (NPC)	New Delhi
4	National Institute of Financial Management	Faridabad
5	Institute for Financial Management & Research	Chennai
6	HCM Rajasthan Institute of Public Administration	Jaipur
7	UP Academy of Administration	Nainital
8	Y.B. Chavan Academy of Developmental Administration	Pune
9	Assam Administrative Staff College	Guwahati
	Private Sector & Autonomous Organisations	
1	Indian Institute of Management	Bangalore
2	Indian Institute of Management	Ahmedabad
3	Indian Institute of Management	Kolkata
4	Indian Institute of Management	Lucknow
5	Indian Institute of Management	Indore
6	Indian Institute of Management	Kozikode
7	Tata Consultancy Services (TCS)	Mumbai
8	ORG-MARG Research Limited	Mumbai
9	Tata Management Training Centre	Pune
10	Xavier Institute of Management	Bhubaneswar
11	Xavier Labour Relations Institute	Jamshedpur
12	Management Development Institute (MDI)	Gurgaon
13	Institute of Development Studies (IDS)	Jaipur
14	Symbiosis Institute of Management	Pune

Components of Technical Assistance

5. Since the training packages to be used at various training institutions would be quite similar in terms of content, one of the premier institutions, say the Indian Institute of Management, Ahmedabad (IIM-A) may be assigned the responsibility of developing the training packages and also for training the trainers at other select training institutions. The Ministries/Departments and other State Governments may, thereafter, select the training institutions from the illustrative list of institutions. This component may require funds to the extent of Rs.100 lac (US$ 200,000). As and when re-engineering groups are established in other Ministries/ Departments, the technical assistance will need to be expanded to also cover such Ministries/Departments.

6. In the first phase, capacity building through training may be taken up for the six select Ministries/Department and 10 States. As per review, IIM Ahmedabad would review the results of trainings conducted by other institutions. The technical assistance requirement for training, at an average of 8 person-months for each Ministry/Department and 12 person-months for each State, is estimated at 168 person-months and is likely to cost around Rs. 200 lac (US$ 400,000), including the expenses on resource personnel, training material, visits, travel and other miscellaneous expenses.

7. The re-engineering groups in the Ministries/Departments of Government of India would also propose generic re-engineering of regulatory processes at the State level, to be fine-tuned in consultation with States for state specific response. The States would require technical assistances from identified institutions for the actual re-engineering of their regulatory processes. It is expected that on an average, technical assistance of around 30-40 person-months would be required by each State for actual re-engineering of regulatory processes. At an estimated average cost of Rs. 50,000 per person-month, the total expenditure would be around Rs. 15-20 lac for each State. The estimated cost for covering 10 States in the first phase would be around 150-200 lac (US$ 300,000-400,000).

8. The National Institute of Smart Governance, Hyderabad (NISG) could act as the nodal point for re-engineering of

regulatory processes at the State level. Assistance of IIM Ahmedabad may be taken to embody the principles of IT mode in the re-engineered processes at the State level. The re-engineered processes would be subject to peer review jointly by NISG and IIM, Ahmedabad.

Funds Requirement

While the actual funds requirement for the technical assistance through capacity building and actual re-engineering of the regulatory processes may be worked out in consultation with the concerned institutions, an indicative requirement of funds has been worked out as under

S. No.	*Component*	*Estimated amount*
a.	Preparation of training package and training of trainers	US$ 200,000
b.	Training of the personnel-Central and State level	US$ 400,000
c.	Re-engineering of regulatory processes at Central level	US$ 240,000
d.	Re-engineering of regulatory processes at State level	US$ 400,000
	Total	US$ 1,240,000

10. The expenditure on actual re-engineering of the regulatory processes in the Ministries/Departments of the Government of India will be met by the concerned Ministry/Department from their plan provisions as the Ministries/Departments are required to earmark 3 per cent of their plan funds for IT. Government of India may provide assistance to the States under technical assistance for actual re-engineering of the regulatory processes at the State level. The Government of India could meet the expenditure on the preparation of training material and training of personnel at the Central and State level.

ANNEX - XII

STEPS TO LAND ACQUISITION

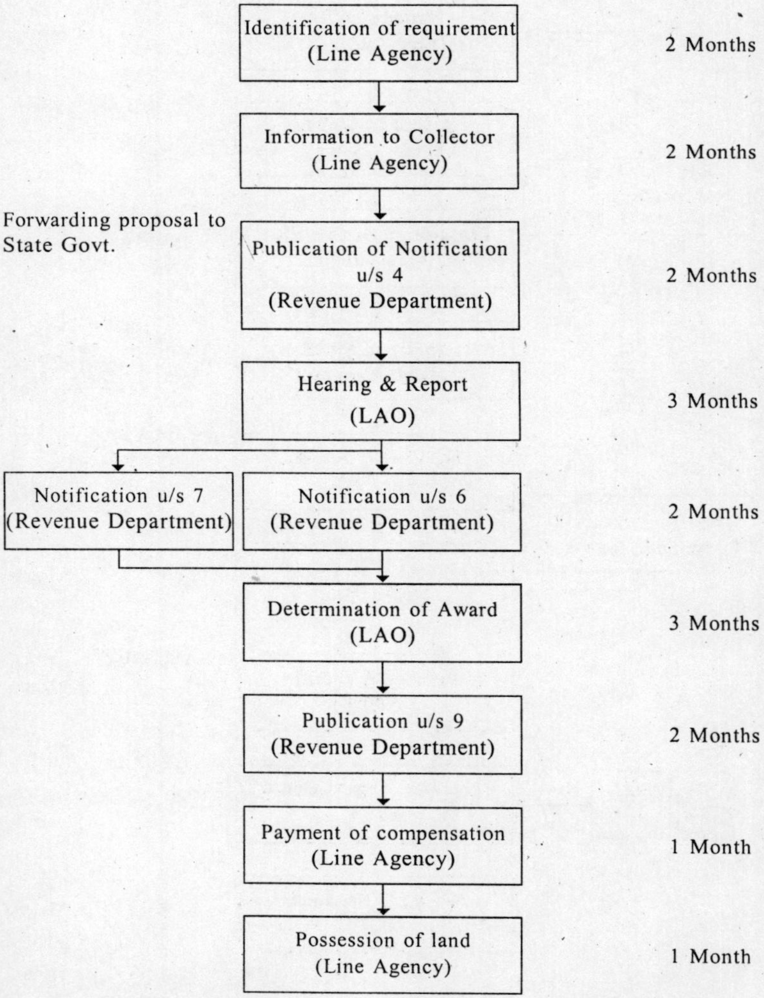

ANNEX – XIII

STEPS TO ENVIRONMENTAL CLEARANCE

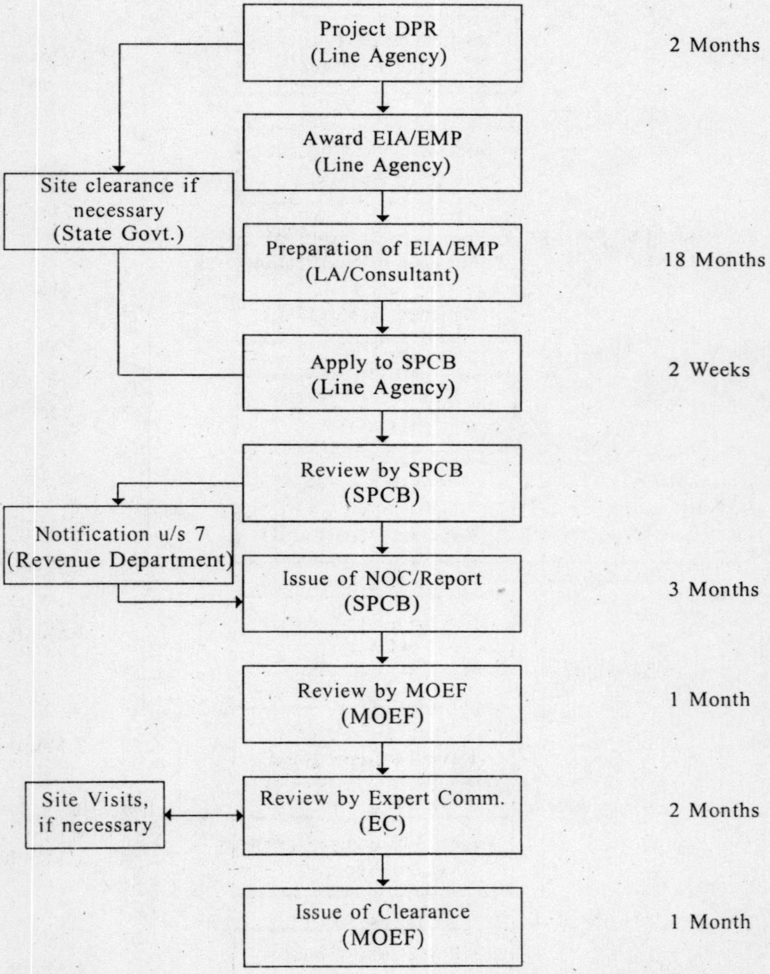

ANNEX – XIV

STEPS TO FOREST ACQUISITION

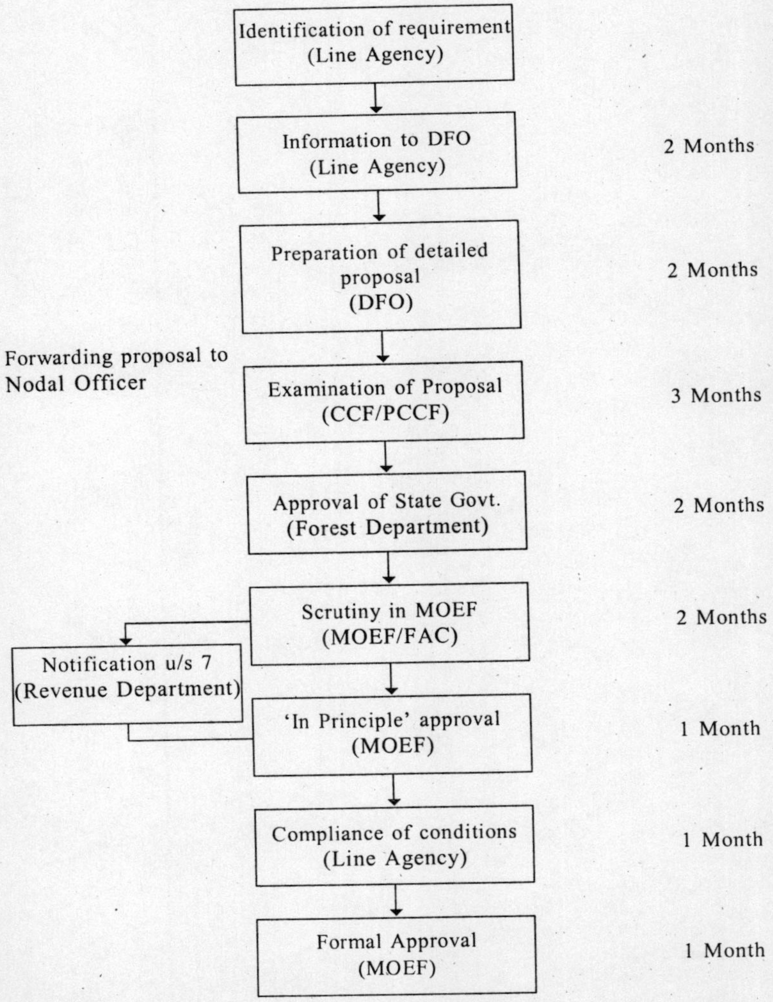

Parliamentary Standing Committee Report on Foreign Direct Investment

Rajya Sabha Secretariat, New Delhi, (May, 2003)

Contents

DEPARTMENT – RELATED PARLIAMENTARY STANDING COMMITTEE ON COMMERCE

(constituted on 1st January, 2003)

1. Shri Kailash Joshi - Chairman

Rajya Sabha

2. Shri K.M. Khan
3. Shri Janardhana Poojary
4. Shri Ashwani Kumar
5. Shri Rishang Keishing
6. Shri Parmeshwar Kumar Agarwalla
7. Shri C.O. Poulose
8. Shri Abu Asim Azmi
9. Shri S.P.M. Syed Khan
10. Shri J. Chitharanjan
11. Shri Ghanshyam Chandra Kharwar
12. Shri Sukhbir Singh
13. Shri Robert Kharshing
14. Shri Korambayil Ahammed Haji
15. Shri Mukhtar Abbas Naqvi

Lok Sabha

16. Shri Mahendra Baitha
17. Shri Girdhari Lal Bhargava
18. Shri Nandkumar Singh Chauhan
19. Shri Gurcharan Singh Galib
20. Shri Pusp Jain
21. Shri Shivaji Vithalrao Kamble
22. Shri Rizwan Zahir Khan
23. Shri N.N. Krishnadas
24. Shri Ramchandra Paswan
25. Shri Deepak C. Patel
26. Shri Dinsha Patel
27. Shri Danve Raosaheb Patil
28. Shri C.P. Radhakrishnan
29. Dr. D.V.G. Shankar Rao
30. Shri Y.V. Rao
31. Shri H.G. Ramulu
32. Shri Pradeep Rawat
33. Shri Balbir Singh
34. Shri Jai Bhadra Singh
35. Shri V.S. Sivakumar
36. Shri M.K. Subba
37. Shri Tarit Baran Topdar
38. Shri Ramakant Yadav

INTRODUCTION

THE Chairman of the Department-related Parliamentary Standing Committee on Commerce, having been authorised by the Committee, present this report of the Committee on Foreign Direct Investment.

2. The Sub-Committee on Industrial Policy and Promotion of the Department-Related Parliamentary Standing Committee on Commerce took up for an indepth study the subject of Foreign Direct Investment. It held three meetings for the purpose. It considered the information on the subject supplied by the Department of Industrial Policy and Promotion, Ministry of Commerce and Industry, besides the other papers/documents received during the course of deliberations. It also heard the views of the Secretary, Department of Industrial Policy and Promotion. It visited some units having participation of Foreign Direct Investment at Noida/Greater Noida, Bangalore, Pune, Mumbai, Chennai, Hyderabad, Gurgaon, Rewari, Jaipur and Udaipur and held discussions with their representatives on the subject.

3. The Sub-Committee considered and adopted the report at its sitting held on 18th December, 2002.

4. The Committee considered and adopted the report at its sitting held on 17th February, 2003.

Kailash Joshi
Chairman
Parliamentary Standing
Committee on Commerce

New Delhi
February 17, 2003.

REPORT

1. Foreign Direct Investment (FDI) today is seen as an instrument to facilitate and support domestic investment for achieving a higher level of economic development, since it benefits both the domestic industry as well as the consumer, by providing opportunities for technological upgradation, access to global managerial skills and practices, optimal utilisation of human and natural resources, making industry internationally competitive, opening up export markets, providing backward and forward linkages and access to international quality goods and services. In the wake of current era of globalisation a transnational economic regime has emerged. With the establishment of a global economic order in the form of World Trade Organisation (WTO), let the nations of the world moved towards integrating their economies. The economic activities in any country need substantial investments and the FDI tends to bridge the investment-saving gap to achieve sustained growth. Besides, the long-term additional capital that it brings in, FDI also tends to facilitate upgradation and transfer of technology and introduction of modern production and management practices.

2. In the face of the Balance of Payment (BOP) crisis in 1991, Government took recourse to Structural Adjustment Programme (SAP) and to open up the economy by initiating economic reforms. Since 1991, the Government policy on FDI aimed at encouraging foreign investment, especially in the core and infrastructure sectors. While the restrictions on FDI were eased in a phased manner, the following steps were taken to increase the inflow of FDI in the Country:-

- There are two modalities for FDI approval: automatic route and the Foreign Investment Promotion Board (FIPB)/ Government approval route;
- All items/activities, except a small negative list, qualify for automatic approval, as per sector specific policy for FDI;
- The remaining activities require approval of FIPB/ Government. FIPB endeavours to dispose of applications for FDI within a time frame of 30 days;

- At present FDI is not permissible in sectors such as agriculture (including plantations), housing and real estate, domestic trading, print media, etc;
- Comprehensive guidelines for consideration of FDI proposals by FIPB have been notified to ensure greater transparency in decision making;
- Full repatriation of original investment and returns is generally allowed;
- Liberal access to foreign technology is available through the automatic route, which permits lumpsum payments upto US $2 million and royalty @ 5 per cent for domestic sales and 8 per cent for exports (subject to a total payment of 8 per cent on sales). Cases not falling under the automatic route approval are considered by FIPB or Project Approval Board (PAB). While applications for financial and technical collaboration are considered by FIPB, applications for technical collaboration are considered only by the Project Approval Board; and
- Liberal External Commercial Borrowings (ECBs) and debt servicing norms have been notified and no ceiling has been placed on raising Global Depository Receipts (GDRs)/American Depository Receipts (ADRs)/Foreign Currency Convertible Bonds (FCCBs).

3. The extant FDI policy in the specified sectors was as under:

Retail Trading: Foreign Direct Investment is not permitted in retail trading.

I. *Agriculture sector (including Plantation)*: No FDI/NRI/OCB investment is permitted other than Tea sector, where FDI is permitted up to 100 per cent in tea sector, including tea plantations with prior Government approval and subject to the following conditions:

1. Compulsory divestment of 26 per cent equity in favour of Indian partner/Indian public within a period of five years; and
2. Prior State Government approval required in case of any future land use change.

The above dispensation would be applicable to all fresh investments (FDI) made in this sector.

II. *Print Media*: Government has announced Print Media policy recently. The policy & guidelines in respect of this sector is notified by the Ministry of Information & Broadcasting.

III. *Housing and Construction sector*: No foreign investment is permitted in the Housing and Real Estate sector except for development of integrated townships and settlements where FDI upto 100 per cent is permitted with prior Government approval. NRIs/OCBs are allowed to invest in the following activities:

a. Development of serviced plots and construction of built-up residential premises.

b. Investment in real estate covering construction of residential and commercial premises including business centers and offices.

c. Development of townships.

d. City and regional level urban infrastructure facilities, including both roads and bridges.

e. Investment in manufacture of building materials, which is also open to FDI.

f. Investment in participatory ventures in (a) to (e) above.

g. Investment in housing finance institutions, which is also open to FDI as an NBFC.

IV. *Electronic Media: Broadcasting*

(a) TV Software Production - 100 per cent foreign investment is allowed subject to (i) all future laws on broadcasting and no claim of any privilege or protection by virtue of approval accorded, and (ii) not undertaking any broadcasting from Indian soil without Government approval.

(b) setting up hardware facilities, such as uplinking, HUB, etc., - Private companies incorporated in India with permissible FDI/NRI/OCB/PIO equity within the limits (as in the case of telecom sector FDI limit up to 49 per cent inclusive of both FDI and portfolio investment) to set up uplinking hub (teleports) for leasing or hiring out their facilities to broadcasters*.

(c) Cable Network - Foreign investment allowed up to 49 per cent (inclusive of both FDI and portfolio investment) of paid up share capital. Companies with minimum 51 per cent of paid up share capital held by Indian citizens are eligible under the Cable Television Network Rules (1994) to provide cable TV services.

(d) Direct-to-Home - Company with a maximum of foreign equity including FDI/NRI/OCB/FII of 49 per cent would be eligible to obtain DTH License. Within the foreign equity, the FDI component not to exceed 20 per cent.

(e) Terrestrial Broadcasting FM - The licensee shall be a company registered in India under the Companies Act. All share holding should be held by Indians except for the limited portfolio investment by FII/NRI/PIO/OCB subject to such ceiling as may be decided from time to time. Company shall have no direct investment by foreign entities, NRIs and OCBs. As of now, the foreign investment is permissible to the extent of 20 per cent portfolio investment.

(f) Terrestrial TV - No private operator is allowed in terrestrial TV transmission.

In all the above cases automatic route is not available.

V. *Coffee and Tea Plantation*: Under Agriculture sector, No FDI is permitted in any plantation other than Tea Plantation. The details of FDI in tea plantation sector are given under Agriculture sector.

VI. Mineral Sector: *Atomic Minerals*: The following three activities are permitted to receive FDI/NRI/OCB investments through FIPB on exploitation of beach sand minerals (as per the detailed guidelines issued by Department of Atomic Energy vide

---

* As regards satellite broadcasting, all TV Channels irrespective of the ownership or management control to uplink from India provided they undertake to comply with the broadcast (Programme and advertising) code.

Resolution No. 8/1(1)/97-PSU/1422 dated 6.10.98): (i) Mining and mineral separation, (ii) value addition per se to the products of (i) above. (iii) Integrated activities (comprising of both (i) and (ii) above. Further FDI participation is permitted (a) upto 74 per cent in both pure value addition and integrated projects. (b) For pure value addition projects as well as integrated projects with value addition upto any intermediate stage. FDI is permitted upto 74 per cent through joint venture companies with Central/State PSUs in which equity holding of at least one PSU is not less than 26 per cent. (c) in exceptional cases, FDI beyond 74 per cent will be permitted subject to clearance of the Atomic Energy Commission before FIPB approval. The rights to mine any mineral vests with the Government. No individual or company, domestic or foreign can extract any mineral from the ground without the explicit permission of the Government.

VII. Consumer goods industries: FDI upto 100 per cent is permitted under the automatic route.

VIII. Tourism: FDI upto 100 per cent is permissible in the sector on the automatic route. Tourism related industry include travel agencies, tour operating agencies and tourist transport operating agencies, units providing facilities for cultural, adventure and wild life experience to tourists, surface, air and water transport facilities to tourists, leisure, entertainment, amusement, sports and health units for tourists and Convention/Seminar units and organization.

IX. Mining: (i) For exploration and mining of diamonds and precious stones FDI is allowed up to 74 per cent under automatic route. (ii) For exploration and mining of gold and silver and minerals other than diamonds and precious stones, metallurgy and processing FDI is allowed up to 100 per cent under automatic route. (iii) Press Note No. 18 (1998 Series) dated 14.12.98 would not be applicable for setting up 100 per cent owned subsidiaries in so far as the mining sector is concerned, subject to a declaration from the applicant that he has no existing joint venture for the same area and/or the particular mineral.

X. *Food Processing*: FDI upto 100 per cent is permitted in this sector under the automatic route.

XI. *Pharmaceutical Sector*: FDI upto 100 per cent is permitted on the automatic route for manufacture of drugs and pharmaceutical, provided the activity does not attract compulsory licensing or involve use of recombinant DNA technology and specific cell/tissue targeted formulations. FDI proposals for the manufacture of licensable drugs and pharmaceuticals and bulk drugs produced by recombinant DNA technology and specific cell/tissue targeted formulations will require prior Government approval.

Major Initiatives to Attract FDI

4. In pursuance of Government's commitment to further facilitate Indian industry to engage in various activities unhindered, Government have permitted, except for a negative list, access to the automatic route for Foreign Direct Investment. Under this automatic route, the foreign investors need to inform the Reserve Bank of India, within 30 days of bringing in their investment, and again within 30 days of issuing any shares. The negative list includes the following:-

- All proposals that require an industrial licence because the activity is licensable under the Industries (Development and Regulation) Act, 1951, cases where foreign investment is more than 24 per cent in the equity capital of units manufacturing items reserved for small scale industries, and the activities that require an industrial license in terms of the location policy, notified by Government under the Industrial Policy of 1991;
- All proposals in which the foreign collaborator has a previous venture/tie-up in India;
- All proposals relating to acquisition of shares in a existing Indian company in favour of a foreign Non-Resident Indian (NRI)/Overseas Corporate Body (OCB) investor;
- All proposals falling outside notified sectoral policy caps or under sectors in which FDI is not permitted and/or whenever any investor chooses to make an application to the Foreign Investment Promotion Board and not to avail of the automatic route;
- Foreign Institutional Investors (FIIs) can invest in a company under the portfolio investment route up to 24

per cent of the paid up capital of the company. This can be increased to 40 per cent with the approval of the General body of the shareholders by a special resolution and the limit has been increased to 49 per cent; and

- Foreign Direct Investment (FDI) in Non-Banking Financial Companies (NBFCs) is permitted on a case-by-case basis upto 100 per cent but with a condition that a minimum of 25 per cent of their holding is divested in the domestic market. This condition is being removed, provided the foreign investors bring in a minimum of US $50 million. FDI in NBFCs will now be put on the automatic route, subject to RBI guidelines.
- In the process of liberalisation of FDI policy, Government have further announced the following policy changes:-
- 100 per cent FDI has been permitted for B to B e-commerce;
- Condition of Dividend Balancing on 22 consumer items has been removed;
- Cap on foreign investment in the Power sector has been removed;
- 100 per cent FDI has also been permitted in oil-refining.
- Automatic Route is available to proposals in the Information Technology sector, even when the applicant company has a previous joint venture or technology transfer agreement in the same field.
- Automatic Route of FDI upto 100 per cent is allowed in all manufacturing activities in Special Economic Zones (SEZs), except for the following activities:-
  - Arms and ammunition, explosives and allied items of defence equipment, defence aircraft and warships;
  - Atomic substances;
  - Narcotics and psychotropic substances and hazardous chemicals;
  - Distillation and brewing of alcoholic drinks; and

  - Cigarettes/cigars and manufactured tobacco substitutes.

- FDI upto 100 per cent is allowed with some conditions for the following activities in the Telecom sector:-
- ISPs not providing gateways (both for satellite and submarine cables);
- Infrastructure Providers providing dark fiber (IP Category I);
- Electronic Mail;
- Voice Mail.
- Payment of royalty upto 2 per cent on exports and 1 per cent on domestic sales is allowed under automatic route on use of trademarks and brand names of the foreign collaborator without technology transfer;
- Payment of royalty upto 8 per cent on exports and 5 per cent on domestic sales by wholly owned subsidiaries to off-shore parent companies is allowed under the automatic route without any restriction on the duration of royalty payments;
- Off-shore Venture Capital Funds/Companies are allowed to invest in domestic venture capital undertakings as well as other companies through the automatic route, subject only to SEBI regulations and sector specific caps on FDI;
- Existing companies with FDI are eligible for automatic route to undertake additional activities covered under automatic route; and
- FDI upto 26 per cent is eligible under the automatic route in the Insurance sector, as prescribed in the Insurance Act, 1999, subject to their obtaining licence from Insurance Regulatory and Development Authority.

Capital Account Liberalisation

5. Until about 10 years ago, all the foreign exchange transactions were tightly controlled by Government and the RBI. Government have progressively loosened these controls and made the current account completely convertible. Government have also liberalised the capital account for certain purposes.

5.1 The following measures have also been taken for liberalising the Capital Account:-

- Indian companies wishing to invest abroad, may now invest up to US$ 50 million on an annual basis through the automatic route, without being subject to the three year profitability condition;
- Companies which have issued ADRs/GDRs may henceforth make foreign investments up to 100 per cent of these proceeds;
- Companies with proven track record, wishing to invest larger amounts, may now get a block allocation, in advance, from the RBI for investments overseas;
- Indian companies that have issued ADRs/GDRs may acquire shares of foreign companies up to an amount of US $100 million or an amount equivalent to ten times of their exports in a year, whichever is higher;
- ADRs/GDRs would be provided two-way fungibility. Converted local shares may be reconverted to ADRs/GDRs while being subject to sectoral caps, wherever applicable.

5.2 Government are continuously making additional reforms for further liberalisation of FDI. Such measures include ending of State monopoly in insurance, opening up of banking and manufacturing industry to competition and gradual disinvestment of public sector enterprises. Foreign investors are being allowed to own bigger stakes in projects like chemicals and chemical products, basic metals and metal products, electricity production and distribution, construction, transport and storage and advertising, where the ceiling on foreign ownership has been raised to 74 per cent from 51 per cent. Foreign equity of upto 51 per cent is permitted in textiles and telecommunication services. Wholly foreign owned ventures are now allowed in mining and the film industry. India is gradually moving to a regime where, except for a short negative list, most investment proposals are given automatic approval, provided the proposed foreign equity is within the specified ceiling. Foreign exchange controls have also been relaxed.

5.3 For non-fund based activities, minimum capitalisation norm of US$ 0.5 million is applicable in respect of all the permitted non-fund based NBFCs with foreign investment. Foreign investors can set up 100 per cent operating subsidiaries (without any restriction on the number of subsidiaries) without the condition to disinvest a minimum of 25 per cent of their equity to Indian entities, subject to bringing in US$ 50 million, out of which US$ 7.5 million to be brought upfront and the balance in 24 months. Joint venture operating NBFCs that have upto 75 per cent foreign investment, would also be allowed to set up subsidiaries for undertaking other NBFCs activities, subject to the subsidiaries complying with the applicable minimum capital inflow. FDI up to 49 per cent from all sources is permitted in the private banking sector on the automatic route subject to conformity with RBI guidelines.

5.4 FDI upto 74 per cent is permitted for the following telecom services, subject to licensing and security requirements (proposals with FDI beyond 49 per cent shall require prior Government approval):

(i) Internet services providers with gateways;

(ii) Radio paging; and

(iii) End-to-end bandwidth

5.5 Payment of royalty upto 2 per cent on exports and 1 per cent on domestic sales is allowed under automatic route on use of trademarks and brand names of the foreign collaborators, without technology transfer. Payment of royalty up to 8 per cent on exports and 5 per cent on domestic sales by wholly owned subsidiaries to offshore parent companies is allowed under the automatic route, without any restriction on the duration of royalty payments. Offshore Venture Capital Funds/Companies are allowed to invest in domestic venture capital undertakings as well as other companies through the automatic route, subject only to SEBI regulations and sector specific caps on FDI. Existing companies with FDI are eligible for automatic route, to undertake additional activities covered under automatic route. FDI upto 26 per cent is eligible under Automatic Route in the insurance sector, as prescribed under the insurance Act, 1999, subject to their obtaining licence from

Insurance Regulatory and Development Authority. FDI upto 100 per cent is permitted in airports, with FDI above 74 per cent requiring prior approval of Government. FDI upto 100 per cent is permitted with prior approval of Government in courier services, subject to existing laws and exclusion of activities relating to distribution of letters. FDI up to 100 per cent is permitted with prior approval of Government for development of integrated township, including housing, commercial premises, hotels, resorts, city and regional level urban infrastructure facilities such as roads and bridges, mass rapid transit systems and manufacture of building material in all metros, including associated commercial development of real estate. Development of land and providing allied infrastructure will form an integral part of townships' development. FDI up to 100 per cent is permitted on the automatic route for Mass Rapid Transport Systems in all metropolitan cities, including associated commercial development of real estate.

5.6 The defence industry sector has been opened upto 100 per cent Indian private sector participation, with FDI permitted up to 26 per cent, both subject to licensing. FDI up to 100 per cent is permitted on the automatic route in hotel and tourism sectors. NRI investment in foreign exchange has been made fully repatriable, whereas investments made in Indian rupees shall remain non-repatriable. International Financial Institutions like ADB, IFC, DEG, etc., have been allowed to invest in domestic companies through the automatic route, subject to SEB/RBI guidelines and sector specific caps on FDI. Industrial licences/ letter(s) of intent issued by the Secretariat for Industrial Assistance (SIA) in the past, carrying the condition of export obligation, have been exempted from the operation of this condition for items which stand de-reserved by an appropriate notification.

6. According to the Department the UNCTAD's World Investment Report, 2002 indicated India's ranking in the performance index at 119, as compared to the ranking of Pakistan (114) and China (47). The ranking was based on UNCTAD's new FDI benchmarking tools which measured performance by standardizing a country's inflows to the size of its economy and measured potential by using a set of economic and policy factors, of importance to foreign investors. However, the World Investment Report (WIR), 2002 had rated countries' performance for the

period 1998-2000, based on a ratio of a countrys' share in global FDI flows, to its share in global GDP and not on the performance relating to absolute FDI inflows, in which India had outperformed most countries in 2001. Further, in contrast to the downward trend in the world FDI inflows, India received US$4.06 billion (excluding ADRs/GDRs) during 2001-02, as against US$2.46 billion received in 2000-01, registering a growth of 66 per cent. The upward trend in FDI inflows had been sustained during the current financial year as well. The first quarter of the financial year 2002-2003 witnessed inflows of US $1.35 billion (net of ADRs/GDRs), representing a growth of 106 per cent, as compared to the first quarter of the previous year. According to the UNCTAD's report, China, Malaysia, India and Philippines had been identified as the four developing countries in Asia, which were expected to witness increased FDI inflows. Further, the cumulative FDI inflows from January, 1991 to June, 2002 was around US $30.6 billion, inclusive of ADRs/GDRs and around US$ 25.02 billion net of ADRs/GDRs. The realisation rate against FDI approvals had risen from 17 per cent in 1992 to 72 per cent in 2001. The FDI figures stated above did not include reinvested earnings and other direct capital flows, which actually formed part of FDI, as per international reporting practices (IMF BPM5). According to a recent study conducted by the International Finance Corporation (IFC), adoption of international standards for computation of FDI would raise India's net annual FDI inflows, from the present level of US $2-3 billion to about US $8 billion, which works out to approximately 1.7 per cent of India's GDP and was not far behind the 2 per cent level achieved in China.

Foreign Investment Promotion Board (FIPB)

7. The Foreign Investment Promotion Board (FIPB) has been constituted by Government with a view to promote and attract foreign investment in India. The FIPB is empowered to consider proposals for investment in India which do not fall within the parameters of the existing policy. The functions of the Boards include:-

(a) Expenditious clearance of proposals;

(b) Establishment of contacts with and inviting select international companies for investment in the country in appropriate ventures and to periodically review implementation of the projects cleared;

(c) The Board's programmes of investment include a variety of activities such as marketing, designing and export promotion, energy conservation. technology upgradation and modernisation, infrastructure development, better utilisation of raw materials and natural resources and substantial increase in employment.

Changing Role of FIPB

8. Government are keen to gradually reduce the quantum of projects being referred to the FIPB and instead ensure that the bulk of foreign investment proposals are approved automatically by RBI. The aim being to bring only selected large or sensitive projects for clearance to the FIPB. The role of FIPB is being altered from merely issuing clearances to carrying out policy.

8.1 The Foreign Investment Implementation Authority (FIIA) has been set up in the Ministry of Commerce & Industry. It has the mandate to provide translation of Foreign Direct Investment (FDI) approvals into implementation, provide a pro-active one-stop after-care service to foreign investors, by helping them obtain necessary approvals, sort out operational problems and meet various Government agencies to find solutions to problems and maximising opportunities through a partnership approach. The FIIA may co-opt other Secretaries to the Government of India, like Chief Commissioner (NRI), top functionaries of financial institutions and professional experts from industry and commerce, as and when necessary. The Secretariat for Industrial Assistance (SIA) in the Department of Industrial Policy & Promotion functions is the Secretariat of the FIIA. For conducting meeting of FIIA, the country had been divided into four regions. So far eight meetings of FIIA have been held. The region-wise break-up of the meetings is northern (3), western (2), southern (2) and Eastern (1).

9. The cumulative approval of FDI, from January, 91 to April, 2001 was upto Rs. 258,707.29 crore (US $ 70.96 billion) and the total inflows upto April, 2001 were Rs. 94,882.14 crore (US $ 24.94 billion) (both are including ADRs/GDRs of FIPB), giving a success rate of around 36.68 per cent in Rupee term (35.15 per

cent in US $ term). The realisation rate of inflows during the calendar year 1999 was 59.46 per cent as compared to 1998 which works out 43.29 per cent, in terms of Rupees. During the year 2000 (Jan.-Dec.), the realisation rate of Inflows worked out to over 52 per cent. The top five States getting FDI approvals during the period from August, 1991 to April, 2001 were Maharashtra followed by Delhi, Karnataka, Tamil Nadu and Andhra Pradesh. Following is a brief statement of sectorwise inflows during January, 1999 to December, 2001 and January, 2002 to 31st August, 2002:-

Sector wise Inflows from 01/01/1999 to 31/08/2002

(In Rs. Crore)

S.No.	*Sector*	*1999*	*2000*	*2001*	*Total (1999-2001)*	*From 1.1.02 to 31.8.02*
1.	Metallurgical Industries	164.18	65.41	124.64	354.23	164.38
2.	Fuels (Power and Oil refinery)	748.46	484.02	536.88	1769.35	2729.05
3.	Boilers and Steam Generating Plants	0.29	0.00	0.00	0.29	
4.	Prime Movers other than Electrical	6.26	0.00	0.00	6.26	
5.	Electricals Equipment (Incl. s/w & elec)	703.61	1201.22	1875.73	3780.56	1740.27
6.	Telecommunications	215.56	685.54	4227.25	5128.34	346.34
7.	Transportation Industry	1130.20	1225.98	1143.68	3499.86	223.10
8.	Industrial Machinery	99.34	29.97	74.90	204.21	42.44
9.	Machine Tools	9.99	10.37	13.66	34.02	12.46
10.	Agricultural Machinery	51.07	15.65	0.00	66.71	5.00
11.	Earth-Moving Machinery	0.10	0.00	0.48	0.58	0.43
12.	Miscellaneous Mechanical & Engineering	62.91	109.85	299.00	471.76	110.41
13.	Commercial, Office & Household Equipment	67.77	55.05	13.54	136.36	10.07
14.	Medical and Surgical Appliances	9.17	10.11	186.45	205.73	9.59
15.	Industrial Instruments	0.63	0.00	0.10	0.73	0.26
16.	Scientific Instruments	3.14	23.81	10.47	34.71	0.15
17.	Fertilizers	0.00	0.50	0.00	0.50	80.75
18.	Chemicals (other than Fertilizers)	475.62	538.07	163.98	1177.66	134.88

(Contd...)

(...Contd...)

S.No.	*Sector*	*1999*	*2000*	*2001*	*Total (1999-2001)*	*From 1.1.02 to 31.8.02*
19.	Photographic Raw Film and Paper	0.24	0.00	0.00	0.24	1.70
20.	Dye-Stuffs	0.00	4.50	0.00	4.50	0.87
21.	Drugs and Pharmaceuticals	75.73	207.99	147.23	430.95	62.49
22.	Textiles (include Dyed, Printed)	124.88	8.10	18.29	151.27	25.91
23.	Paper and Pulp Including Paper Product	51.36	259.95	50.14	361.46	54.96
24.	Fermentation Industries	0.00	68.88	29.80	98.69	0.25
25.	Food Processing Industries	404.70	222.45	146.81	773.96	138.02
26.	Vegetable Oils and Vanaspati	8.60	0.00	0.00	8.60	..
27.	Soaps, Cosmetics and Toilet Preparations	2.42	0.00	0.00	2.42	..
28.	Rubber Goods	17.76	16.20	3.07	37.03	177.86
29.	Leather, Leather Goods and Pickers	0.15	13.25	31.57	44.97	0.30
30.	Glass	171.81	145.64	22.50	339.95	214.66
31.	Ceramics	3.75	8.28	10.04	22.06	1.10
32.	Cement and Gypsum products	9.34	317.83	590.95	918.12	32.74
33.	Consultancy Services	21.42	14.83	234.00	270.25	87.30
34.	Service Sector	402.38	186.15	781.42	1369.95	820.72
35.	Hotel & Tourism	40.54	52.40	36.25	129.19	149.48
36.	Trading	98.05	123.98	201.64	423.67	14.83
37.	Miscellaneous Industries**	3729.69	3986.39	4867.29	12583.37	910.56
38.	NRI RBI Scheme*	348.80	348.85	229.74	927.39	11.08
39.	Sugar					4.12
40.	Mathematical, Surveying and Drawing					0.02
41.	Euro Issues (GDR)**					762.80
42.	Acquisition of Shares					4115.40
43.	Advance of Inflow					769.54
	Total	**9259.90**	**10441.20**	**16071.50**	**35772.60**	**13970.79**

Note:

(i) * Special NRI schemes administered by RBI from 01/01/1999 to 31/12/2001.

(ii) ** Misc. Industries includes the amount of acquisitions of shares.

10. In his deposition before the Sub-Committee, the Secretary, Department of Industrial Policy and Promotion informed that as India was opening up its economy and treading on the path of delicensing, deregulation and removal of restrictions on industry, a large number of restrictions which existed earlier, were getting dismantled. They were working in this direction to remove sectoral caps, for opening up all sectors of the economy for Foreign Direct Investment. In the last nine years since 1991, the inflow of FDI was of the order of $21.7 billion. But comparing this flow of Foreign Direct Investment into India with some other countries in the Asian region, it was far less than that in China, Thailand, Taiwan, Singapore besides some other countries in the region. A large portion of the Foreign Direct Investment took place in developed countries, some proportion in the developing countries and very little in the least developing countries. Some of the benefits which accrued through Foreign Direct Investment are that it supplemented the requirement of capital, especially in a country like India. India's domestic saving is around 23 per cent of its Gross Domestic Product (GDP). India had witnessed a growth in its economy at the approximate rate of six (6) per cent in its GDP. To alleviate poverty, it has been calculated that the GDP growth rate must hover around 8 per cent or more. Therefore, India had a gap of 2 per cent in its growth rate which has to be supplemented by additional investment to the tune of US $ 10 billion a year. It's a target that had been set by Government with regard to attraction of Foreign Direct Investment. But the inflow had remained range bound with only 3.5-4 billion dollars per year. In the previous year, India received a foreign direct investment of 4.02 billion dollars. Up to the end of July this year India received 2.5 billion dollars. By the end of the year, India was expected to be able to touch the figure of almost 4 billion dollars as the macro economic indicators were sound, the rupee had stabilised against the dollar and the industry, though a little sluggish, was also showing signs of growth. A large number of constraints were holding back foreign investment. Some of the important ones were the slow pace of economic reforms and the question of subsidies, wrangled in the complex bureaucratic controls and various other measures for privatization of PSUs needed to be introduced very fast in the economy, so that foreign investment could find a smooth inflow in to the country. Some foreign investors were complaining about

the excess time taken in the approval of some projects and their implementation, both at the Centre and the States. A project, which normally should take about 12 to 15 months, stretched to three to four years to get completed in India. There was a lack of infrastructure such as pathetic conditions of ports, not conducive for fast movement of goods traffic and containers, telecom services not up to the standard and the air connectivity within the country needing improvement. Apart from these, the banking system also required reforms. To redress these issues and other related issues, the Department had set up a Foreign Investment Implementation Authority, which met periodically, interacted with the foreign investors who were already in India, listened to their grievances and problems and tried to remove the constraints.

11. The Sub-Committee visited Noida/Greater Noida, Bangalore, Pune, Mumbai, Chennai, Hyderabad, Gurgaon, Rewari, Jaipur and Udaipur for an on-the-spot assessment of the impact of Foreign Direct Investment (FDI) in the industrial units. List of units visited is at Annexure-I.

11.1 During visits, the following problems/suggestions were highlighted by the representatives of various units as well as the trade and industry:-

(I) That there was inconsistency between what had been announced in EXIM Policy of the Government of India and what procedures the Customs actually followed through their notifications. India had taken very good policy decisions but their incomplete or slow implementation had added to the problems for the industry. There was also lack of co-ordination in the Customs and Excise Departments;

(II) That they were getting exemptions from local Sales Tax but were compelled to pay Central Sales Tax first, which was reimbursed later and that was a very time consuming process. Tax laws, especially the provisions regarding Income Tax exemptions on R&D activities, were not clear. There were artificial barriers of State taxes, which made movement of goods difficult. A uniform policy of taxes needed to be followed all over the country, for efficient business. The impact of domestic taxes, such as Excise Duty,

Sales Tax, Octroi, Turnover Tax should always be appreciably less than the effective Import Duty levied on similar items, to encourage investment for setting up manufacturing facilities. Further, multiplicity of domestic taxes called for greater amount of procedural formalities, to comply with. The procedure regarding MODVAT of Excise Duty also needed simplification, to avoid denial of MODVAT benefit on flimsy grounds. Further, there should be single Duty at the manufacturing point and the Duty paid on inputs should be adjusted against final Duty, as long as the manufacturers submitted proof of Excise Duty paid;

(III) That the procedures for inter-unit transfer, i.e. from one EOU to another, were very complicated and needed simplification;

(IV) That many Departments, which were created during the Licence Raj, were still continuing. Mere existence of those Departments was coming in the way of efficient operations of the industry. So, those Department, needed to be cut in size. There was general corruption in the Central and the State Government departments;

(V) That lack of adequate infrastructure added to operating costs, e.g. frequent telecommunications failures proved very costly to the industry. For Industrial Development, the country needed a unified approach, as had been followed by China. Whatever development in infrastructure had taken place was not consistent;

(VI) That there was a lack of transportation facilities due to bad roads, insufficient air connections for cargo facilities. Airports in major cities needed to be brought on the international air route, to make movement easy;

(VII) That the interest rates may be brought down;

(VIII) That selling to Government was very difficult, due to bureaucratic procedures and non transparency;

(IX) That the labour laws were quite old. There were the problems of labour unions. Labour laws were not conducive to export promotion, as there was no exit policy. System of contract labour needed to be introduced at greater scales. Some social security measures were required. In order to protect the interests of labour, contractor companies should be notified/registered/licensed with the respective State Governments, who would ensure that such company provides the labour with all the facilities, as required under the labour laws. Many industrial units, which, over the time, had become unproductive and uneconomic, cannot be closed due to labour laws. Hence, it was not only harming the interests of the industry, but also of the labour engaged in units. This was also blocking the capital for unproductive uses, creating unnecessary shortage of capital of these sectors;

(X) That VAT was not fully implemented;

(XI) That the FDI may be invited freely; it should not have any strings with it. FDI may also be attracted in the manufacturing sector;

(XII) That the time lag for completion of projects or policies was too long in India. There was a large gap between formulation of the policy and its implementation;

(XIII) That there was great potential of FDI in tourism sector, which needed attention; Development of Ports and Airports was required;

(XIV) That the Central and State policies were not consistent. The State Governments needed more freedom to implement their industrial policies;

(XV) That for Industrial Development, investment in backward areas of the country was also needed, especially in the form of small industries, developing road, and other infrastructure facilities. FDI in small-scale industries may also be attracted;

(XVI) That Rail density in some parts of the country was very low, as compared to northern States. New rail links to nearby ports, airports, cities, etc, needed to be created, for more industrial development and to attract more FDI;

(XVII) That more EPZs may be established. It would enhance the exports by attracting more FDI;

(XVIII) That the existing FDI projects, with an investment exceeding Rs. six billion and having 100 per cent foreign equity (which have been already cleared by CCFI), should be allowed for further induction of foreign equity for expansion of capacity through automatic route, provided the items of manufacture did not fall under the compulsory licensing. The capital goods for the projects should be levied the minimum Import Duty. Further, in order to reduce the initial capital outlay, levy of additional Duty, which was equivalent to Excise Duty and later on refunded through MODVAT, should not be charged. This involved a lot of documentation and procedural drill, to comply with;

(XIX) That a foreign company, which is investing, would like to place its own persons in certain key areas. For foreigners to work in India, they needed employment visas. The Indian Missions in different countries did not follow uniform procedures in that behalf. Foreigners employed in India, holding employment visas, invariably found it difficult to get them renewed and had to go back to their countries for securing extensions. Renewal of employment visas in India took a very long time as the applications are first processed in the Foreigner's Registration Office (FRO) in the region/by the State Government, before it goes to Delhi for their decision. The reply also comes through the same route. The Home Ministry should be advised to lay down a simplified procedure to obtain extension of employment visas in India, so that the companies/foreigners are not made to run from pillar to post, for getting the necessary permissions;

(XX) That the devaluation of rupee over the time was reducing the value of NRI's investment. The total capital of NRIs in India was decreasing in dollar terms, because they had brought their capital in India. They were no more willing to come to India because of requirement of many clearances, changing policies of Government and infrastructure bottlenecks. In fact, they were trying to go back;

(XXI) That inland ports may be developed on the lines of Singapore. Inland movement of containers was very slow; it had to be accelerated. Penalty may also be introduced if the containers are not delivered on time. It would decongest the ports;

(XXII) That there was perennial power shortage. Setting up of small captive power plants would help in setting up of the industries;

11.2 In order to accelerate the flow of FDI on a sustained basis, the following suggestions were offered:-

A. Investment Policy

(I) That there was no definite and transparent investment policy in India, which could be applicable to both the foreign and the domestic investments. Government should, therefore, spell out such policy framework clearly;

(II) The Government should announce a negative list of sectors. It would not be in the interest of the country to make a restrictive policy on Foreign Direct Investment, only to the select areas, on case-to-case basis, and that too, after inordinate delays;

(III) That the States may be given some incentives for their efforts to attract FDI. This could activate the lesser-developed States to make extra efforts to attract FDI. It was suggested that one percent of total divisible pool of Central Government revenues could be allocated for the purpose;

(IV) That Government could consider establishing joint venture companies, with foreign investors. The management of the company could rest with the foreign investor, while Government should contribute land, by way of their equity contribution and should take responsibility for land acquisition and other clearances, including environment;

(V) That mergers and amalgamations should be favourably considered, as it was attracting huge amounts of FDI;

(VI) For attracting FDI, Government should target the foreign companies, e.g. Fortune 500 companies, and not the countries or foreign Governments;

(VII) For the foreign investors to come into the country, it would be necessary to create enabling conditions for them. It was being observed that the waiting period for companies, to put up their business in Free Trade Zones (FTZs), was about 8-9 years. No foreign investor could afford to wait that long. In the matter of foreign investment approvals, etc., Government officials should not be allowed to be policing. They should become facilitators.

(VIII) That any incentives offered for FDI should not be at the expense of domestic industry.

B. Infrastructure

(IX) Special procedural provisions needed to be created for infrastructure projects, to ensure their effective execution and completion. Treating such projects as National Priority Projects would enable special considerations to be made in the following areas:-

a) *Land Acquisition*: There should be a time-bound land acquisition system which does not allow inordinate delays due to frivolous tactics. An appellate authority should be created to ensure just and effective implementation of land acquisition within a stipulated period, which could be six months at the maximum; Courts should not have powers to grant injunctions on continuance of such projects, once the tribunal's decision-making procedure was complete.

b) *Environmental Clearance*: In the case of environmental clearance, there should be a single appellate tribunal, similar to that proposed above for land acquisition. Further, there should be a single clearance system instead of the current requirement of clearance from both the Central and the State Governments.

c) *Project Finance:* Financial/lending institutions should be made to appraise and complete documentation procedures within a period of six months, from the date of application.

C. Taxation Issues

(X) Government should pursue long-term taxation policy, as the short-term tinkering in the policy was discouraging the foreign investors. Until three years ago, India had competitive tax rates, compared to most of the countries, which were keen to attract investment. While other countries had reduced their tax rates to encourage economic growth, India had gradually increased the same, by adding surcharge, which was supposed to be temporary but had become a permanent feature. The tax rate on distribution of profits had increased from 10 per cent to 22 per cent, now. The combined effect of these tax rates was 49.5 per cent, which was amongst the highest, compared to other countries. Such non-competitive tax rates sometimes made other destinations more attractive for the foreign investors. Increase in Duty Draw-back rates, to improve international market competitiveness and Government support to levy anti-dumping Duty, through WTO forum, for supplies by Korean/Chinese companies, below the cost price, was definitely needed. Multiplicity in taxation was a major source of making the products uncompetitive, as the cost increases were passed on to the ultimate consumer. A single taxation policy would help to bring a spurt in the industrial activity.

11.3 It was also suggested that a FDI Promotion Body should be set up, similar to the Economic Development Board of Singapore. Setting up of such a Body would bring together the key policy makers and the representatives of business. There should be a committee to sanction proposals for FDI, within twenty-four hours. To attract FDI inflows, the country needed to improve its image as a favourable location for FDI projects, and put itself on the map of investors. For an effective image changing, appropriate dissemination of information was vital. Information about investment opportunities and the regulatory framework was particularly important as, without such information, a country may simply not be considered in the investment-location decisions, for a range of projects. In the WTO era, efforts ought to be made to bring forth the legislations which could facilitate Foreign Direct Investment.

11.4 Liberalisation of the economy and shaping of FDI policy was an on-going process and the policy framework should facilitate growth and progress. It should harness the strength of the economy by optimally utilizing the economic and human resources of India for this purpose.

12. The Sub-Committee had invited the views of various ministries/Departments also on the subject, which are summarized as under:-

Ministry of Power

13. Ministry of Power vide their communication of 3rd January, 2001, highlighted the main reasons for power shortages in the country:-

(i) Exceeding demands:- Though there had been substantial increase in the generation capacity over the years, the growth in demand for power had outstepped the generation capacity. There had been inadequate capacity addition, to match the growing demand for electricity. The energy and peak demand shortages for the period April to October, 2000 were 6.9 per cent and 10.8 per cent, respectively;

(ii) High T&D Losses:- the high transmission and distribution losses (around 24.55 per cent) were one of the main reasons, contributing to power shortages;

(iii) Inadequate utilisation of present installed capacity:- The average Plant Load Factor (PLF) of thermal power plants had generally been below the desired level, although there was an improvement and some of the power plants had shown high PLF in the past few years. At the same time, greater attention was needed for the renovation and modernisation (R&M) of existing thermal plants.

(iv) Inadequate investment in hydro electric power:- The optimal thermal hydro mix for the country should be to the tune of 60:40, which at present, was round 76:24. Over the years, investment in hydro electric power projects, which can suitably address the problem of peaking power, has been less than desired. The main reasons for low investment included opposition to hydro plants due to environmental problems, problems relating to rehabilitation of displaced persons, to and geological surprises, etc. Due to these problems, the vast hydro potential in the country could not be fully tapped;

(v) High tariffs:- Of late, there has been a general reluctance on the part of some States to off-take power from some of the new power plants, based on liquid fuels, due to the high tariff. The high tariff was again due to the increase in global prices of liquid fuels, coupled with steady depreciation in the value of rupee vis-a-vis US dollar;

(vi) Inadequate investment in transmission, leading to pockets of surplus and deficits.

13.1 Government had taken various steps for private sector participation in the power sector. Government formulated a policy in 1991, with the objective to encourage greater investment, including foreign, by private enterprises in the electricity sector. The Electricity (Supply) Act, 1948 was amended in 1991, to provide a legal framework for facilitating investments. The policy allowed 100 per cent foreign investment in the power sector.

13.2 So far, 57 projects, having capacity of around 29,375 MW had been given techno-economic clearance by the CEA. Out of these, 10 projects, having a total capacity of around 3500 MW, had been fully commissioned. Seven projects for a total capacity of around 2500 MW, had achieved financial closure and were presently under construction. Five more projects, accorded TEC, had also started construction, though they were yet to achieve financial closure.

13.3 There were some other projects also which did not require the TEC of CEA and had been commissioned/started construction. Since 1991, in all, 24 projects of capacity of around 5200 MW, had been fully commissioned (including 10 TEC projects mentioned above) and 18 projects of around 5400 MW were in various stages of construction (including 12 TEC projects).

13.4 Private participation in distribution:- Participation of private sector in the distribution area was possible even before announcement of the Policy in 1991 and license companies had been operational in a few of the States. Companies like Kolkata

Electric Supply Company in Kolkata, Ahmedabad Electric Company in Ahmedabad, Tata Electric Company and Bombay Suburban Electric Supply Company (BSES) in Mumbai and Noida Power Company in Noida were already operational. In the recent past, Orissa was the only State which had privatized distribution by divesting 51 per cent share holding. BSES had taken over three Zones, while M/s AES Ltd. of US had taken over the Central Zone. The initial reports indicated that the revenue collection had gone up by 20 per cent and T&D losses were coming down.

13.5 The Committee feel that inspite of some steps taken by Government, the availability of adequate power still seemed to be a distant dream. Its inadequate availability worked as a dampener on inflow of FDI. There was a need to achieve, quantum jump in the production/generation of electricity.

13.6 Even though the Power sector had been able to attract inflow of FDI to some extent, yet it had stagnated due to the lack of transparency in operations and governance. Functioning of the State Electricity Boards needed to be improved and Government should lay down clear policy guidelines in respect of purchasing electricity from the private power generating companies. Clear policy guidelines with respect to power should be governed by the canons of economics, rather than that of the regional interests and other extraneous considerations.

Ministry of Communications

14. The Ministry of Communications vide their communication of 4th January, 2001, highlighted that telecom infrastructure was vital for economic growth of the country. Government had realized way back in 1994 that efforts of Government alone would not be able to achieve the objectives of rapid expansion in the Telecom infrastructure in the country and hence, envisaged private sector participation in supplementing the Government's efforts, and announced National Telecom Policy 1994. Since then, Government had taken a number of steps for improving the Telecom infrastructure in the country. Some of the important decisions taken are as under:

i) six private companies had been licensed to operate telecom services in the circles of Madhya Pradesh,

Gujarat, Rajasthan, Maharashtra, Andhra Pradesh and Punjab, in addition to DoT (now Bharat Sanchar Nigam Ltd.) and MTNL;

ii) a number of licenses had been issued for providing various value-added services, including Cellular Mobile Service, throughout the country/various Telecom Circles;

iii) The New Telecom Policy, 1999 (NTP'99) was the most important landmark in the Telecom reforms in India. There aimed at creating an ideal investment environment, to enable establishment of a world class Telecom Infrastructure. It also aimed at creating a level playing field, strengthening the regulator, attracting Private Investment, creating for convergence and leveraging on technological advancements;

iv) Through migration package, existing licenses have been allowed to migrate from fixed licence fee regime to a revenue share regime;

v) Independent regulator, Telecom Regulatory Authority of India (TRAI), which has been empowered to make recommendations on various aspects related to the functioning of Telecom Service Providers and to discharge regulatory functions, has been set up. For adjudication of disputes, a Telecom Dispute Settlement and Appellate Tribunal (TDSAT) has also been set up;

vi) National Long Distance Services have been opened up for private sector participation. Government have also decided to prepone monopoly of VSNL over International Voice Telephony from April, 2002;

vii) Foreign Direct Investment policy for telecom sector is quite liberal and investor friendly. As per the guidelines of Government, 100 per cent Foreign Direct Investment (FDI) is permitted in the telecom manufacturing sector, and 49 per cent in the telecom services, excepting a few services listed below, where 100 per cent FDI is permitted:-

a) ISPs not providing gateways (both for satellite and submarine cables);

b) Infrastructure Providers providing dark fibre (IP Category I);

c) Electronic Mail; and

d) Voice Mail

The above would be subject to the following conditions:-

a) FDI upto 100 per cent is allowed subject to the conditions that such companies would divest 26 per cent of their equity in favour of Indian public in five years, if these companies are listed in other parts of the world;

b) The above services would be subject to licensing and security requirements, wherever required;

c) Proposals for FDI beyond 49 per cent shall be considered by FIPB, on case to case basis.

viii) Telecom sector has been given a number of incentives in respect of taxation/duties. Such incentives include tax holiday under section 80-IA, amortization of telecom license fees under section 35ABB, rebate on subscription on shares and debentures in the telecom sector under (xvi) and (xvii) of section 88, tax exemptions on financing through venture capital, external borrowing and long term borrowing to telecom sector under sections 10(15)(iv), 10(23 F) and 10(23 G), as well as under section 36(1)(viii) and exemptions provided in respect of capital gains tax under section 54EA and 54EB of the Income Tax Act. Import of some of the infrastructure equipment are also allowed at concessional rate of Customs Duty of 5 per cent.

14.1 The Committee feel that telecommunication sector was already in the process of making quantum jump in telecommunication facilities/connectivity and hope that whatever deficiencies are there, the same would be overcome in the near future.

Ministry of Railways

15. The Ministry of Railways vide their communication of 5th January, 2001, highlighted that as regards FDI in the Railways,

the Railways were a strategic sector and, being fully owned by Central Government at present, are not open to FDI. As per the present guidelines of the Government of India, Railways, as an industry, is Reserved for the Public Sector.

15.1 The Ministry, however, submitted that in view of the limitations on availability of funds for investment, the Ministry can only consider construction of specific project-oriented new lines, which provide the necessary internal rate of return to the Railways. Development of rail transport infrastructure is normally only justified in case the project involves large scale movement of coal, minerals and ores, petroleum products or the setting up of new industries for e.g., a steel plant, a cement factory, a fertilizer plant, power house, etc., which have significant rail transport requirement or in the case of new port.

15.2 During the recent years, a major investment in expansion of the network in southern States had been the construction of the Konkan Railway. In addition, a number of new line projects were sanctioned in the Southern States of Andhra Pradesh, Karnataka, Tamil Nadu and Kerala. Many of the projects were not financially viable, although they may be considered socially desirable and completion of those projects would depend upon the availability of funds and level of funding from year to year. The completion of the sanctioned projects will improve the rail route density in southern States.

15.3 In order to develop rail infrastructure, the Ministry of Railways had been able to effectively persuade some State Governments to share cost of investments and had also entered into public-private partnership schemes. In the case of Mumbai, Chennai and Kolkata, the State Governments have agreed to share the cost of upgrading/extending suburban services in these metropolitan cities. In the case of Mumbai, a Mumbai Railway Vikas Corporation (MRVC) had been formed, for execution of projects with 51 per cent equity holding with the Ministry of Railways and the balance equity with the Government of Maharashtra. Initiatives had also been taken for providing rail connectivity to certain ports in the State of Gujarat, with private sector involvement/contribution for infrastructure development, for providing access to new ports.

15.4 For the development of Railway projects in the State of Karnataka, action had been initiated for the formation of a Corporation for rail infrastructure Development, with equity partnership of the Ministry of Railways, Government of Karnataka, Financial Institutions/banks and others. The following four projects had been identified for execution by this Corporation:

- Hubli-Ankola New Line;
- Hospet-Guntakal Double line;
- Hassan-Mangalore Gauge Conversion;
- Sholapur-Gadag Gauge Conversion;

15.5 The Sub-Committee is constrained to note that inadequate infrastructure in Railway hampers flow of FDI into the country.

15.6 The Committee opine that the goods traffic was becoming highly competitive and Government must take adequate steps to guard their interest in goods traffic by way of increasing the rail density in the areas, which had attractted more FDI and take steps to provide adequate rail linkages to ports, airports and railway stations. The railways needed to modernise in all the spheres and develop as a reliable transporter, compared to standard of services being provided by the Railways in other developed/ developing countries.

Ministry of Road Transport and Highways

16. The Ministry of Road Transport and Highway vide their communication dated 1st January, 2001, highlighted that India had 3.3 million kilometers of road network, which was the second largest in the world. Roads occupied an eminent position in transportation as per the present estimate, carried nearly 65 per cent of freight and 87 per cent of passenger traffic. Traffic on roads was growing at a rate of 7 to 10 per cent per annum, while the vehicle population growth, for the past few years, was of the order of 12 per cent per annum.

16.1 The different categories of roads and authorities responsible for them are:

- National Highways
  - * Central Government through Ministry of Road transport and Highways;

- State Highways and Major District Highways
  * State Governments (PWDs);
- Rural Roads and Urban Roads
  * Rural Engineering Organisations, Local authorities, like Panchayats and Municipalities.

16.2 At the Centre, Ministry of Road Transport and Highways was directly responsible for development of National Highways, which aggregate of 57737 kms, which, although was only 1.7 per cent of total length, carried about 45 per cent of the road traffic. The National Highways are thus the lifeline of the country, connecting the farthest corners and the remotest border areas.

16.3 The resource requirement for removal of deficiencies on National Highways is estimated to a whooping Rs. 165,000 crore. Mobilising such funds is a big challenge. This is being done by traditional budgetary allocations, as well as, innovative measures like revamping of Central Road Fund, funding from multi-lateral agencies, private sector participation, market borrowings, etc.

16.4 To meet the challenges of accelerated funding requirement for all the categories of roads in the country, the Central Road Fund has been revamped, by enactment of the Central Road Fund Act, 2000 by the Parliament. The Ministry of Road Transport and Highways is the administrative Ministry for the Central Road Fund.

16.5 The Committee recommend that adequate funds may be placed at the disposal of the National Highways Authority of India so that the express highways are built at the earliest, reducing the time being taken by the vehicles in reaching destinations, and increasing the speed of movement of the goods traffic. Private participation in the realm of increasing the density of roads and modernization of the highways should be encouraged through Built, Operate, Lease and Transfer (BOLT) system. Tax holidays should be provided to the companies, who invest in modernisation of highways and in creating new and efficient road networks.

Ministry of Personnel, Public Grievances and Pensions

17. The Ministry of Personnel, Public Grievances and Pensions vide their communication dated 9th January, 2001, highlighted the following points:-

1. The Department of Personnel and Training had a major role in combating corruption in public administration. The Department is the nodal Department, responsible for formulation and implementation of the Central Government's policy in the field of vigilance, integrity in public services and anti-corruption and to provide guidance and coordination to Ministries and Departments of the Government of India in such matters. The Department also provides administrative support to the major organisations engaged in combating corruption, viz., CBI and Central Vigilance Commission;
2. The work of the Central Government in the field of combating corruption in public administration has been considerably stepped up during the last few years, the main step being to reduce the role of State in society, as in doing away with the licensing system. The Annual Action Plan prepared by the Ministry of Personnel, Public Grievances and pensions envisages three-pronged strategy, comprising preventive vigilance, surveillance and detection, and deterrent punitive action. It was initially launched in 1985-86 and is being continued on annual basis;
3. As far as prevalence of corruption in State Governments is concerned, that was within the sphere of responsibility of the State Governments;
4. Government had also taken measures to bring more transparency and accountability in their functioning. A large number of Ministries/Departments/Organizations, with considerable public interface, had introduced Citizen's Charters, indicating broadly the quality of service the public would be entitled to, within a specified time-frame.

17.1 The Committee feel that there was a need to effect attitudinal change in the bureaucracy, so that they act as facilitators of Foreign Investment, rather than the obstructers.

Ministry of Civil Aviation

18. The Ministry of Civil Aviation, vide their communication dated 10th January, 2001, highlighted the following initiatives,

aimed at increasing FDI in India, by way of leasing of four airports at Delhi, Mumbai, Chennai and Kolkata, through Global tendering system. Disinvestment of Air India and Indian Airlines was also under process, in which they expected direct FDI participation. Another step initiated by the Ministry was to develop new International Airports at Bangalore, Hyderabad and Goa, with major private sector participation. This was besides four other airports, namely Ahmedabad, Cochin, Amritsar and Guwahati having been declared as International Airports. They thus, expected that these steps would improve the quality of passenger services.

18.1 The Committee feel that there was a need for adequate domestic as well as international air connectivity as per the expectations of foreign investors. The Committee are constrained to note that development work at the Bangalore Airport was wrangled in bureaucratic impediments and lack of clear announcement on the part of Government was adding to the woes of the investors there. Addition of the Bangalore and other Airports on the international aviation map would improve international connectivity and would facilitate enhanced in flow of FDI in India. Therefore, the Committee recommend that the Department should take up the case of the airports frequented by foreign investors with the concerned Departments/Ministries to facilitate easy access for them.

Ministry of Shipping

19. According to the Ministry of Shipping vide their communication dated 18th January, 2001, guidelines for foreign investment in the ports sector had been further liberalised. Automatic approval would be accorded for foreign equity participation upto 100 per cent in construction activities, in the area of ports and harbours. In addition to this, automatic approval would be given for majority foreign equity upto 51 per cent support services, like operation and maintenance of Piers and loading and discharging of Vessels. The automatic approval route would be available, where FDI did not exceed Rs. 6 billion. Higher investments would be approved by FIPB.

19.1 Foreign investors can be considered for private sector projects if they had the necessary FIPB/Competent Authority clearance and had been registered as a company under the Indian

Companies Act or had the FIPB/competent authority clearance and proposed to be registered as a company under the Indian Companies Act.

Achievements of the Ministry during the Ninth Five Year Plan Period:

(i) 15 private sector projects, with 57.30 million tonnes capacity and Rs. 4376 crore investment, had been approved and some projects had been completed and other were at various stages of implementation;

(ii) After the delegation of powers from Ministry of Environment and Forests in July, 1997, to accord environmental clearance for the projects in the Coastal Regulation Zone of the existing ports (major and minor), environmental clearance was accorded to 39 projects;

(iii) Bill to amend Major Port Trusts Act, to enable Joint Venture formation, had been approved by Parliament;

(iv) Ennore Port Limited had been incorporated for management of Ennore Port;

(v) The procedure for procurement of cargo handling equipments had been simplified;

(vi) Ports had been delegated enhanced financial powers.

19.2 The development of ports had not kept pace with the needs of the time. As on date, not a single port in the country was equipped to accommodate mother ships. In the era of open and competitive economy, lack of infrastructure, in the form of insufficient facilities, and delays at ports in shipment and trans-shipments of cargo and containers would definitely hold the prospective investors, thus jeopardizing the future of FDI in India. To overcome such a situation, the Committee recommend that development of ports should receive due attention and a blue print for future growth and modernisation should be drawn up and implemented especially to facilitate accommodating the mother ships. The Committee hope that the Ministry would accelerate its efforts in further developing the shipping as a reliable mode of transport as per the requirements of foreign investors.

19.3 At the same time, there was an urgent need to develop more Inland Container Depots, for expenditious movement of containers, from the depots to the ports.

Department of Revenue

20. The Department of Revenue submitted that the Double Taxation Avoidance Agreements (DTAA) promoted Foreign Direct Investment (FDI) between countries. The tax treaties provided foreign investors a certainty of a tax regime prevailing in the country. They also provided a framework for sharing taxes and mutual cooperation between the two tax regimes. The country had treaty with 62 countries. These treaties could generally favour the flow of Foreign Direct Investment. It provided for taxation of business income of a foreign company if it had a permanent establishment (PE) in India. Further profit attributable to the permanent establishment was alone taxed. Payment relating to royalty, fees for technical services and interest were subjected to withholding tax at a lower rate than stipulated in the domestic law. Tax paid in one country could be credited against the tax payable in the country of residence and in case a resident of a country was aggrieved with the interpretation of treaties in the other country, the competent authorities of both the countries would try to resolve the issue by mutual consultation.

20.1 The Department acknowledged that there was need to minimize burden in the matter of compliance of various Customs and Central Excise rules and procedures, on the part of various assesses and other parties concerned with import/exports/ manufacture, etc. As a matter of conscious policy, the Central Board of Excise & Customs had been trying to simplify various rules & procedures by taking up critical reviews. The actions/ steps taken recently for procedural simplification, were as follows:-

20.2 Central Excise duties levied on indigenously manufactured goods on ad valorem basis, were being valued in accordance with the provisions of Section 4 and 4A of the Central Excise Act. The valuation till recently (under Section 4) was on the basis of concept of normal price at which the goods were ordinarily sold in wholesale lots to any class of buyers and different 'normal' prices were accepted for different classes of buyers. On the other hand, Valuation of goods on import, where duties were levied on ad valorem basis, had been based since 1988 on GATT, and since 1995, on WTO valuation agreement. Till the 2000 Budget, there was not much similarity between the valuation practices followed on the Customs & Central Excise sides. Whereas Customs was adopting the transaction value as the basis, for Central Excise purposes, notional whole sale 'normal price' had to be determined for arriving at same uniform incidence of excise for goods cleared to same class of buyers. The valuation rules and Section 4 governing the valuation in different situations were subject matter of different interpretation and disputes. As a measure of simplification and in tune with practice of valuation on the customs side, the concept of 'transaction value'-between the manufacturer and the Customers has been made the basis of valuation for excise duty purposes. Certain revised Valuation Rules had also been framed for valuation in different situations e.g. where sales were between related persons, or where there was no sale, etc. Some of the principles and practices adopted on the Customs valuation had also been adopted for Central Excise side and there was greater similarity and coordination in valuation principles for charging Customs & Central Excise duties, on commodities on ad valorem basis than what it used to be before the year 2000.

20.3 Prior to 1994, there were as many as 21 ad valorem rates of excise duty, which had been brought down to 11 by 1998 and in 1999 Budget, the 11 rates of excise duty were further compressed into 3 rates of 8 per cent, 16 per cent and 24 per cent alongwith special excise on a few items at three different rates. In the 2000 Budget, in a historic step, a uniform CENVAT rate of 16 per cent had been introduced on almost all excisable goods with few exceptions. In Budget 2001, even the special duty of excise had been brought to a uniform rate of 16 per cent.

20.4 In tune with international practice of system of collection of VAT on periodic basis and not consignment-wise, with effect from 1st April, 2000, all assesses of Central Excise were allowed to pay duty on fortnight basis, except the small scale industries who will continue to pay duty on monthly basis.

20.5 In order to minimise disputes and for more simple valuation system, MRP (Maximum Retail Price) based excise levy was introduced in the 1997 Budget for certain commodities. The scheme provided for fixing the taxable value of a product as a percentage of the MRP after giving due abatements for all the taxes payable on the product and reasonable trade margins.

20.6 With effect from 1st April, 2000, a new CENVAT (Central Value Added Tax) simplified rules had replaced erstwhile MODVAT scheme under which the credit of CENVAT duty on all raw materials, consumables, parts and components and capital goods had been allowed where these were used in the manufacture of dutiable excisable goods. In the Budget 2001-2002, these rules were further liberalised so as to allow CENVAT credit of special duty of excise paid on all the inputs.

20.7 As a measures of further simplification for industries and improved scrutiny of accounts, the requirement of maintaining several statutory records in prescribed format under Central excise law had been dispensed with. The private record of the assessee, which should contain certain minimum information as indicated in the Central Excise Rules, would now be accepted.

20.8 In the Budget 2001-2002, new Central Excise Rules, 2001 had been announced replacing the Central Excise Rules, 1944. In the new rules, simplified procedures have been specified. There rules had come into effect from 1st July, 2001. Provisions have been made for prior approval of senior level officers before any show cause notices is issued under the Central Excise and Customs law. The Government had set up a Settlement Commission for Settlement of certain categories of disputes relating to customs and excise duties. An authority for Advance Tax Rulings for excise and customs in view of the need for foreign investors to be assured in advance of their likely indirect tax liability was also being set-up.

20.9 The Department further submitted that in the Budget 2001-2002, certain amendments were proposed aiming at early finalisation/resolution of disputes, namely,-

(a) Charging of interest in all cases of demands, starting from the date the duty ought to have been paid.

(b) No interest to be charged in case where the assessee pays the duty within 30 days of the issue of any Section 37 B order.

(c) All cases of adjudication were to be completed, as far as possible, within 6 months from the date of the notice.

(d) Powers of Commissioner (Appeals) to remand case for de novo adjudication had been withdrawn.

20.10 Rules had also been framed to facilitate computerization of records by assesses and steps were underway to introduce electronic submission of return/information etc.

20.11 In order to make identification of Central Excise assesses more systematic, to create comprehensive data base on computer system to facilitate profiling of assesses, and share information with other government agencies, new Excise Control Code Number would be given to all assesses and registered on the Permanent Account Number of Income Tax Department was introduced.

20.12 Consequent to the process of economic reforms initiated in the early 1990s, it was realized that harmonization and rationalisation to domestic trade tax system in the country needed urgent reforms. The process of discussions amongst State Governments which started in early 1994 came to its fruition on 16th November, 1999 when all the Chief Ministers took a consensus decision to implement uniform floor rates of sales tax and phase out sales tax based incentives by January 1, 2000. It was also decided to go in eventually for a unified Value Added Tax (VAT) system all over the country. A view was also taken to rationalize the Central Sales Tax in the meanwhile. The measures were intended not only to prevent the 'rate wars' between the different States (thus checking revenue leakage through unhealthy competition) but also a significant move in the direction of transforming indirect taxation into a harmonized system.

20.13 Subsequently, a Conference of Chief Ministers/State Finance Ministers of all the States/Union Territories was held on 22nd June, 2000 to discuss the progress achieved by the States and Union Territories on the above decisions and reforms in the Central Sales tax. In pursuance of the decision taken in the Conference, an Empowered Committee of Finance Ministers of 10 States had been constituted by the Central Government to monitor the implementation of the above decisions. The Empowered Committee has decided that all the States/Union Territories would introduce Value Added Tax by 1.4.2002, the interim period would be used for preparation, training, computerisation, and Publicity.

20.14 Introduction of Value Added Tax was basically intended as a measure of tax rationalization, which would lead to transparency, simplicity and equity in the domestic trade tax structure in the country. According to the Department, in a federal fiscal system, as in operation in our country, multiplicity of taxes hitherto had been hindering Foreign Direct Investment (FDI). Reforms in Central Sales Tax (CST) and the introduction of Value Added Tax by the States would facilitate the process of tax restructuring which would be industry-friendly and act as a catalyst for FDI.

20.15 The Committee feel that a coherent tax system should be evolved. Greater transparency and immediate actions are required in the domain of tax regime. The process of realisation of tax should be simple and transparent. The duties imposed should be rationalised so that investing in India becomes a lucrative proposition.

20.16 The Committee recommend that the Department of Revenue may be persuaded to set up a mechanism to receive feedback from the prospective investors so that various tax laws are updated continuously to make them investor-friendly.

Ministry of Labour

21. The Ministry of Labour submitted their views on the points affecting in flow of FDI in the Country. Commenting on the issue regarding obsolete Labour Laws, the Ministry of Labour informed that it was seized of the matter and had taken steps to rationalise and simplify labour laws for greater industrial harmony, enhance production and productivity and to create an environment for stimulating growth and attracting domestic and foreign investments. Under the present Industrial Relations Labour Laws, there were no such provisions, which prohibited closing of uneconomic and unproductive units. The appropriate Governments, under the existing laws, have been granting permission for closure to such unviable and perennially sick units. However, to protect the interests, of workers, the Government of India had also permitted VRS/VSS, on attractive pecuniary package, to employees of such unviable units, before closure. The Government had already amended the Trade Unions Act, 1926, with a view to reducing multiplicity of trade unions, orderly growth of trade unions and promoting internal

democracy. The draft Industrial Relations Bill and Contract Labour Bill, 2000 could not be carried through, as the National Commission on Labour was in the process of examining the various facets of labour laws, in the context of liberalization and globalisation of the industry and trade. Since, NCL had submitted its report, Government was actively considering amendment of these laws, taking into consideration the recommendations of the Commission.

21.1 On the basis of the Commissions' report, efforts were afoot to bring fresh legislations/amendments on wages and bonus, umbrella legislation for unorganised sector, social security, worker-management relations, small enterprises, child & women welfare, etc. By integrating and re-grouping of existing labour acts, the number of legislations would be reduced and made more simple and transparent.

Exit Policy vis-a-vis Labour Laws for Export Promotion:-

21.2 The Ministry further submitted that there had been demand from the Indian employers to have a right to hire and fire. This involved amendment in Chapter V-B of the Industrial Disputes Act, 1947. The National Commission on Labour had already given its recommendation on this point. The feasibility of implementing all such recommendations was being examined, in consultation with social partners in the Ministry of Labour.

Outsourcing of Labour Laws in EPZs:-

21.3 The Ministry had received proposals from the Ministry of Commerce and Industry, for exempting EPZs from application of the provisions of Contract Labour (Regulation & Abolition) Act, 1970. The powers under Section 31 of this Act were that of the State Governments, where the EPZs were located. Therefore, the Central Government was not an appropriate Government for granting exemptions from applicability of labour laws to such EPZs. However, in case of intermittent employment not exceeding 120 days in a year and where less than 20 workmen were employed, no such exemption was required, if the employment was not in the category of prohibited employment under the Act. Besides, a proposal to amend the Contract Labour (Regulation & Abolition) Act, 1970, to facilitate outsourcing of certain activities by an establishment was already under consideration of Government.

21.4 Government were seriously thinking to reduce the number of inspections under the labour laws and permit self-certification on labour laws by employers. Inspections would be permitted by Government in such cases, where there was demand from workers' organizations, not satisfied with the compliance by the employers or on complaints of wrong information by the employers.

On Contract Labour System:-

21.5 The Contract Labour (Regulation & Abolition) Act, 1970 sought to regulate the employment of contract labour in certain establishments, to provide for its abolition in certain circumstances and for matters connected therewith. The Act applied to every establishment/contractor, employing 20 or more contract labour. The Act was administered by the Central and State Governments, within the respective spheres of their jurisdiction. The Central and State Governments were required to set up Advisory Boards to advise the respective Governments, on matters connected with the administration of the Act and to perform other functions assigned to them. The establishments covered under the Act were required to be registered as the principal employer and every contractor had to obtain a licence, subject to certain conditions relating to payment of wages, etc., for the welfare and health of contract labour. The contractor had to provide amenities like canteen, rest rooms, first aid, latrines and urinals. Contravention of the provisions of the Act and the Rules, invited maximum penalty of upto Rs. 1000 or imprisonment upto three months, or both. The appropriate Government could exempt any establishment/ contractor from the provisions of the Act or Rules, in case of an emergency.

21.6 Section 10 of the Act empowered the "Appropriate Government" to prohibit employment of contract labour, after consultation with the Central Board or the State Board, in any process, operation or other work in any establishment, falling under the State sphere or the Central sphere, as the case may be. Establishments, in which work of an intermittent, casual or seasonal nature only was performed, did not fall within the purview of the Act. Instances of engagement of contract labour in perennial nature of activities, brought to the notice of the Government by way of complaints, directions of the Court, inspections, etc., were dealt with in accordance with section 10 and appropriate action was taken. In the Central Sphere, 58 prohibitory notifications had been issued so far, under Section 10 of the Act.

21.7 In the wake of economic liberalization and keeping in view various proposals received from the social partners, as well as court judgements on contract labour, a need had been felt to enact a new law on contract labour. The proposal made by the Ministry of Labour, with a view to facilitate outsourcing of certain activities of an establishment, at the same time to protect the interests of contract labour in terms of wages, social security, welfare, health and safety, was submitted to the Cabinet Secretariat in February, 2000, after approval by the Committee of Secretaries (COS). The Hon'ble Prime Minister constituted a Group of Ministers (GOM) to examine these proposals, before the same could be brought before the Cabinet. The Group of Ministers had been reconstituted recently and matter was presently, before them for consideration and finalisation.

21.8 The Committee feel that in the face of emerging global economic situation, particularly after introduction of new economic policy in 1991, the entrepreneur-labour relationships were getting sore day by day, both pointing the accusing finger for one's malaise to the other. Cordial entrepreneur-labour relationships is therefore, vital for improving the investment climate in the Country. The Committee, therefore, recommend that Government should make earnest efforts to ensure harmonious entrepreneur-labour relations, to make the country an investor-friendly destination for the foreign investors. For this purpose, Government should initiate the necessary reforms in the Labour Laws.

22. Further, there should be a single-window clearance system, consisting of officials of both the Central and State Governments, especially in the field of infrastructure projects, to prevent the delays and to ensure that no administrative hassles come in way of the foreign investors, after the clearances.

23. India already had been left behind in the field of FDI; Moreover the country was now in a precarious position, especially in light of the negotiations at the Fourth Ministerial conference at Doha, in which, irrespective of the fact that India rejected the Draft ministerial Declaration, there was a move to frame multilateral rules on Investment, Competition, which would be

binding on all the WTO member States. The Committee feel that the Ministry of Commerce and Industry should be able to foresee the consequences of such binding multilateral rules on investment, which can result in flight of FDI to more favourable destinations than India and prepare an advance contingency strategy, to meet such a situation.

24. In a developing country like India, the FDI policy should focus on maximisation of its contribution to India's development, rather than maximisation of the magnitude of inflows by itself.

25. Ever since the process of liberalisation and structural reforms was launched a decade ago, the inflow of foreign capital has never matched the targets envisaged. Instead of liberalising the FDI policies further, Government should try to change the mindset of State Governments, which still had not changed with the times.

26. The FDI inflows in India were too meager. Till now, India had attracted less than one per cent of its Gross Domestic Product (GDP), in terms of FDI, ever since the reforms process was set in motion. The macro economic and organisational framework should be improved, so that the FDI policy looks more coherent. The pace of improvement in infrastructure should be hastened, to convert intent into action in a global market, where everybody is out to woo investors. Bold and proactive moves, embedded in reality and governed with a will to improve the economic environment of the country were needed, to bring about radical changes.

27. Government should strive to obviate any scope for differential interpretation of the provisions of Exim Policy, by any agency. The controversial provisions, if any, should be looked into immediately and prompt clarifications should be issued, clarifying the contradictions.

28. There were many more areas which needed to be improved to ensure greater FDI inflows into the country viz., the Regulatory Framework must improve to reduce the delays and the resultant frustration; various State Governments must follow through in implementing their own declared policies; the large gap between high profile policy statements on the one hand and their implementation on the other, to be streamlined; large scale

maintenance of different records was a big blockade and impediment to business operations and, therefore, be simplified.

29. The Committee feel that one of the major factors affecting the steady flow of FDI into India was that the majority of investors preferred export-oriented FDI. The Committee recommend that the Department should accentuate its policy on Foreign Direct Investment, so as to facilitate and attract Foreign Investors towards export-oriented FDI, so as to boost the level of FDI, as in China, where large amount of FDI inflow was in the form of export-oriented FDI.

30. Foreign Direct Investment is also regulated/facilitated by the Group of Ministers (GOMs). The GOM's meet regularly to decide on the FDI access to various sectors. It looked very strange that on the one hand the Department was working towards facilitating single window clearances and on the other, there were a multiplicity of bodies like FIPB/GOM's, to facilitate FDI. The Committee recommend that Government should strive to set up a single body for dealing with FDI matters, so as to negate the confusion/complexity of Foreign investors, who want to invest in the country.

Table – 1

Sector Specific Guidelines for Foreign Direct Investment

Sl. No.	*Sector*	*Guidelines*
1.	Private Sector Banking	49% from all sources on the automatic route subject to guidelines issued by RBI from time to time.
	Non Banking Financial Companies (NBFC)	a. FDI/NRI/OCB investments allowed in the following 19 NBFC activities shall be as per levels indicated below: i. Merchant Banking ii. Underwriting iii. Portfolio Management Services iv. Investment Advisory Services v. Financial Consultancy vi. Stock Broking vii. Venture Capital viii. Custodial Services x. Factoring xi. Credit Reference Agencies xii. Credit Rating Agencies xiii. Leasing & Finance xiv. Housing Finance xv. Forex Broking xvi. Credit Card Business xvii. Money Changing Business xviii. Micro Credit xix. Rural Credit b. Minimum capitalization norms for fund based NBFCS: i) For FDI up to 51%-US$ 0.5 million to be brought upfront. ii) For FDI above 51% and up to 75% - US$ 5 million to be brought upfront. iii) For FDI above 75% and up to 100% - US $ 50 million out of which US $ 7.5 million to be brought upfront and the balance in 24 months. c. Minimum capitalization norms for non-fund based activities:

(Contd...)

(...Contd...)

Sl. No.	*Sector*	*Guidelines*
		Minimum capitalization norm of US$ 0.5 million is applicable in respect of all permitted non-fund based NBFCs with foreign investment.
		d. Foreign investors can set up 100% operating subsidiaries without the condition to disinvest a minimum of 25% of its equity to Indian entities, subject to bringing in US$ 50 million as at b) (iii) above (without any restriction on number of operating subsidiaries without bringing in additional capital).
		e. Joint Venture operating NBFCs that have 75% or less than 75% foreign investment will also be allowed to set up subsidiaries for undertaking other NBFC activities, subject to the subsidiaries also complying with the applicable minimum capital inflow i.e. (b) (i) and (b) (ii) above.
		f. FDI in the NBFC sector is put on automatic route subject to compliance with guidelines of the Reserve Bank of India. RBI would issue appropriate guidelines in this regard.
	Insurance	FDI up to 26% in the insurance sector is allowed on the automatic route subject to obtaining licence from Insurance Regulatory & Development Authority (IRDA).
2.	Domestic Airlines	(Detailed guidelines have been issued by Ministry of Civil Aviation) in the domestic Airlines
		i. FDI up to 40% permitted subject to no direct or indirect equity participation by foreign airlines.
	Airports	ii. 100% investment by NRIs/OCBs.
		iii. The automatic route is not available. Up to 100% with FDI beyond 74% requiring Government approval.
3.	Telecommunication	i. In basic, cellular, value added services and global mobile personal communications by satellite, FDI is limited to 49% subject to licensing and security requirements and adherence by the companies (who are investing and the companies in which the investment is being made) to the licence conditions for foreign equity cap and lock-in period for transfer and addition of equity and other licence provisions.

(Contd...)

(...Contd...)

Sl. No.	*Sector*	*Guidelines*
		ii. In ISPs with gateways, radio-paging and end-to-end bandwidth, FDI is permitted up to 74% with FDI, beyond 49% requiring Government approval. These services would be subject to licensing and security requirements. iii. no equity cap is applicable to manufacturing activities. iv. FDI upto 100% is allowed for the following activities in the telecom sector: a. ISPs not providing gateways (both for satellite and submarine cables). b. Infrastructure Providers providing dark fibre (IP Category I) c. Electronic Mail; and d. Voice Mail The above would be subject to the following conditions: a. FDI up to 100% is allowed subject to the condition that such companies would divest 26% of their equity in favour of Indian public in 5 years, if these companies are listed in other parts of the world. b. The above services would be subject to licensing and security requirements, wherever required. c. Proposals for FDI beyond 49% shall be considered by FIPB on case to case basis.
4.	Petroleum (other than Refining)	a. Under the exploration policy, FDI up to 100% is allowed for small fields through competitive bidding; upto 60% for unincorporated JV; and up to 51% for incorporated JV with a No Objection Certificate for medium size fields. b. For petroleum products and pipeline sector, FDI is permitted up to 51%. c. FDI is permitted up to 74% in infrastructure related to marketing and marketing of petroleum products. d. 100% wholly owned subsidiary (WOS) is permitted for the purpose of market study and formulation. e. 100% wholly owned subsidiary (WOS) is permitted for investment/financing.

(Contd...)

(...Contd...)

Sl. No.	*Sector*	*Guidelines*
		f. For actual trading and marketing, minimum 26% Indian equity is required over 5 years. The automatic route is not available.
	Petroleum (Refining)	a. FDI is permitted up to 26% in case of public sector units (PSUs). PSUs will hold 26% and balance 48% by public. Automatic route is not available. b. In case of private Indian companies, FDI is permitted up to 100% under automatic route.
5.	Housing & Real Estate	No foreign investment is permitted in this sector except for development of integrated townships and settlements where FDI up to 100% is permitted with prior Government approval. NRIs/OCBs are allowed to invest in the following activities. a. Development of serviced plots and construction of built up residential premises b. Investment in real estate covering construction of residential and commercial premises including business centers and offices. c. Development of townships. d. City and regional level urban infrastructure facilities, including both roads and bridges. e. Investment in manufacture of building materials, which is also open to FDI. f. Investment in participatory ventures in (a) to (e) above. g. Investment in housing finance institutions, which is also open to FDI as an NBFC.
6.	Coal and Lignite	i. Private Indian companies setting up or operating power projects as well as coal or lignite mines for captive consumption are allowed FDI up to 100%. ii. 100% FDI is allowed for setting up coal processing plants subject to the condition that the company shall not do coal mining and shall not sell washed coal or sized coal from its coal processing plants in the open market and shall supply the washed or sized coal to those parties who are supplying raw coal to coal processing plants for washing or sizing. iii. FDI up to 74% is allowed for exploration or mining of coal or lignite for captive consumption.

(Contd...)

(...Contd...)

Sl. No.	Sector	Guidelines
		iv. In all the above cases, FDI is allowed up to 50% under the automatic route subject to the condition that such investment shall not exceed 49% of the equity of a PSU.
7.	Venture Capital Fund (VCF) and Company (VCC)	Offshore Venture Capital Funds/Companies are allowed to invest in domestic venture capital undertaking as well as other companies through the automatic route, subject only to SEBI regulations and sector specific caps on FDI.
8.	Trading	Trading is permitted under automatic route with FDI up to 51% provided it is primarily export activities, and the undertaking is an export house/ trading house/super trading house/star trading house. However, under the FIPB route:- i. 100% FDI is permitted in case of trading companies for the following activities: * exports; * bulk imports with ex-port/ex-bonded warehouse sales; * cash and carry wholesale trading; * other import of goods or services provided at least 75% is for procurement and sale of goods and services among the companies of the same group and not for third party use or onward transfer/distribution/sales. ii. The following kinds of trading are also permitted, subject to provisions of EXIM Policy; a. Companies for providing after sales services (that is not trading per se) b. Domestic trading of products of JVs is permitted at the wholesale level for such trading companies who wish to market manufactured products on behalf of their joint ventures in which they have equity participation in India. c. Trading of hi-tech items/items requiring specialized after sales service d. Trading of items for social sector e. Trading of hi-tech, medical and diagnostic items.

(Contd...)

(...Contd...)

Sl. No.	*Sector*	*Guidelines*
		f. Trading of items sourced from the small scale sector under which, based on technology provided and laid down quality specifications, a company can market that item under its brand name. g. Domestic sourcing of products for exports. h. Test marketing of such items for which a company has approval for manufacture provided such test marketing facility will be for a period of two years, and investment in setting up manufacturing facilities commences simultaneously with test marketing. i. FDI up to 100% permitted for e-commerce activities subject to the condition that such companies would divest 26% of their equity in favour of the Indian public in five years, if these companies are listed in other parts of the world. Such companies would engaged only in business to business (B2B) e-commerce and not in retail trading.
9.	Investing Companies in Infrastructure/ Service Sector	In respect of companies in infrastructure/ service sector, where there is a prescribed cap for foreign investment, only the direct investment will be considered for the prescribed cap and foreign investment in an investing company will not be set off against this cap provided the foreign direct investment in such investing company does not exceed 49% and the management of the investing company is with the Indian owners. The automatic route is not available.
10.	Atomic Minerals	The following three activities are permitted to receive FDI/NRI/OCB investments through FIPB on exploitation of beach sand minerals (as per detailed guidelines issued by Department of Atomic Energy vide Resolution No. 8/1(1)/97-PSU/1422 dated 6.10.98): a. Mining and mineral separation b. Value addition per se to the products of (a) above c. Integrated activities (comprising of both (a) and (b) above.

(Contd...)

(...Contd...)

Sl. No.	Sector	Guidelines
		The following FDI participation is permitted: i. Up to 74% in both pure value addition and integrated projects ii. For pure value addition projects as well as integrated projects with value addition upto any intermediate stage, FDI is permitted upto 74% through joint venture companies with Central/State PSUs in which equity holding of at least one PSU is not less than 26%. iii. In exceptional cases, FDI beyond 74% will be permitted subject to clearance of the Atomic Energy Commission before FIPB approval.
11.	Defence and Strategic Industries	Foreign Direct Investment, including NRI/OCB investment, is permitted up to 26% with prior Government approval subject to licensing and security requirements. Detailed guidelines for participation of private sector and foreign investors in this sector are given in Appendix-B.
12.	Agriculture (including Plantation)	No FDI/NRI/OCB investment is permitted other than Tea sector, where FDI is permitted up to 100% in tea sector, including tea plantations with prior Government approval and subject to the following conditions: * Compulsory divestment of 26% equity in favour of Indian partner/Indian public within a period of five years; and * Prior State Government approval required in case of any future land use change. The above dispensation would be applicable to all fresh investments (FDI) made in this sector.
13.	Print Media	Government has announced Print Media policy recently. The policy & guidelines in respect of this sector will be notified by the Ministry of Information & Broadcasting in due course.
14.	Broadcasting	a) TV Software production 100% foreign investment allowed subject to: (i) all future laws on broadcasting and no claim of any privilege or protection by virtue of approval accorded; and (ii) not undertaking any broadcasting from Indian soil without Government approval. b) Setting up hardware facilities, such as uplinking, HUB, etc.

(Contd...)

(...Contd...)

Sl. No.	*Sector*	*Guidelines*
		Private companies incorporated in India with permissible FII/NRI/OCB/PIO equity within the limits (as in the case of telecom sector FDI limit up to 49% inclusive of both FDI and portfolio investment) to set up uplinking hub (teleports) for leasing or hiring out their facilities to broadcasters*.
		c) Cable Network
		Foreign investment allowed up to 49% (inclusive of both FDI and portfolio investment) of paid up share capital. Companies with minimum 51% of paid up share capital held by Indian citizens are eligible under the Cable Television Network Rules (1994) to provide cable TV services.
		d) Direct-to-Home
		Company with a maximum of foreign equity including FDI/NRI/OCB/FII of 49% would be eligible to obtain DTH License. Within the foreign equity, the FDI component not to exceed 20%.
		e) Terrestrial Broadcasting FM
		The licensee shall be a company registered in India under the Companies Act. All share holding should be held by Indians except for the limited portfolio investment by FII/NRI/PIO/OCB subject to such celling as may be decided from time to time. Company shall have no direct investment by foreign entities, NRIs and OCBs. As of now, the foreign investment is permissible to the extent of 20% portfolio investment.
		f) Terrestrial TV
		No private operator is allowed in terrestrial TV transmission. In all the above cases automatic route is not available.
15.	Power	Up to 100% FDI allowed in respect of projects relating to electricity generation, transmission and distribution, other than atomic reactor power plants. There is no limit on the project cost and quantum of foreign direct investment.

* As regards satellite broadcasting all T.V. Channels irrespective of the ownership or management control to uplink from India provided they undertake to comply with the broadcast (programme and advertising) code.

(...Contd...)

Sl. No.	Sector	Guidelines
16.	Drugs & Pharmaceuticals	FDI up to 100% is permitted on the automatic route for manufacture of drugs and pharmaceutical, provided the activity does not attract compulsory licensing or involve use of recombinant DNA technology and specific cell/ tissue targeted formulations. FDI proposals for the manufacture of licensable drugs and pharmaceuticals and bulk drugs produced by recombinant DNA technology and specific cell/tissue targeted formulations will require prior Government approval.
17.	Roads & Highways, Ports and Harbours	FDI up 100% under automatic route is permitted in projects for construction and maintenance of roads, highways, vehicular bridges, toll roads, vehicular tunnels, ports and harbours.
18.	Hotels & Tourism	100% FDI is permissible in the sector on the automatic route. The term hotels include restaurants, beach resorts, and other tourist complexes providing accommodation and/or catering and food facilities to tourists. Tourism related industry include travel agencies, tour operating agencies and tourist transport operating agencies, units providing facilities for cultural, adventure and wild life experience to tourists, surface, air and water transport facilities to tourists, leisure, entertainment, amusement, sports, and health units for tourists and Convention/ Seminar units and organisations. For foreign technology agreements, automatic approval is granted if: i. up to 3% of the capital cost of the project is proposed to be paid for technical and consultancy services including fees for architects, design, supervision, etc; ii. up to 3% of net turnover is payable for franchising and marketing/publicity support fee; and iii. up to 10% of gross operating profit is payable for management fee, including inventive fee.
19.	Mining	i. For exploration and mining of diamonds and precious stones FDI is allowed up to 74% under automatic route; ii. For exploration and mining of gold and silver and minerals other than diamonds and precious stones, metallurgy and processing FDI is allowed up to 100% under automatic route;

(Contd...)

(...Contd...)

Sl. No.	*Sector*	*Guidelines*
		iii. Press Note No. 18 (1998 series) dated 14.12.98 would not be applicable for setting up 100% owned subsidiaries in so far as the mining sector is concerned, subject to a declaration from the applicant that he has no existing joint venture for the same area and/or the particular mineral.
20.	Postal Services	FDI up to 100% is permitted in courier services with prior Government approval excluding distribution of letters, which is reserved exclusively for the state.
21.	Pollution Control and Management	FDI up to 100% in both manufacture of pollution control equipment and consultancy for integration of pollution control systems is permitted on the automatic route.
22.	Advertising and Films	a) Advertising sector FDI up to 100% allowed on the automatic route b) Film sector (film production, exhibition and distribution including related services/products) FDI up to 100% allowed on the automatic route with no entry-level condition
23.	Mass Rapid Metro Transit System	FDI up to 100% is permitted on the automatic route in mass rapid transport system all metros including associated real estate development.
24.	Township Development	FDI up to 100% is permitted for development of integrated townships including houses, commercial premises, hotels, resorts, city and regional level urban infrastructure facilities such as roads and bridges, mass rapid transit system; and manufacture of building materials. Development of land and providing allied infrastructure will form an integral part of township's development. FDI in this sector would be permissible with prior Government approval. Detailed guidelines regarding investment in this sector are given at Appendix-C.
25.	Establishment & operation of Satellites	FDI up to 74% is permitted with prior Government approval.
26.	Lottery Business, Gambling & Betting	Government has reiterated prohibition of foreign direct investment (FDI) foreign technical collaboration (FTC) in any form in Lottery business, gambling & betting sector.

Table – II

Break up of FDI Financial and Technology Cases Approved by Government During April, 2001, to October 2002

Sl. No.	Country	2001-02 April-March				2002-03 April-October				Total (April 2001 to October 2002)			
		Number			Amount	Number			Amount	Number			Amount
		TOT	FIN	TECH	FDI	TOT	FIN	TECH	FDI	TOT	FIN	TECH	FDI
1	2	3	4	5	6	7	8	9	10	11	12	13	14
1.	Australia	35	30	5	84.85	18	16	2	25.43	53	46	7	110.28
2.	Austria	13	7	6	7.82	9	7	2	16.30	22	14	8	24.12
3.	Bahamas	2	2	0	0.05	0	0	0	0.00	2	2	0	0.05
4.	Bahrain	4	4	0	1.12	1	1	0	2.00	5	5	0	3.12
5.	Belgium	18	11	7	28.34	13	11	2	347.76	31	22	9	376.10
6.	Bermuda	6	6	0	52.67	6	6	0	0.05	12	12	0	52.72
7.	Brazil	1	1	0	0.01	0	0	0	0.00	1	1	0	0.01
8.	Canada	25	21	4	177.37	17	15	2	150.13	42	36	6	327.50
9.	Cayman Island	6	6	0	124.80	5	5	0	26.14	11	11	0	150.94
10.	Channel Island	6	6	0	139.77	1	1	0	0.01	7	7	0	139.78
11.	China	5	1	4	0.00	4	1	3	0.01	9	2	7	0.01
12.	Croatia	0	0	0	0.00	1	1	0	0.96	1	1	0	0.96
13.	Czech Republic	3	3	0	0.03	1	1	0	0.19	4	4	0	0.22
14.	Cyprus	8	8	0	21.53	3	3	0	3.23	11	11	0	24.76
15.	Denmark	21	17	4	60.61	13	11	2	20.19	34	28	6	80.80
16.	Finland	6	5	1	17.43	1	1	0	-11.05	7	6	1	6.38
17.	France	61	54	7	782.75	32	26	6	305.56	93	80	13	1088.31
18.	Germany	161	127	34	350.73	96	75	21	166.81	257	202	55	517.55
19.	Hongkong	35	35	0	49.64	20	20	0	5.79	55	55	0	55.43
20.	Hungary	1	1	0	0.00	1	1	0	0.10	2	2	0	0.10
21.	Indonesia	3	3	0	1.05	4	4	0	110.41	7	7	0	111.46

(Contd...)

1	2	3	4	5	6	7	8	9	10	11	12	13	14
22.	Ireland	6	4	2	8.64	3	3	0	0.71	9	7	2	9.35
23.	Isle of Man	3	3	0	1.56	0	0	0	0.00	3	3	0	1.56
24.	Israel	9	6	3	8.75	4	3	1	0.06	13	9	4	8.80
25.	Italy	59	37	22	107.84	28	22	6	17.88	87	59	28	125.72
26.	Japan	107	77	30	849.56	80	52	28	470.60	187	129	58	1,320.16
27.	Korea (North)	1	0	1	0.00	0	0	0	0.00	1	0	1	0.00
28.	Lebanon	0	0	0	0.00	1	1	0	0.20	1	1	0	0.20
29.	Korea (South)	34	23	11	51.40	23	18	5	28.55	57	41	16	79.95
30.	Kuwait	3	3	0	15.47	4	4	0	0.31	7	7	0	15.77
31.	Luxembourg	4	4	0	0.89	2	2	0	0.02	6	6	0	0.90
32.	Malaysia	24	24	0	104.00	16	16	0	353.58	40	40	0	457.58
33.	Mauritius	245	244	1	2,878.24	131	130	1	1,093.53	376	374	2	3,971.77
34.	NRI	115	115	0	698.08	47	47	0	73.90	162	162	0	771.98
35.	Netherlands	112	102	10	1,591.62	86	52	34	224.91	198	154	44	1,816.53
36.	New Zealand	2	2	0	110.40	3	3	0	0.58	5	5	0	110.98
37.	Nigeria	1	1	0	0.01	3	3	0	3.65	4	4	0	3.66
38.	Norway	6	6	0	24.90	2	2	0	2.02	8	8	0	26.92
39.	Oman	5	5	0	7.78	2	2	0	16.68	7	7	0	24.46
40.	Panama	0	0	0	0.00	1	1	0	0.68	1	1	0	0.68
41.	Philippines	3	3	0	1.93	1	1	0	0.03	4	4	0	1.96
42.	Portugal	1	1	0	0.24	1	1	0	0.04	2	2	0	0.28
43.	Russia	4	4	0	0.16	3	3	0	0.10	7	7	0	0.26
44.	Saudi Arabia	4	2	2	1.15	4	4	0	0.36	8	6	2	1.50
45.	Singapore	118	115	3	271.85	57	55	2	180.76	175	170	5	452.62
46.	Scotland	4	2	2	7.48	0	0	0	0.00	4	2	2	7.48
47.	South Africa	4	3	1	1.99	1	1	0	0.01	5	4	1	2.00
48.	Spain	6	5	1	0.38	5	4	1	26.01	11	9	2	26.38
49.	Sri Lanka	9	9	0	4.04	2	2	0	0.18	11	11	0	4.22
50.	Sweden	27	21	6	142.28	12	9	3	13.09	39	30	9	155.37
51.	Slovenia	1	1	0	6.77	0	0	0	0.00	1	1	0	6.77
52.	Switzerland	54	42	12	115.20	40	36	4	49.38	94	78	16	164.59

(Contd...)

1	2	3	4	5	6	7	8	9	10	11	12	13	14
53.	Taiwan	3	3	0	356.89	6	5	1	0.28	9	8	1	357.17
54.	Thailand	7	3	4	1.17	1	1	0	0.01	8	4	4	1.18
55.	Turkey	2	1	1	0.00	0	0	0	0.00	2	1	1	0.00
56.	U.A.E.	31	29	2	65.03	26	26	0	42.94	57	55	2	107.97
57.	U.K.	202	174	28	1,128.31	108	94	14	956.99	310	268	42	2,085.30
58.	U.S.A.	657	594	63	3,962.84	345	314	31	605.41	1002	908	94	4,568.25
59.	Ukraine	2	1	1	3.03	1	1	0	0.01	3	2	1	3.04
60.	Euro Issues (GDR)	7	7	0	5,847.27	0	0	0	0.00	7	7	0	5,847.27
61.	British Virginia	18	18	0	27.38	17	17	0	67.82	35	35	0	95.19
62.	West Indies	2	2	0	0.00	3	3	0	0.28	5	5	0	0.28
63.	Yogoslavia	0	0	0	0.00	2	1	1	0.00	2	1	1	0.00
64.	Unindicated Country	6	6	0	1.68	2	2	0	0.02	8	8	0	1.70
65.	Iran	4	4	0	2.13	0	0	0	0.00	4	4	0	2.13
66.	Tanzania	1	1	0	0.53	0	0	0	0.00	1	1	0	0.53
67.	Georgia	0	0	0	0.00	1	1	0	0.50	1	1	0	0.50
68.	Gibraltar	1	1	0	0.05	4	4	0	0.02	5	5	0	0.07
69.	Jordon	0	0	0	0.00	1	1	0	0.00	1	1	0	0.00
70.	Ice Land	1	1	0	0.18	0	0	0	0.00	1	1	0	0.18
71.	Kenya	3	3	0	1.34	1	1	0	0.03	4	4	0	1.37
72.	Yaman	1	1	0	0.00	0	0	0	0.00	1	1	0	0.00
73.	Cuba	2	0	2	0.00	1	0	1	0.00	3	0	3	0.00
74.	Liberia	1	1	0	0.25	0	0	0	0.00	1	1	0	0.25
75.	Costa Rica	1	0	1	0.00	0	0	0	0.00	1	0	1	0.00
76.	Myanmar	1	1	0	0.21	0	0	0	0.00	1	1	0	0.21
77.	Guernsey	1	1	0	0.50	0	0	0	0.00	1	1	0	0.50
78.	Zambia	1	1	0	0.46	0	0	0	0.00	1	1	0	0.46
79.	Palestine Authority	1	1	0	0.05	0	0	0	0.00	1	1	0	0.05
80.	Moracco	0	0	0	0.00	1	1	0	78.40	1	1	0	78.40
81.	Columbia	0	0	0	0.00	1	1	0	0.01	1	1	0	0.01
82.	British Isles	0	0	0	0.00	1	1	0	0.03	1	1	0	0.03
83.	Vanuatu	0	0	0	0.00	1	1	0	0.10	1	1	0	0.10

Table – III

Country-wise Actual Inflow of FDI Received during the Financial Years 2001-2002 and 2002-2003 (upto October, 2002)

Amount in Rs. crore

Sl.No.	Country	Amount of Inflow	
		2001-02 (April-March)	2002-03 (April-October)
1.	Australia	61.02	46.84
2.	Austria	12.53	10.44
3.	Bahamas	0.00	1.44
4.	Bahrain	0.00	1.44
5.	Belgium	170.68	18.55
6.	Bermuda	73.36	15.75
7.	Iran	0.00	0.10
8.	Tanzania	0.53	0.53
9.	Gibraltar	0.05	0.02
10.	Kenya	1.34	0.03
11.	Brazil	0.01	0.06
12.	Costa Rica	0.00	0.01
13.	Canada	69.59	23.36
14.	Cayman Island	137.37	53.93
15.	China	0.00	0.01
16.	Croatia	0.00	0.96
17.	Channel Island	0.88	0.00
18.	Czech Republic	1.78	0.19
19.	Cyprus	40.79	27.53
20.	Denmark	13.68	21.43
21.	Finland	15.68	0.00
22.	France	420.80	157.22
23.	Germany	360.76	348.67
24.	Hongkong	29.62	23.80
25.	Hungary	0.00	0.10
26.	Indonesia	0.98	100.41
27.	Ireland	8.64	0.81
28.	Isle of Man	4.48	1.90
29.	Israel	1.04	0.00
30.	Italy	136.21	4.62
31.	Liechtenstein	6.07	4.53
32.	Japan	647.43	293.62
33.	Korea (North)	0.00	0.02
34.	Korea (South)	4.50	66.66
35.	Kuwait	3.58	0.91
36.	Luxembourg	64.88	4.50
37.	Malaysia	10.81	77.46
38.	Mauritius	9010.23	1937.71

(Contd...)

Sl.No.	Country	Amount of Inflow 2001-02 (April-March)	2002-03 (April-October)
39.	NRI	32.51	1.34
40.	Netherlands	335.70	352.53
41.	New Zealand	0.00	0.68
42.	Nigeria	1.20	3.65
43.	Norway	21.80	0.79
44.	Oman	8.72	17.73
45.	Panama	16.63	0.78
46.	Philippines	0.12	0.00
47.	Portugal	0.99	0.04
48.	Russia	142.88	0.05
49.	Saudi Arabia	1.28	0.41
50.	Singapore	247.87	112.77
51.	South Africa	7.60	0.57
52.	Spain	1.23	24.80
53.	Sri Lanka	1.29	0.13
54.	Sweden	157.08	7.17
55.	Switzerland	29.84	78.83
56.	Taiwan	1.71	0.28
57.	Thailand	0.57	0.55
58.	U.A.E.	49.03	48.40
59.	U.K.	211.72	994.21
60.	U.S.A.	1629.12	649.35
61.	Ukraine	3.03	0.01
62.	British Virginia	24.19	21.50
63.	West Indies	0.00	1.57
64.	Yugoslavia	0.00	0.31
65.	St. Vincent	6.23	0.00
66.	Zambia	0.46	0.00
67.	Malta	0.68	0.00
68.	Bangladesh	5.58	0.00
69.	British Isles	0.00	0.02
70.	Unindicated Country	0.00	0.06
71.	Euro Issues (GDR)**	2136.88	465.51
72.	Acquisition of Share#	4235.21	3094.76
73.	Advance of Inflow	706.61	862.16
74.	NRI RBI Schemes*	167.95	0.49
	GRAND TOTAL	**21497.67**	**9983.46**

Note:

* Special NRI Schemes Administered by RBI from 01/04/2001 to 31/08/2002, no country-wise details are available with RBI.

** The amount of inflows raised through GDRs/ADRs/FCCBs against the FDI approvals accorded by FIPB during the period from April 2001 to October 2002 on the basis of information furnished by RBI.

\# Reported by RBI, Mumbai-Transfer of shares from resident to non-resident under FEMA during April 2001 to October 2002.

Annexure – I

Units Visited by the Subcommittee

S.No.	*Unit & Place*
1.	Daewoo Motors India Ltd., Greater Noida (U.P.)
2.	Moser-Bear India Ltd., Greater Noida (U.P.)
3.	International Technology Park Ltd., (ITPL), Bangalore (Karnataka)
4.	G.E. Technology Centre Private Ltd., White field, Bangalore (Karnataka)
5.	Wipro GE, White field, Bangalore (Karnataka)
6.	Mercedes Benz India Ltd. (MBIL), Pune (Maharashtra)
7.	Alfa Laval Agri India Ltd., Pune (Maharashtra)
8.	Global Tele System Ltd., Thane (Maharashtra)
9.	Hyundai Motor India Ltd., Sri Perumbudur (Tamil Nadu)
10.	Saint-Gobain Glass India, Sri Perumbudur (Tamil Nadu)
11.	Kirby Building Systems India Ltd., Medak (Andhra Pradesh)
12.	BPL Engineering Ltd., Hyderabad (Andhra Pradesh)
13.	Honda Motorcycle and Scooter India (Pvt.) Ltd. (HMSI), Manesar (Haryana)
14.	Norcool, Manesar (Haryana)
15.	Sony India Pvt. Ltd., Dharhera (Haryana)
16.	Beckten and Dicken Pvt. Ltd., Bawal Growth Centre, (Haryana)
17.	Asahi India Safety Glass Ltd., Jaliawas (Haryana)
18.	Echon Industries Ltd., Udaipur (Rajasthan)
19.	Secure Meters Ltd., Udaipur (Rajasthan)
20.	Asia Pack Ltd., Udaipur (Rajasthan)
21.	Pink City Color Stores (P) Ltd., Jaipur (Rajasthan)
22.	Podder Pigments Ltd., Jaipur (Rajasthan)
23.	Genus Overseas Electronics Ltd., Jaipur (Rajasthan)

OBSERVATIONS AND RECOMMENDATIONS AT A GLANCE

- The Committee feel that inspite of some steps taken by Government, the availability of adequate power still seemed to be a distant dream. Its inadequate availability worked as a dampener on inflow of FDI. There was a need to achieve, quantum jump in the production/ generation of electricity. (para 13.5)
- Even though the Power sector had been able to attract inflow of FDI to some extent, yet it had stagnated due to the lack of transparency in operations and governance. Functioning of the State Electricity Boards needed to be improved and Government should lay down clear policy guidelines in respect of purchasing electricity from the private power generating companies. Clear policy guidelines with respect to power should be governed by the canons of economics, rather than that of the regional interests and other extraneous considerations. (para 13.6)
- The Committee feel that telecommunication sector was already in the process of making quantum jump in telecommunication facilities/connectivity and hope that whatever deficiencies are there, the same would be overcome in the near future. (para 14.1)
- The Committee opine that the goods traffic was becoming highly competitive and Government must take adequate steps to guard their interest in goods traffic, by way of increasing the rail density in the areas, which had attracted more FDI and take steps to provide adequate rail linkages to ports, airports and railway stations. The railways needed to modernised in all the spheres and develop as a reliable transporter, compared to standard of services being provided by the Railways in other developed/developing countries. (para 15.6)
- The Committee recommend that adequate funds may be placed at the disposal of the National Highways Authority of India so that the express highways are built at the earliest, reducing the time being taken by the vehicles in reaching destinations, and increasing the speed of movement of the goods traffic. Private participation in

the realm of increasing the density of roads and modernization of the highways should be encouraged through Built, Operate, Lease and Transfer (BOLT) system. Tax holidays should be provided to the companies, who invest in modernisation of highways and in creating new and efficient road networks, (para 16.5)

- The Committee feel that there was a need to effect attitudinal change in the bureaucracy, so that they act as facilitators of Foreign Investment, rather than the obstructers. (para 17.1)
- The Committee feel that there was a need for adequate domestic as well as international air connectivity as per the expectations of foreign investors. The Committee are constrained to note that development work at the Bangalore Airport was wrangled in bureaucratic impediments and lack of clear announcement on the part of Government was adding to the woes of the investors there. Addition of the Bangalore and other Airports on the international aviation map would improve international connectivity and would facilitate enhanced inflow of FDI in India. Therefore, the Committee recommend that the Department should take up the case of the airports frequented by foreign investors with the concerned Departments/ Ministries to facilitate easy access for them. (para 18.1)
- To overcome such a situation, the Committee recommend that development of ports should receive due attention and a blue print for future growth and modernisation should be drawn up and implemented especially to facilitate accommodating the mother ships. The Committee hope that the Ministry would accelerate its efforts in further developing the shipping as a reliable mode of transport as per the requirements of foreign investors. (para 19.2)
- At the same time, there was an urgent need to develop more Inland Container Depots, for expeditious movement of containers, from the depots to the ports. (para 19.3)
- The Committee feel that a coherent tax system should be evolved. Greater transparency and immediate actions are

required in the domain of tax regime. The process of realisation of tax should be simple and transparent. The duties imposed should be rationalised so that investing in India becomes a lucrative proposition. (para 20.15)

- The Committee recommend that the Department of Revenue may be persuaded to set up a mechanism to receive feedback from the prospective investors so that various tax laws are updated continuously to make them investor-friendly. (para 20.16)
- The Committee, therefore, recommend that Government should make earnest efforts to ensure harmonious entrepreneur-labour relations, to make the country an investor-friendly destination for the foreign investors. For this purpose, Government should initiate the necessary reforms in the Labour Laws. (para 21.8)
- Further, there should be a single-window clearance system, consisting of officials of both the Central and State Governments, especially in the field of infrastructure projects, to prevent the delays and to ensure that no administrative hassles come in way of the foreign investors, after the clearances. (para 22)
- The Committee feel that the Ministry of Commerce and Industry should be able to foresee the consequences of such binding multilateral rules on investment, which can result in flight of FDI to more favourable destinations than India and prepare an advance contingency strategy, to meet such a situation. (para 23)
- In a developing country like India, the FDI policy should focus on maximisation of its contribution to India's development, rather than maximisation of the magnitude of inflows by itself. (para 24)
- Ever since the process of liberalisation and structural reforms was launched a decade ago, the inflow of foreign capital has never matched the targets envisaged. Instead of liberalising the FDI policies further, Government should try to change the mindset of State Governments, which still had not changed with the times. (para 25)

- The FDI inflows in India were too meager. Till now, India had attracted less than one per cent of its Gross Domestic Product (GDP), in terms of FDI, ever since the reforms process was set in motion. The macro economic and organisational framework should be improved, so that the FDI policy looks more coherent. The pace of improvement in infrastructure should be hastened, to convert intent into action in a global market, where everybody is out to woo investors. Bold and proactive moves, embedded in reality and governed with a will to improve the economic environment of the country were needed, to bring about radical changes. (para 26)
- Government should strive to obviate any scope for differential interpretation of the provisions of Exim Policy, by any agency. The controversial provisions, if any, should be looked into immediately and prompt clarifications should be issued, clarifying the contradictions. (para 27)
- There were many more areas which needed to be improved to ensure greater FDI inflows into the country viz. the Regulatory Frame work must improve to reduce the delays and the resultant frustration; various State Governments must follow through in implementing their own declared policies; the large gap between high profile policy statements on the one hand and their implementation on the other, to be streamlined; large scale maintenance of different records was a big blockade and impediment to business operations and, therefore, be simplified. (para 28)
- The Committee recommend that the Department should accentuate its policy on Foreign Direct Investment, so as to facilitate and attract Foreign Investors towards export-oriented FDI, so as to boost the level of FDI, as in China, where large amount of FDI inflow was in the form of export-oriented FDI. (para 29)
- The Committee recommend that Government should strive to set up a single body for dealing with FDI matters, so as to negate the confusion/complexity of Foreign investors, who want to invest in the country. (para 30)

Report of the Committee on Compilation of Foreign Direct Investment in India

(October, 2002)

Contents

PREFACE

ACCORDING to International Monetary Fund (IMF) definition contained in the Balance of Payments Manual, Fifth Edition (BPM-5), FDI has three components, viz., equity capital, reinvested earnings and other direct capital. A large number of countries, including several developing countries report FDI inflows in accordance with the IMF definition, which include reinvested earnings and other direct capital flows, besides equity capital. The Reserve Bank of India (RBI) reports FDI inflows only on the basis of investments received from non-residents on equity and preference share capital under the FDI scheme. As FDI data released by RBI do not capture reinvested earnings and other capital, these inflows to India do not fully comply with standard international coverage and are, therefore, not comparable with FDI data released by many other countries of the world.

With a view to bringing the present FDI reporting system of RBI in alignment with the international reporting system, Government, in consultation with RBI, had constituted a Committee comprising officials from RBI and the Department of Industrial Policy and Promotion (DIPP), Government of India (GoI) in May 2002 to study the conceptual and methodological issues, including data gaps involved and make necessary recommendations to strengthen the collection, compilation and reporting of FDI data.

The Committee was constituted with the following members:

1. Shri I. Srinivas, Director, Department of Industrial Policy and Promotion (DIPP), Government of India.
2. Dr. R.K. Pattnaik, Director, Division of International Finance, Department Economic Analysis and Policy (DEAP), RBI.
3. Shri M.R. Rangachari, Deputy General Manager, Exchange Control Department (ECD), RBI.

The terms of reference of the Committee were as follows:

1. Study the international definition of FDI;
2. Analyse current practices prevailing in different countries;

3. Analyse current data compilation and reporting practices in India and identify gaps in collection and compilation of FDI data; and
4. Make appropriate recommendations to put the FDI reporting system in alignment with international reporting practices.

The Committee had several rounds of deliberations on the subject, including consultations with technical experts from RBI. The Committee also referred to available published material on the subject.

The Committee is immensely benefited from the guidance received from Shri V. Govindarajan, Secretary, DIPP, Shri M.S. Srinivasan, Joint Secretary, DIPP, Government of India and Dr. Narendra Jadhav, Officer-in-Charge, Department of Economic Analysis and Policy, RBI. The Committee places on record its acknowledgment for the technical assistance rendered by Shri Brijesh Pazhayathodi and Smt. Atri Mukherjee from the Division of International Finance, DEAP, RBI in its work.

(R.K. Pattnaik) **(M.R. Rangachari)** **(I. Srinivas)**

Mumbai
16th October, 2002

INTRODUCTION

DURING the nineties, Foreign Direct Investment (FDI) accounted for an increasing share of private capital flows to developing countries. According to the World Investment Report 2002 (WIR02) published by United Nations Conference on Trade and Development (UNCTAD), developing countries received 28 per cent of the world FDI inflows in 2001. Global FDI inflows have, however, declined by 51 per cent in 2001, which also affected the flow to developing countries. Developing countries witnessed a 14 per cent decline in FDI inflows in 2001 to US$ 205 billion from US$ 238 billion in 2000. A few developing countries like China and India, however, registered increased FDI inflows in 2001, which is indicative of their attractiveness for international investment.

With the opening up of the Indian economy in the early nineties, FDI inflows have shown a consistent growth, bringing in US$ 4 billion in 2001-02 as compared with US$ 129 million in 1991-92 (*Annex-I*). Several independent surveys have rated India among the favourite destinations for FDI. The WIR02 projects bright prospects for FDI in the Asia-Pacific region over the next three to five years with China topping the list, followed by Indonesia and Thailand. Another survey ranks India, Malaysia and Singapore as favoured destinations. The WIR02, however, ranks India at 119th position in terms of Inward FDI Performance Index, which is the ratio of a country's share in global FDI flows to its share in global GDP. This raises the issue of international comparability of cross-country data on FDI. For example, FDI data released by Reserve Bank of India (RBI) comprises equity and preference share capital only and do not include reinvested earnings and other direct capital flows, which otherwise form part of FDI as per International Monetary Fund (IMF) classification. As such, these data are not readily available in India. Hence, it has become imperative to strengthen the reporting arrangements in order to facilitate proper international comparisons.

Constitution of the Committee on FDI Computation

As per the existing practice, RBI disseminates information on FDI inflows mainly on the basis of issue/transfer of equity/

preference shares of Indian companies to foreign direct investors. The present system of FDI data dissemination by RBI is in line with the format, definition and classification of balance of payment (BoP) laid down by IMF in the Balance of Payments Manual 5th Edition (BPM5) in so far as equity capital is concerned. Due to non-availability of contemporaneous data, this figure, however, excludes reinvested earnings and other direct capital flows, which are important components of FDI.

In view of the above there is a need to align the reporting system with the international reporting practices so as to facilitate proper international comparisons in respect of FDI flows. Following this, a Committee comprising representatives of Department of Industrial Promotion and Policy (DIPP), Ministry of Commerce, Government of India (GoI) and RBI was constituted by GoI to go into the definitional and methodological issues relating to FDI with a view to aligning the present reporting system in India with the international reporting practices. The constitution and terms of reference of the Committee have been given in the preface to the report.

Structure of the Report

The remainder of the Report is organised into five sections. *Section II* discusses the methodological issues involved in the compilation of FDI. *Section III* presents the country practices with regard to reporting FDI data. *Section IV* deals with the present system, the divergences of the Indian practice from the international definition and conceptual issues regarding the present FDI data collection and reporting mechanism in India. The recommendations of the committee are contained in *Section V* of the report. *Section VI* by way conclusion presents the summary of the Report.

SECTION II

METHODOLOGICAL ISSUES

Definition of Foreign Direct Investment

FDI is the process whereby residents of one country (the home country) acquire ownership of assets for the purpose of controlling the production, distribution and other activities of a firm in another country (the host country).

IMF Definition

According to the BPM5, Foreign Direct Investment is the category of international investment that reflects the objective of obtaining a lasting interest by a resident entity in one economy in an enterprise resident in another economy. The lasting interest implies the existence of a long-term relationship between the direct investor and the enterprise and a significant degree of influence by the investor on the management of the enterprise.

UNCTAD Definition

The WIR02 defines FDI as 'an investment involving a long-term relationship and reflecting a lasting interest and control by a resident entity in one economy (foreign direct investor or parent enterprise) in an enterprise resident in an economy other than that of the FDI enterprise, affiliate enterprise or foreign affiliate. FDI implies that the investor exerts a significant degree of influence on the management of the enterprise resident in the other economy. Such investment involves both the initial transaction between the two entities and all subsequent transactions between them and among foreign affiliates, both incorporated and unincorporated. Individuals as well as business entities may undertake FDI.

Flows of FDI comprise capital provided (either directly or through other related enterprises) by a foreign direct investor to an FDI enterprise, or capital received from an FDI enterprise by a foreign direct investor. FDI has three components, viz., equity capital, reinvested earnings and intra-company loans.

- Equity capital is the foreign direct investor's purchase of share of an enterprise in a country other than its own.

- Reinvested earnings comprise the direct investors' share (in proportion to direct equity participation) of earnings not distributed as dividends by affiliates, or earnings not remitted to the direct investor. Such retained profits by affiliates are reinvested.
- Intra-company loans or intra-company debt transactions refer to short- or long-term borrowing and lending of funds between direct investors (parent enterprises) and affiliate enterprises.

OECD Benchmark Definition of Foreign Direct Investment (Third Edition)

FDI reflects the objective of obtaining a lasting interest by a resident entity in one economy (direct investor) in an entity resident in an economy other than that of the investor (direct investment enterprise). The lasting interest implies the existence of a long-term relationship between the direct investor and the enterprise and a significant degree of influence on the management of the enterprise. Direct investment involves both the initial transaction between the two entities and all subsequent capital transactions between them and among affiliated enterprises, both incorporated and unincorporated.

As is evident from the above definitions, there is a large degree of commonality between the IMF, UNCTAD and OECD definitions of FDI. Since the IMF definition is followed internationally, the Committee is in favour of following the IMF definition.

Direct Investment Enterprise

OECD Definition

OECD recommends that a direct investment enterprise be defined as an incorporated or unincorporated enterprise in which a foreign investor owns 10 per cent or more of the ordinary shares or voting power of an incorporated enterprise. The numerical guideline of ownership of 10 per cent of ordinary shares or voting stock determines the existence of a direct investment relationship. An effective voice in the management, as evidenced by an ownership of at least 10 per cent, implies that the direct investor is able to influence or participate in the management of an enterprise; it does not require absolute control by the foreign investor.

Although not recommended by the OECD, some countries may still find it necessary to treat the 10 per cent cut-off point in a flexible manner to fit the circumstances. In some cases, the ownership of 10 per cent of the ordinary shares or voting power may not lead to the exercise of any significant influence while, on the other hand, a direct investor may own less than 10 per cent but still have an effective voice in the management. OECD does not recommend any qualifications to the 10 per cent rule. Consequently, countries that choose not to follow the 10 per cent rule in all cases should identify, wherever possible, the aggregate value of transactions not falling under the 10 per cent cut-off rule, so as to facilitate international comparability. In India, the holding by each foreign institutional investor (FII)/Securities and Exchange Board of India (SEBI) approved sub-account of FII cannot exceed 10 per cent of the total paid-up equity capital or 10 per cent of the paid-up value of each series of convertible debentures issued by an Indian company and the total holdings of all FIIs/sub-accounts of FIIs put together cannot exceed 24 per cent of the paid-up equity capital or paid-up value of each series of convertible shares. However, there is a provision to raise the total FII holding to the level prescribed for FDI subject to the Indian company passing a Board Resolution followed by a special resolution to that effect by its General Body.

Some countries consider that the existence of elements of a direct investment relationship may be indicated by a combination of factors such as:

- Representation on the board of directors;
- Participation in policy-making processes;
- Material inter-company transactions;
- Interchange of managerial personnel;
- Provision of technical information; and
- Provision of long-term loans at lower than existing market rates.

Other relationships may exist between enterprises in different economies, which exhibit the characteristics set out previously, although there is no formal link with regard to shareholding. For example, two enterprises, each operating in different economies, may have a common board and common policymaking and may share resources, including funds, but with neither having a shareholding in the other of 10 per cent or more. In such cases where neither is a direct investment enterprise of the other, the transactions could be treated as between related subsidiaries. These are not regarded as direct investment in India.

Balance of Payments Manual Definition

A direct investment enterprise is defined in the IMF Manual as an incorporated or unincorporated enterprise in which a direct investor, who is resident in another economy, owns 10 per cent or more of the ordinary shares or voting power (for an incorporated enterprise) or the equivalent (for an unincorporated enterprise). Direct investment enterprises comprise those entities that are subsidiaries (a non-resident investor owns more than 50 per cent), associates (an investor owns 50 per cent or less) and branches (wholly or jointly owned unincorporated enterprises) either directly or indirectly owned by the direct investor. Subsidiaries in this connection also may be identified as majority owned affiliates. Although the 10 per cent criterion is specified in the Manual, some countries may choose to allow for two qualifications that involve a degree of subjective judgment.

First, if the direct investor owns less than 10 per cent (or none) of the ordinary shares or voting power of the enterprise but has an effective voice in management, the enterprise may be included.

Second, if the investor owns 10 per cent or more but does not have an effective voice in management, the enterprise may be excluded. Although the application of these two qualifications is not recommended in BPM5, the manual says that the countries that apply such qualifications should identify the aggregate value of transactions in order to facilitate international comparability.

Direct investors may be individuals, incorporated or unincorporated private enterprises; associated groups of individuals or enterprises; governments or government agencies; or estates, trusts, or other organisations that own direct investment enterprises in economies other than those in which the direct investors reside.

The components of direct investment capital transactions are recorded on a directional basis (i.e., resident direct investment abroad and non-resident direct investment in the recording economy).

Standard Statistical Requirements
(IMF, UNCTAD and OECD)

Countries are expected to compile and disseminate FDI data according to the standard components of balance of payments (BoP). These components are (a) direct investment income, (b) direct investment transactions and (c) direct investment position.

The direct investment income component is divided into two categories for (i) income on equity and (ii) income on debt.

Direct investment transactions are sub-classified into (i) equity, (ii) reinvested earnings (iii) other capital (inter-company transactions) and (iv) financial derivatives.

Equity capital is the foreign direct investors' purchase of shares of an enterprise in a country other than its own. Equity capital comprises equity in branches, all shares in subsidiaries and associates (except non-participating, preferred shares that are treated as debt securities and included under direct investment in other capital category) and other capital contributions.

Reinvested earnings comprise the direct investors' share (in proportion to direct equity participation) of earnings not distributed as dividends by affiliates or earnings not remitted to the direct investor. Such retained profits by affiliates are reinvested. Because undistributed (reinvested) earnings result in additions to direct investors' equity in subsidiaries and branches, these earnings are included as direct investment capital transactions in amounts equal to the corresponding entries recorded under direct investment income.

Other capital covers the borrowing and lending of funds, including debt securities and suppliers' credits between direct investors and subsidiaries, branches and associates.

Direct investment position data are also divided into four categories such as, (i) equity capital (ii) reinvested earnings (iii) other capital and (iv) financial derivatives.

One distinguishing feature of FDI from the viewpoint of direct investors is that direct investment enterprises often represent units in a multinational operation, the overall profitability of which depends on the advantage to be gained by deploying the various resources available to the investors in units located in different economies. Direct investors are thereby in a position to derive benefits in addition to the investment income that may accrue on the capital that they invest (e.g., the opportunity to earn management fees or other sorts on income). Such extra benefits are likely to be derived from the investors' associations with the enterprises over considerable period of time.

SECTION III

COUNTRY PRACTICES

Methodology

A study of the country practices reveals that almost all countries while compiling the FDI data for BoP purposes follow the IMF Manual (BPM5). According to BPM5, the direct investment data should be presented as follows:

Standard Components of BOP as per BPM5
(Direct Investment)

Components	*Credit*	*Debit*	*Net*
1. Direct Investment Abroad			
1.1. Equity Capital			
1.1.1. Claims on affiliated enterprises			
1.1.2. Liabilities to affiliated enterprises			
1.2. Reinvested Earnings			
1.3. Other Capital			
1.3.1. Claims on affiliated enterprises			
1.3.2. Liabilities to affiliated enterprises			
1.4. Financial Derivatives			
1.4.1. Claims on affiliated enterprises			
1.4.2. Liabilities to affiliated enterprises.			

2. Direct Investment in Reporting Country
   2.1. Equity Capital
      2.1.1. Claims on direct investors
      2.1.2. Liabilities to direct investors
   2.2. Reinvested Earnings
   2.3. Other Capital
      2.3.1. Claims on direct investors
      2.3.2. Liabilities to direct investors
   2.4. Financial Derivatives
      2.4.1. Claims on direct investors
      2.4.2. Liabilities to direct investors

An analysis of the coverage and methodology/definitions adopted by select countries – developed, developing and least-developed - is presented in *Annex 2A* and *2B*. A brief resume is in order in the following paragraph.

It may be observed that in the reporting format of Balance of Payments Year Book 2001 that the Asian countries like China, Hong Kong and Japan have provided the FDI data with the break up of equity capital, reinvested earnings and other capital as per the BPM5. However Indonesia, Republic of Korea and Thailand have not provided FDI data under the reinvested earning category. On the other hand Pakistan has not provided FDI data under the other capital category. Other than Asian countries, Germany, Mexico, USA, UK, Russia, Australia, France and Switzerland have provided FDI data under all three categories. South Africa, Belgium-Luxembourg, Brazil, Euro area and New Zealand have not provided data under reinvested earning category. Chile has not provided data under other capital category and Canada has not provided data under equity capital category. It may be mentioned in this context that India's current practice does not capture FDI data both under reinvested earning and other capital category. Therefore, the FDI data for India consist only of equity capital. Same is the case with Singapore and Mauritius.

Institutional Practices

A review of the institutional practices followed in select countries - developed, developing and least-developed - reveals that in most of the countries the central bank compiles and disseminates the FDI data with few exceptions, where FDI data are compiled and disseminated by governments and other agencies. For example, the central banks compile and disseminate FDI data in countries like China, Germany, India, Indonesia, Mexico, South Africa, Republic of Korea, Thailand, Mauritius, Russia, Belgium-Luxembourg, Brazil, Chile, France, Euro area, Philippines, Pakistan and Switzerland. On the other hand in countries like USA, UK, Singapore, Hong Kong, it is the government which collects and disseminates the FDI data. In Japan, the Ministry of Finance is responsible for the compilation of statistics, but the actual preparation of statistics (including data collection) is entrusted to the central bank.

Source

In case of Hong Kong, South Africa, Russia, Belgium-Luxembourg, Chile and USA, data on FDI are obtained from annual sample surveys/reports filed by the recipient entities. In Indonesia, data on direct investment are derived from semi-annual reports provided by FDI enterprises. In Thailand, FDI data are compiled on the basis of information obtained from International Transactions Reporting System (ITRS), bank reports and non-bank debt surveys.

SECTION IV

PRESENT INDIAN PRACTICE AND DIVERGENCES

Present Data Reporting Mechanism in India

Status of Data Reporting

Following the methodology prescribed in BPM5, data on fresh inflows of foreign direct investment are being captured through reporting of these transactions by the companies who receive these funds. Under the general reporting system, Authorised Dealers (ADs) have to report the inflows and outflows of foreign investment through R-returns. The companies who receive the Foreign Direct Investment are required to report these receipts with full details (i.e., name of the investor and investee company, country from where investment is received, amount, and currency, etc.) to the regional office of the Exchange Control Department (ECD). The reporting of data by the companies is done in two stages. In the first stage when a company brings in the funds through automatic route, it has to report to the ECD the receipt of the funds within 30 days. In the second stage, the company has to file FC-GPR after issuing of shares.

RBI publishes foreign investment data on a monthly basis in the RBI Bulletin, which provides component-wise details of direct investment and portfolio investment. Direct investment comprises of inflows through (i) Government (SIA/FIPB) route, (ii) RBI automatic route, (iii) NRI, and (iv) acquisition of shares. Portfolio investment covers: (i) GDRs/ADRs (ii) FIIs, and (iii) offshore funds and others.

The cash component of direct investment, as indicated above, is published on a monthly basis in the RBI Bulletin, while the cash and non-cash components (provision of capital goods) of direct investment are included in the direct investment data in table for 'India's Overall Balance of Payments' every quarter in the RBI Bulletin. The data on reinvested earnings are available with a lag since such data are collected from annual surveys on FDI companies. The latest available survey on 'Finances of Foreign Direct Investment Companies' relating to 1999-2000 was published in May 2001 issue of RBI Bulletin. In view of the lag in availability of reinvested earnings data, the direct investment transactions data disseminated in the BoP statistics for the first time do not include reinvested earnings. The inclusion of reinvested earnings also necessitates adjustment in other items of BoP in addition to changes in the inflow of FDI. The data on 'other capital' are not separately compiled since such transactions are not reported.

In India, the BoP statistics including that of FDI are compiled on a quarterly basis by the RBI, using an international transactions reporting system (ITRS) as the principal source of information. Data on foreign direct investment obtained under various routes (i.e. RBI, SIA/FIPB, NRI/OCB, and mergers and acquisitions) are captured from investee companies who receive these funds. The companies who receive the FDI report send these receipts with full details to the concerned regional office of the ECD. Based on the consolidated reports sent by the Regional offices, the Central office of RBI compiles the data on FDI. The data reported by the companies to the RBI are used as a benchmark for final compilation and monitoring of these data.

Divergence from the International Practices

The reporting format as prescribed by BPM5 and the present practice in India are set out in the table given below: -

	BPM5 Requirements	*Present Practice*
1	**Equity Capital**	
	Claims on direct investors	Included
	Liabilities to direct investors	Included
2	**Reinvested Earnings**	
	Claims on direct investors	Not Included
	Liabilities to direct investors	Not Included
3	**Other Capital**	
	Claims on direct investors	Not Included
	Liabilities to direct investors	Not Included

Reinvested Earnings and Other Capital

As alluded to earlier, according to the international definition (i.e. BPM5 and OECD definition), reinvested earning is a part of FDI. But as per the present practice in India, reinvested earnings are not captured in its FDI data. Furthermore, according to the international definition, there is a category of other capital, which covers the borrowing and lending of funds-including debt securities and suppliers credits between direct investors and subsidiaries, branches and associates.

Swap

The investment made by foreign investor/entity on swap basis is also not captured by the present system

Venture Capital

FDI investment by international bodies in Indian companies as venture capital funds is not captured, as it placed under Schedule 6 of Foreign Exchange Management Act (FEMA) Regulations

20/2000 dated May 3, 2000, which is not covered by the FC-GPR reporting system.

External Commercial Borrowing (ECB): Inter-Company Debt Transactions

As of now, the data regarding inter-company debt transactions are included under ECB. Conceptually, this component should be captured under other capital in FDI.

Conceptual Issues

Inclusion of ADR/GDR under FDI

According to BPM5, foreign portfolio investment includes, in addition to equity securities and debt securities in the form of bonds and notes, money market instruments and financial derivatives such as options. Equity securities cover all instruments and records acknowledging, after the claims of all creditors have been met, claims to the residual values of incorporated enterprises. Shares, stocks, participation, or similar documents – such as ADRs – usually denote ownership of equity.

Following the above definition, notwithstanding the treatment of ADR/GDR as FDI under FEMA, RBI publishes ADRs/GDRs as portfolio investment. DIPP, however, treats this as FDI.

Balance of Payments Effect

At a conceptual level, it is important to recognize that the flow of FDI in terms of reinvested earnings has neutral effect on overall BOP position. The amount recorded under reinvested earnings included in the capital account has a contra entry under the investment income in the current account. It means that depending on inflow/outflow in the capital account there will be an offsetting entry in the current account. For example, if the reinvested earnings recorded an inflow under capital account, it will be an outflow under the current account and vice versa.

Grants

At present the grants given by the parent company to the subsidiaries in India do not get reported under FC-GPR. However, this should form part of FDI, as it is a financial assistance from the parent company to its Indian subsidiary without any repayment obligation.

Investments in Unincorporated Entity

It may be noted that more and more unincorporated entities are getting registered. In unincorporated entities like branches, project offices, liaison offices, etc., substantial foreign interest is involved. But the data on this category are not captured in the present FDI data.

Foreign Currency Convertible Bonds

In India as per the present practice, foreign currency convertible bonds are included in FDI only when it is converted into equity. Otherwise an FCCB is treated as ECB.

Control Premium, Non-competition Fee

The reporting format for FDI prescribed under FEMA 1999 by RBI does not capture control premium/non-competition fee, etc. paid by the foreigner and as a result the FDI data is underestimated to that extent.

SECTION V

RECOMMENDATIONS

Recording comprehensive, comparable and up to date statistics on FDI is a crucial prerequisite for economic analysis and policy making. The objective of the Committee is not only to suggest detailed operational and conceptual definition of FDI, but also to determine what should be the ideal coverage of the data. Against the backdrop of the analysis presented in the preceding sections, the recommendations of the Committee are set out below.

Coverage

Reinvested Earnings

It may be mentioned that RBI has started capturing data on reinvested earnings through surveys. However, it may be noted that there are some basic constraints to base the FDI compilation on reinvested earnings data derived through the existing survey method. Some of the major limitations in doing so are as follows:

- The responses from the companies are very poor.
- The survey does not give any weightage to the companies according to their share in the total reinvested earnings.
- The composition of companies in the survey differs from year to year. This creates a problem of composition for example, if the companies reported in one year do not report in the next year, the reinvested earnings data obtained on the basis of survey will not be comparable.

In view of the above, the committee recommends a mandatory reporting system for all the companies for which the following alternatives could be considered:

a. Through the modification of FEMA for making it mandatory for the companies to report these data. OR

b. The Committee understands that DIPP is contemplating a system of mandatory registration for all FDI companies. DIPP may include such reporting requirement under the IDR Act of 1956 for making it mandatory for the companies to report these data.

c. With a view to improving the response from the FDI companies in the immediate time frame, DIPP may issue a press note calling upon the companies to cooperate with the questionnaire sent by the RBI.

Other Capital

Since the component other capital of the FDI cover the borrowing and lending of funds, including debt securities and suppliers credit between direct investors and subsidiaries, branches and associates; short term and long term commercial loans incurred by a resident company where the foreign lender has a stake of 10 per cent or more; and the debt incurred by resident subsidiaries, branches and associates of the FDI investor from the parent foreign direct investment enterprise abroad, the same may be treated as other capital under FDI. Efforts by RBI may be undertaken to initiate a comprehensive reporting mechanism for the same.

Swap

The approvals for foreign investment granted by RBI on a Swap basis may be used to capture the value of the FDI in Indian enterprises and included in the FDI data.

Venture Capital

Foreign investment in Indian venture capital is presently not being captured in the FDI data, as the reporting of the same is not in place. *Schedule 6 of FEMA* may be brought under *schedule 1* so that data on venture capital would automatically be captured under the present reporting system.

Investments in Unincorporated Entity

RBI may device a suitable reporting mechanism to capture these data either through the entities themselves or through authorised dealers.

Grant, Control Premium, Non-Competition Fee, etc.

The format for reporting the FDI data viz., FC-GPR prescribed under FEMA, may be amended to capture these data.

Treatment of ADRs/GDRs

The Committee examined both arguments in favour and against the inclusion of ADRs and GDRs in FDI data. It was noted that ADRs/GDRs were in some ways distinct from portfolio investment because they do not attract 10 per cent ceiling and also permit automatic acquisition of shares on retirement of GDRs/ ADRs. However, taking into account the principles of long-term relationship and management interest, the Committee is of the view that the present practice of treating ADRs/GDRs as portfolio investment may continue. The Committee is also of the view that the present conflict between FEMA categorisation of ADRs/GDRs as FDI and IMF definition may be removed by deleting ADRs/ GDRs from Schedule I to FEMA Regulations and placing it under a separate schedule.

SECTION VI

CONCLUSION

In the view of the Committee, the present system of capturing FDI data by the RBI may be supplemented by the implementation of the recommendations mentioned in the previous section. The recommendations are summarised as given in the table below.

	Divergence from the international definition	*Present Practice*	*Recommendations*
1.	Reinvested earnings and other capital	Not included	Should be captured through survey by RBI by making the reporting system mandatory for the companies through modification of FEMA or IDR Act.
2.	Swap	Not included	Should be captured on the basis of existing valuation approval by RBI.
3.	Venture capital	Not included	Schedule 6 of FEMA may be brought under schedule 1.
4.	External Commercial Borrowing (ECB) between related entities	Shown under external commercial borrowings	RBI should devise a suitable reporting mechanism.
5.	Investment in unincorporated entities	Not included	RBI should device a suitable reporting mechanism.
6.	Control premium, non-competition fee, etc.	Not included	FC-GPR form may be modified suitably to incorporate this information.

Proposed Modifications in Data Capturing/Monitoring

Comprehensive Reporting Format

The Committee at a technical level understands that the present reporting system in respect of FDI does not comprehensively and sufficiently capture the requirements of international standards regarding compilation of FDI. Furthermore, the present enterprise survey of assets and liabilities does not meet adequately the BPM5 requirements. In view of this, the Committee recommends that the present survey formats and reporting system need to be modified. In the Committee's view, a suitable survey model may be developed in the line with the quarterly survey method adopted in Hong Kong and Australia (Australian Bureau of Statistics).

The Committee understands that there is a trade-off between comprehensive reporting as indicated in BPM5 and the burdens associated with such reporting. This involves delicate balancing of trade-off so that efficient monitoring is achieved. In view of this, the group recommends that reporting system besides having "most timely" data should also have "most comprehensive" statistics. For this purpose, the group recommends that a technical group involving officials from DEAP, ECD and DESACS from RBI may finalise the format and other technical details of the survey.

Legal Framework

As alluded to earlier, at present FDI data are generated through specific reporting by FDI companies, which does not meet the statistical requirements of BPM5. Thus, there is an urgent need to strengthen the reporting arrangements from the FDI companies so as to collect the additional inputs. The Committee recommends that for timely and comprehensive reporting, there should be adequate legal framework for collection of data.

At the conceptual level, there are a number of broad principles, which need to be considered in the compilation of FDI statistics. The first and foremost is the adoption of clear concepts and definitions; capital flows like FDI should be clearly defined so as to facilitate external account recording. It is important that the concepts, definitions and classifications used are internally consistent and support comparability of these statistics with other compilers. Secondly, the compilation of FDI statistics has to be based on internationally accepted BPM5. Moreover, BPM5 has to be consistent and integrated with other accounts, viz., national accounts, monetary and fiscal accounts, for which internationally acceptable methodological standards are available. The advantage of these systems is that these data are consistent with the 1993 System of National Accounts (SNA). Thirdly, the compilation of these statistics has to be in accordance with international special data dissemination standards (SDDS) and International Investment Position (IIP). The IIP is the balance sheet of the stock of a country's financial asset and liabilities, which is also based on BPM5. The compilation of international investment data as part of the broader set of accounts allows for checks on coherence and consistency.

ANNEXURE

Annexure 1

Recent FDI Trends in India

Fiscal 2001-02 witnessed FDI inflows of US$ 4.06 billion (net of ADRs/GDRs). Compared with US$ 2.46 billion received in 2000-01, this represents 66 per cent growth. The upward trend has been sustained during the first quarter of fiscal 2002-03 with FDI inflows of US$ 1.35 billion (net of ADRs/GDRs) as against US$ 0.63 billion (net of ADRs/GDRs) in the corresponding period of fiscal 2001-02, representing 106 per cent growth. It is pertinent to note that this growth has been achieved at a time when global FDI inflows have been experiencing a steep decline of 51 per cent (during 2001).

The cumulative FDI inflows from January 1991 to June 2002 are around US$ 25.02 billion net of ADRs/GDRs. The realisation rate against FDI approvals has risen from 17 per cent in 1992 to 72 per cent in 2001. The sectors that account for maximum FDI are fuel (power, oil refineries, gas); telecom; electronic goods, IT and software; automobiles; and services. The major investing countries are Mauritius (mainly routed from developed countries), USA, Japan, UK, Germany, the Netherlands and South Korea. The States that account for maximum FDI are Maharashtra, Delhi, Tamil Nadu, Karnataka and Gujarat.

During the first half of 2002 the FDI inflows went mainly into transportation industry, services, telecom and electronics/IT/ software.

Some of the factors that explain the recent spurt in FDI inflows into India are:

- Progressive liberalisation of FDI policy has strengthened investor confidence – opening up of new sectors (integrated townships, defence industry, tea plantations, etc.); removal of FDI caps in most sectors, including advertising, airports, private sector oil refining, drugs and pharmaceuticals, etc. and greater degree of automaticity for investment.
- Liberalisation of foreign exchange regulations by way of simplification of procedures for making inward and outward remittances.

- Sectoral reforms, especially in sectors such as telecom, information technology and automobiles have made them attractive destination for FDI.
- Policy to allow foreign companies to set up wholly owned subsidiaries in India has enabled foreign companies to convert their joint ventures into wholly owned subsidiaries. The percentage of FDI through merger and acquisition route has increased to around 30 per cent (from around 10 per cent in 1999), which is still much lower than the global percentage of 70-80 per cent.
- Public sector disinvestment has finally emerged as an important means to promote FDI.
- Liberal policy towards Foreign Venture Capital Investment (FVCI) has given an impetus to investments in technology and infrastructure projects.
- Various investment facilitation measures taken by DIPP such as facility for electronic filing of applications, online chat facility with the applicants, online status on registration/disposal of applications, dedicated e-mail facility for investment related queries, etc., have also contributed substantially to improving investor confidence. On an average about 2,000 responses in a year are given to investors and potential investors.
- Government has set up an inter-ministerial Committee to examine the extant procedures for investment approvals and implementation of projects, and suggest measures to simplify and expedite the process for both public and private investment. The Committee, which was set up in September 2001, has submitted Part I of its report to the Government, which is under examination. A sub-Group of the Committee is specifically looking into simplification of procedures relating to private investment. The sub-Group will submit its report shortly.
- The Foreign Investment Implementation Authority (FIIA) has been activated and now meets at regular intervals to review and resolve investment-related problems. A recent study conducted by FICCI, FIIA acknowledges that has emerged as a problem-solving platform.

Annexure 2A

Table – 1

FDI Coverage and Methodology for Select Countries

Sr. No.	*Country*	*Items/Components*	*FDI during 2000 (US $ Million)*	*Percentage to Total*
1	Australia	Equity Capital	4019	34.9
		Re-Invested Earnings	3910	33.9
		Other Capital	3599	31.2
		Total	11528	100
2	Belgium-Luxembourg	Equity Capital	40627	47.0
		Re-Invested Earnings	0	0.0
		Other Capital	45871	53.0
		Total	86498	100
3	Brazil	Equity Capital	30016	91.6
		Re-Invested Earnings	0	0.0
		Other Capital	2763	8.4
		Total	32779	100
4	Canada	Equity Capital	0	0
		Re-Invested Earnings	7994	12.8
		Other Capital	54222	87.2
		Total	62216	100
5	Chile	Equity Capital	2904	79.0
		Re-Invested Earnings	771	21.0
		Other Capital	0	0
		Total	3675	100
6	China Mainland	Equity Capital	20841	54.3
		Re-Invested Earnings	16022	41.7
		Other Capital	1536	4.0
		Total	38399	100
7	China Hong Kong	Equity Capital	35479	55.1
		Re-Invested Earnings	20275	31.5
		Other Capital	8679	13.5
		Total	64433	100
8	Euro Area	Equity Capital		
		Re-Invested Earnings		
		Other Capital		
		Total	304570	100
9	France	Equity Capital	26650	61.7
		Re-Invested Earnings	3220	7.5
		Other Capital	13300	30.8
		Total	43170	100

(Contd...)

(...Contd...)

Sr. No.	*Country*	*Items/Components*	*FDI during 2000 (US $ Million)*	*Percentage to Total*
10	Germany	Equity Capital	111280	58.8
		Re-Invested Earnings	-4150	-2.2
		Other Capital	82050	43.4
		Total	189180	100
11	India	Equity Capital	2315	100
		Re-Invested Earnings		
		Other Capital		
		Total	2315	100
12	Indonesia	Equity Capital	892	
		Re-Invested Earnings	0	
		Other Capital	-5442	
		Total	-4550	
13	Japan	Equity Capital	7590	92.2
		Re-Invested Earnings	-100	-1.2
		Other Capital	740	9.0
		Total	8230	100.0
14	Republic of Korea	Equity Capital	7735	88.6
		Re-Invested Earnings	0	0.0
		Other Capital	997	11.4
		Total	8732	100
15	Mauritius	Equity Capital	265.6	
16	Mexico	Equity Capital	4781	36.0
		Re-Invested Earnings	3622	27.3
		Other Capital	4884	36.8
		Total	13287	100.0
17	New Zealand	Equity Capital		
		Re-Invested Earnings		
		Other Capital		
		Total	3209	
18	Pakistan	Equity Capital	209	67.9
		Re-Invested Earnings	99	32.1
		Other Capital	0	0.0
		Total	308	100.0
19	Philippines	Equity Capital	1024	50.5
		Re-Invested Earnings	579	28.5
		Other Capital	426	21.0
		Total	2029	100
20	Russia	Equity Capital	948	34.9
		Re-Invested Earnings	95	3.5
		Other Capital	1672	61.6
		Total	2715	100

(Contd...)

(...Contd...)

Sr. No.	*Country*	*Items/Components*	*FDI during 2000 (US $ Million)*	*Percentage to Total*
21	South Africa	Equity Capital	913	95.0
		Re-Invested Earnings	0	0.0
		Other Capital	48	5.0
		Total	961	100
22	Singapore	Equity Capital	6390	100
		Re-Invested Earnings		
		Other Capital		
		Total	6390	100
23	Switzerland	Equity Capital	11238	62.8
		Re-Invested Earnings	5022	28.1
		Other Capital	1642	9.2
		Total	17902	100
24	Thailand	Equity Capital	3402	101.1
		Re-Invested Earnings	0	0.0
		Other Capital	-36	-1.1
		Total	3366	100
25	United Kingdom	Equity Capital	95730	73.7
		Re-Invested Earnings	26080	20.1
		Other Capital	8030	6.2
		Total	129840	100
26	U.S.A.	Equity Capital	216760	75.3
		Re-Invested Earnings	23660	8.2
		Other Capital	47260	16.4
		Total	287680	100

Source: Balance of Payments Statistics Year Book 2001.

Table – 2

FDI Coverage and Methodology for Select Countries

Sr. No.	*Country*	*Institution Compiling BoP*	*Method/ Reporting System*	*Source/Coverage*
1	Australia	The Australian Bureau of Statistics (ABS) compiles and disseminates Australia's BoP.	BPM 5	Data are reported by resident direct investors and direct invest enterprises.
2	Belgium-Luxembourg	The National Bank of Belgium (NBB) is responsible for compiling and publishing the BoP of Belgium-Luxembourg Economic Union (BLEU) and Belgium.	BPM 5	Trade credits and debt securities between affiliated enterprises are registered but are not included indirect investment. Re-invested earnings are not registered. Basic data on DI are verified with other sources and compared with DI survey. Data for direct investment transactions are obtained from yearly DI survey, information published by the enterprises according to legal provisions and from the Supervisory Institution for Financial Markets.
3	Brazil	The Central Bank of Brazil (CBB) is responsible for compiling FDI data.	Differs from the version recommend by the BPM5.	Primary source of the data is exchange records. The classification of the exchange record permits separating funds received directly by enterprises for capital participation from inflows of funds for purchases of equity securities. Investment in goods as reported in export and import statistics is also taken into accounts are conversions of loans into equity and reinvestments of profits.
4	Canada	The BoP Division of Statistics Canada is responsible for the compilation kof Canada's BoP.	BPM 5	Reinvested earnings are obtained from the quarterly survey of the Industrial Organisation and Finance Division of Statistics Canada.

Contd.....

(...Contd...)

5	Chile	Central Bank of Chile (CBC)	In some cases BPM 5 is not adopted Does not always comply with the recommendations of BPM 5	Annual and quarterly data on reinvested earnings are derived from special surveys or financial statements of direct investors and direct investment companies. DI data are based on data provided by the Foreign Exchange Transactions System and by the Foreign Investment Committee and on estimates of reinvested earnings.
6	China Mainland	The State Administration of Foreign Exchange (SAFE) of the People's Bank of China (from 1996). Prior to 1996, data collected from Govt. Agencies, Banks and Safe's internal records.	BPM-5 on the basis of International Transactions Reporting System (ITRS)	Transaction records are supplemented with new surveys.
7	China Hong Kong	The Census and Statistics Dept (C&SD) of the Hong Kong Special Administrative Region (HKSAR).	BPM5	Data on FDI obtained from" Survey of External Claims, Liabilities and Income" (SECLI).
8	Euro Area	The ECB publishes Balance of Payment statistics for Euro Area.	Follows third edition of the OECD Benchmark Definition of FDI. The 10% ownership criterion is used for defining the EURO area data on direct investment	
9	France	The Banque de France (BdF) is responsible for compiling the statistics on France's BoP.	BPM 5	Data on FDI comes from two sources, the direct reporting enterprises and the banks.

(Contd...)

(...Contd...)

10	Germany	The Central Bank (Deutsche Bundesbank).	BPM5	Annual Survey on Foreign Assets and Liabilities of Direct Investors and Direct Investment Enterprises
11	India	The Reserve Bank of India is responsible for compiling the FDI data.	BPM5	Data obtained from exchange control records. Data on non-cash inflows and retained earnings is taken from Survey of Foreign Assets and Liabilities.
12	Indonesia	Bank Indonesia (BI).	Presently BPM4 and will be adjusted to BPM5 gradually.	Data on DI derived from semi-annual reports provided by FDI enterprises.
13	Japan	Ministry of Finance (MOF) is responsible for the compilation of statistics, but the actual preparation of statistics (including data collection) is entrusted to the Bank of Japan. (Supplementary surveys)	Broadly BPM5	Japan's BoP includes all investments by non-residents in unlisted resident companies' stocks in FDI. (As per BPM5 this goes to Portfolio).
14	Republic of Korea	The Bank of Korea (BOK) is responsible for the compilation of the FDI data.	BPM5	Direct Investment depends on the administrative records of the Government
15	Mauritius	The Bank of Mauritius is responsible for compilation of FDI data.		Returns of commercial banks.
16	Mexico	Bank of Mexico is responsible for the compilation of BoP.	In transition between BPM4 and BPM 5	Data for DI is obtained from the financial statements that the direct investment enterprises are obliged to submit to Ministry of Trade and Industrial Development.

(...Contd...)

(...Contd...)

17	New Zealand	Statistics New Zealand (SNZ) compiles New Zealand's BoP.	BPM5.	The DI threshold applied is 10 per cent or more of the equity ownership in an enterprise at the individual investor level. The types of DI investment included are changes in equity capital, unremitted earnings and changes in long and short-term capital.
18	Pakistan	Records of the foreign exchange dept. of State Bank.	BPM4. Preparation under way to adopt BPM5.	Confined to transactions routed through Ads.
19	Philippines	The Department of Economic Research (DER) of the Central Bank of the Philippines (Bangko Sentral ng Pilipinas-BSP) compiles the BoP.	BPM5. However full compliance yet to be achieved.	Data for DI obtained from ITRS.
20	Russia	Compiled by Bank of Russia (BR)	BPM5	Based on Non-Financial enterprises surveys conducted by SSC. A supplemental source of information is the data on privatization provided by the Federal Fund of Property and Customs.
21	South Africa	The South African Reserve Bank is responsible for compiling the BoP.	BPM5.	Main sources of data on inward and outward DI are the quarterly and annual sample surveys.
22	Singapore	Singapore Dept. of statistics (DOS) is responsible for the compilation of the balance of payments.	BPM5	Includes Equity holdings of foreign investors in their subsidiaries and branches. Also included are net purchase of properties by foreigners and a contra-entry to Re-invested earnings by foreign investors. Data are obtained from the survey of foreign equity investments in Singapore and the survey of property transactions.

(Contd...)

(...Contd...)

23	Switzerland	The Swiss National Bank collects data and compiles BoP.		Data on DI in Switzerland cover DI by foreign enterprises in enterprises in Switzerland. The data relate to equity capital, re-invested earnings and inflows and outflows of credit. Data sources are the quarterly and annual surveys carried out by the Swiss National Banks.
24	Thailand	The Bank of Thailand (BOT) compiles theft data.	BPM5	DI compiled from data obtained from ITRS, bank reports, and a non-bank debt survey. Currently, DI does not include reinvested earnings or transactions in debt securities and suppliers' credits between direct investors and subsidiaries, branches.
25	United Kingdom	Office for National Statistics (ONS) and Bank of England.	BPM5	DI includes investors' share of unremitted profits of the subsidiary or associated company. FDI is derived from annual and quarterly inquiries carried out by the ONS and the Bank of England.
26	U.S.A.	The Bureau of Economic Analysis (BEA), Dept of Commerce is responsible for compilation of US BoP.	BPM5	BEA Conducts a number of mandatory surveys for capital flows on data relating to direct investment. Comprehensive benchmark surveys are conducted periodically.

Source : Balance of Payments Statistics Year Book 2001.

Annexure 2B

Table – 3

Definitions Used for Identifying Direct Investment Enterprises Resident in the Reporting Economy

(by number of countries)

Region	*Countries those apply the 10 percent equity threshold*	*Countries those use a percent of ownership different from the 10 percent threshold*	*Countries those apply the 10 percent threshold but allow a qualification to the threshold:*		*Countries those apply a value threshold when identifying FDI enterprises*	*Countries those apply a different treatment for incorporated and unincorporated enterprises*
			Countries those Include enterprises in which the investor has a voice in the management but owns less than 10 percent of ordinary shares or voting power	*Countries those exclude enterprises in which the investor has no voice in the management but owns more than 10 percent of ordinary shares or voting power*		
OECD (29)	24	6	7	2	4	3
Africa (15)	11	2	2	0	-	-
Asia (13)	10	2	-	0	1	-
Europe (16)	14	2	3	-	3	1
Middle East (2)	2	-	-	-	1	-
Western Hemisphere (21)	16	1	2	1	1	1
Total (96)	77	13	14	3	10	5

Note - India also adopts the 10 percent rule (Individual FII limit is 10 per cent and classified as portfolio investment). Figures in brackets represent total numbers of countries in the region.

Source : Report on the Survey of Implementation of Methodological standards for Direct Investment, IMF (March 2000)

Table – 4

The Components of FDI Other Capital Transactions included in the Statistics

(by number of countries)

Region	*Countries those include in their FDI other capital transactions:*				
	Long-term loans	*Short-term loans*	*Financial leasing*	*Trade credits*	*Bonds and money market instruments*
OECD (29)	25	23	13	17	14
Africa (15)	8	8	4	7	4
Asia (13)	10	10	4	7	3
Europe (16)	14	12	6	10	4
Middle East (2)	-	-	-	-	-
Western Hemisphere (21)	13	10	3	12	1
Total (96)	70	63	30	53	26

Note : India does not include long-term/short-term loans, leasing, trade credits and bonds and money market instruments in its FDI data whereas majority of the countries treat long-term/short-term loans and trade credits as FDI. Therefore India's FDI reporting is an underestimation to that extent.

Figures in brackets represent total numbers of countries in the region.

Source : Report on the Survey of Implementation of Methodological standards for Direct Investment, IMF (March 2000)

Table – 5

Components of FDI Equity Capital Transactions included in the Statistics

(by number of countries)

Region	*Countries those include in their FDI equity capital transactions*		
	Transactions in voting and non-voting stocks	*Reinvested earnings*	*Non-cash acquisition of equity*
OECD (29)	28	23	19
Africa (15)	6	6	7
Asia (13)	7	9	7
Europe (16)	11	9	13
Middle East (2)	2	2	2
Western Hemisphere (21)	10	18	18
Total (96)	64	67	66

Note : India does not include reinvested earnings and non-cash equity transactions in its FDI reporting. Figures in brackets represent total numbers of countries in the region.

Source : Report on the Survey of Implementation of Methodological standards for Direct Investment, IMF (March 2000)

Table – 6

Countries that included Indirectly Owned FDI Enterprises in FDI Statistics

(by number of countries)

Region	Countries those include earnings data of indirectly held FDI enterprises	Countries those equity and other group transactions within a group of related entities as FDI without consideration of the percentage of equity held by these enterprises in each other	Countries those apply the fully consolidated system	
			Partially	Fully
OECD (29)	13	13	12	10
Africa (15)	6	5	5	3
Asia (13)	4	4	6	1
Europe (16)	5	6	7	1
Middle East (2)	1	1	1	-
Western Hemisphere (21)	6	2	12	-
Total (96)	35	31	43	15

Note : India does not include earnings data of indirectly held FDI enterprises.

Figures in brackets represent total numbers of countries in the region.

Source : Report on the Survey of Implementation of Methodological standards for Direct Investment, IMF (March 2000)

Technical Monitor Group on Foreign Direct Investment:
First Action Taken Report

(June, 2003)

TECHNICAL MONITORING GROUP ON FOREIGN DIRECT INVESTMENT: FIRST ACTION TAKEN REPORT

(June 2003)

Contents

I. Constitution of the Group

The Committee on Compilation of Foreign Direct Investment (FDI) in India submitted its Report to the Government in October 2002. As a follow up of the submission of the Report, Shri V. Govindarajan, Secretary, DIPP, Government of India advised to constitute a Technical Monitoring Group (TMG) for speedy implementation of the recommendations made by the above Committee. The TMG was constituted by Department of Industrial Policy and Promotion (DIPP) with the representatives from Reserve Bank of India (RBI), DIPP, Department of Economic Affairs (DEA), Department of Company Affairs (DCA) and National Informatics Centre (NIC) with the following terms of reference.

II. Terms of Reference

The terms of reference of TMG were as follows:

1. Review the availability of data for the list of items identified for inclusion in FDI statistics;

2. Take steps for inclusion of available data on immediate basis;
3. Take steps to devise appropriate reporting systems in areas where data are presently not readily available;
4. Create appropriate linkages with SEBI, DEA, Banking and Insurance Division, DIPP, NIC, CMIE, etc. for strengthening the data sources and data collection methods;
5. Recommend on FDI registration for strengthening compliance to compulsory reporting requirements;
6. Lay down the periodicity and timeliness for data collection and reporting; and
7. Suggest suitable legal framework for the proposed data collection methods.

III. Functioning of the Group

The TMG met four times in New Delhi on November 20, 2002, December 10, 2002, January 10, 2003 and April 23, 2003 to deliberate on the various issues relating to the terms of reference referred to earlier. The TMG received technical support from the officials of RBI and DIPP. Officials from NIC, DCA and DEA also participated in the deliberations and provided technical inputs to TMG.

IV. Approach

In line with the terms of reference the broad approach of the TMG was to resolve various operational problems associated with the compilation of the FDI statistics to make it comparable with the international best practice. The main focus of TMG in this context was to identify various components of FDI, which are operationally feasible and to capture these components in a specified institutional framework and within a specified time period. In addition, the TMG focused on compilation process of the identified components such as (a) reinvested earnings by FDI entities, (b) "other capital" in the form of inter-corporate debt transactions, and (c) equity capital of branches of foreign banks operating in India. The components of FDI identified by TMG and the compilation procedure are discussed below.

(a) Components of FDI Identified by TMG

TMG identified the following 14 items, which are required to be included in FDI statistics in order to make the data internationally comparable.

1. Equity Capital

- **a.** Equity in unincorporated entities,
- **b.** Non-cash acquisition against technology transfer, plant and machinery, goodwill, business development and similar considerations.
- **c.** Control Premium
- **d.** Non-Competition Fee.

2. Reinvested Earnings

- **a.** Reinvested Earning of incorporated entities,
- **b.** Reinvested Earning of unincorporated entities,
- **c.** Reinvested Earnings of indirectly held direct investment enterprises.

3. Other Capital

- **a.** Short-term and long-term borrowings,
- **b.** Trade Credit,
- **c.** Suppliers credit,
- **d.** Financial-leasing,
- **e.** Financial derivatives,
- **f.** Debt securities,
- **g.** Land and buildings.

Actions were taken by DIPP and RBI to institutionalise the inclusion of these items. The revised data on FDI include all items indicated under equity capital (except non-cash acquisitions) and reinvested earnings (except reinvested earnings of indirectly held direct investment enterprises. Data under 'other capital' relate to short-term and long-term borrowing, trade credit (more than 180 days) suppliers' credit (more than 180 days), and financial leasing only. Data on short-term trade credit (upto 180 days) have not been included, as these data are not captured separately through the present reporting system. Attempts are being made to capture these data through revised FC-GPR form as well as through integrated forex management system (IFMS).

It may be mentioned that the data on reinvested earnings and equity capital of foreign bank branches in India will be revised on an annual basis, as these are collated from the Balance Sheet data. The data on 'Other Capital' currently included in (ECB) will be updated on a quarterly basis - coterminous with quarterly BoP Statistics.

(b) Compilation Procedure

The compilation procedure to work out (a) reinvested earning by FDI entities, (b) "other capital" in the form of inter-corporate debt transactions, and (c) equity capital of branches of foreign banks operating in India is discussed below.

Reinvested Earnings

The main source of this information has been the annual survey conducted by the Department of Statistical Analysis and Computer Services (DESACS), RBI, on foreign assets and liabilities (including reinvested earnings) of corporates and unincorporated bodies. The population for this survey is constituted by entities, which seek approval from the RBI or Government of India (GoI) for FDI or joint venture abroad. The latest survey (conducted in 2001-02) had a population size of about 7,000 entities. As this survey relates to both assets and liabilities, the entities included in the population cover companies that are involved in joint ventures abroad, accessing portfolio investment, accessing external commercial borrowings, etc. other than FDI companies. Out of the total population of 7,000, around 2,500 companies responded to the questionnaire of which around 1,400 were FDI companies. Reinvested earnings of these companies were calculated by apportioning (according to the non-resident equity holdings) the current appropriation to unencumbered reserves and net profit after tax and dividend. This formed the reinvested earnings of the companies covered under DESACS survey.

Given the inadequate response to the survey, other sources of information were also explored to improve the coverage. Available balance sheet information on 60 non-respondent FDI companies was collected from the Company Finance Division (CFD) of DESACS. Reinvested earning figures of these companies were compiled with the available balance sheet information through the same method as in the case of companies covered under the DESACS survey.

In the next stage, the Center for Monitoring Indian Economy (CMIE) was approached to access the balance sheet information of the FDI companies, which neither responded to the survey nor the balance sheet information was available with CFD. Information relating to more than 200 such companies was available with CMIE and the same was purchased. Reinvested earning figures of these companies were compiled with the available balance sheet information through the same method as in the case of companies covered under the DESACS survey.

A list comprising nearly 600 large non-respondent companies was given to the Bombay Stock Exchange (BSE). Information received from the BSE does not provide detailed non-resident holdings as well as appropriation to unencumbered reserves. In certain cases, information on net profit and dividend remitted abroad/dividend declared are also not available. Given these shortcomings, data provided by BSE could not be utilised to calculate reinvested earnings.

Reinvested earnings with respect to branches of foreign banks have been calculated from the annual accounts of these banks. Though the net profits after tax and provisions are available in the account, figures relating to dividend remitted abroad are not available. Reinvested earnings have been calculated as profit net of appropriation to encumbered reserves.

Reinvested earnings has been compiled on the basis of information collected from DESACS Survey, CFD database, CMIE database and balance sheets of branches of foreign banks operating in India consisting about 1,700 FDI entities.

"Other Capital"

"Other Capital" covers the borrowing and lending of funds – including debt securities and suppliers' credit - between direct investors and subsidiaries branches and associates. At present, FC-GPR is not capturing these details separately. However, some of these details are available in the ECB database. In the present ECB reporting system, there is one column to identify the borrower of ECB whose creditor is holding 10 per cent or more equity capital or not. However, it does not specifically indicate whether the equity holding is in the borrower company or in any other Indian company.

An exercise was carried out to identify the pairs of creditor and borrower who are having direct investor and direct investment enterprise relationship with the help of detailed pairs of direct investor and direct investment enterprise database collected through the Survey of India's Foreign Liabilities and Assets. As the response to the Survey is not encouraging, all such pairs could not be identified in the ECB database. However, with the identified direct investor and direct investment enterprise pairs, the following transactions between borrower and creditor were treated as "Other Capital". Components of "Other Capital" that has been captured from the existing ECB database are given in the table below.

"Other Capital" Component	*Data Availability*
Trade Credit (more than 180 days) (includes Suppliers' Credit)	Available in the ECB Database
Financial Leasing	Available in the ECB Database
Loans	Available in the ECB Database

Equity Capital of Branches of Foreign Banks Operating in India

The current reporting system on FDI only captures FDI inflows in the form of equity investment in corporate entities. Since foreign banks operating in India are branches of foreign banks, they are unincorporated bodies in India. Therefore, FDI inflows with respect to branches of foreign banks are not captured under the present system. FDI inflows in the form of equity capital of branches of foreign have been captured by increment in equity capital during the year. This information has been obtained from balance sheets of individual banks.

V. Revised FDI Figures

On the basis of the compilation process discussed above, the final picture that emerges from the above is as follows.

FDI inflows for the fiscal year 2000-01 and 2001-02 as currently published by RBI stood at US$ 2,342 million and US$ 3,905 million, respectively. With the additional components of FDI compiled under the recommendation of the TMG the FDI figure for the above-mentioned years have been revised to US$ 4,029 million and US$ 6,131 million, respectively.

The following table provides the detailed break-up of FDI inflows to India as derived through the above mentioned compilation procedure.

Table – 1

Foreign Direct Investment Inflows

(US$ Million)

Item/Year	*2000-01*	*2001-02*
I. FDI as Currently Published by RBI	2,342	3,905
II. Additional Components Captured by TMG (A+B+C)	1,687	2,226
A. Banking Capital of the Branches of Foreign Banks	*58*	*190*
B. Reinvested Earnings {(i)+(ii+(iii))}	1,350	1,646
(i) Corporate Sector - Compiled through Survey	605	749
(ii) Corporate Sector - Compiled through Balance Sheet information obtained from CMIE & other sources	389	436
(iii) Branches of Foreign Banks	356	461
C. Other Capital (Inter-company Debt Transactions)	279	390
III. Total Foreign Direct Investment Inflows into India (I+II)	4,029	6,131

Note : (1) Reinvested earnings (item II.B) have been calculated on the basis of information on about 1,700 FDI entities.

(2) "Other capital" (item II.C) includes only inter-company debt transactions such as short-term and long-term borrowings, financial leasing and inter-corporate loan available in ECB database.

The internationally comparable figures on FDI in India would now appear as follows (Table 2) :

Table – 2

Revised FDI Inflows into India

(US $ million)

	Item/Year	*2000-01*	*2001-02*
I.	Equity Capital	2400	4095
II.	Reinvested Earnings	1350	1646
III.	Other capital	279	390
IV.	Total	4029	6131

VI. Conclusion

The figures on FDI indicated above are provisional. Finer data on FDI would be disseminated when reporting system is stabilized to capture data on trade credit, venture capital, financial derivatives etc. Nevertheless, the present coverage is significantly wider than the earlier practice of disseminating FDI data covering the equity capital only. The TMG would continue to function till the remaining items identified by it are included in the FDI compilation. The revision of FDI data will not affect the overall BoP position. However, RBI would make appropriate changes in the current account as well as capital account transactions of BoP. The BoP statistics would be modified accordingly. The Report of the Committee on Compilation of Foreign Direct Investment of India and also First Action Taken Report of the TMG may be placed in the website of RBI and DIPP. For wider dissemination, RBI & DIPP may consider a joint Press Release at the earliest on revised FDI data, as well as methodology of compilation of such data in line with international best practices.